LEARNING FROM EXPERIENCE

LEARNING FROM EXPERIENCE
Toward Consciousness

WILLIAM R. TORBERT

19   72

COLUMBIA UNIVERSITY PRESS / NEW YORK & LONDON

William R. Torbert is a member of the faculty at the Graduate School of Education, Harvard University, Cambridge, Massachusetts. He was formerly Assistant Professor of Organizational Behavior at the School of Business Administration, Southern Methodist University, Dallas, Texas.

Library of Congress Cataloging in Publication Data

Torbert, William R   1944–
  Learning from experience.

  Bibliography: pp. 235–42
  1. Learning, Psychology of.   2. Experience.
I. Title.
LB1051.T652   153.1'524   72-8337
ISBN 0-231-03672-8

Inquiry in action can lead to learning from experience. A simple formula, you say; yet, in my life, questioning and answering long remained separated from daily action. And the process of reconciling questioning, answering, and acting—of attempting inquiry in action—has largely defined my personal, professional, and social life during the past decade.

For two reasons it may be particularly appropriate to share with the reader a few fragments of the personal explorations from which this book developed. I find an irresistible aesthetic parallel between a scientific description of the basis of personal learning—to which I devote the bulk of this book—and a personal description of the origin of this scientific investigation—to which I will devote the preface. Also, I want to illustrate at the outset the active, decisive, and historical qualities of inquiry in action, in order to counterbalance the descriptive, informative, and ontological qualities of learning from experience that are emphasized in the body of the book.

Over a period of several years, a number of conclusions about the relation of questioning to answering to acting began to come into focus for me. First, I realized that despite my intellectual uncertainties I was acting all the time. This realization affected the kinds of questions I asked. Questions like, "Why should I do something when I am not sure it is the right thing for me to do?" which had often plagued me, became secondary. They were reflective questions which sometimes kept me from acting and at other times became the source of sedentary ruminations after an event. Instead, it occurred to me that I would gain considerably more knowledge of the standards I actually used in action, whether or not they were ultimately right, if I could observe myself thinking and feeling while in action. Rather than trying philosophically to decide a priori what was right, why not try the scientific approach and get some actual data on what I was treating as right in day-to-day life? Such data could later inform the more difficult "why" questions. In the meantime, self-observation while in action implied a kind of questioning that would bring me closer to my actions rather than leading me away from action into reflection.

Second, I realized that my emphasis on inquiry could represent an active commitment to social openness as well as a reflective commitment to personal openness. The active, social qualities of inquiry can be exemplified in several ways. In terms of moment-to-moment personal behavior that can influence the tone of a social situation, direct questioning, openness to new information, support of someone who is struggling to formulate a relevant feeling, and confrontation of unresearched or unreasoned decisions all require active and often risky social commitments to inquiry.

Third, I realized that a great deal of social conflict and personal anguish derives from fear of admitting one's own uncertainties to oneself and others. One fears that such an admission will lead to paralysis because of lack of standards for action and will make one vulnerable to possibly untrustworthy people. Such fears are realistic *as long as* one's behavioral repertoire includes no ways of seeking truth in action and no ways of testing and developing trust with others. *And this lack,* I have come to believe, *characterizes almost everyone.* Inquiring behaviors and trust-gauging-and-enhancing behaviors are suppressed rather than modeled in most families, schools, and other formal and informal relationships. On a personal scale, the result of this kind of socialization is an increasing disengagement between one's inner life and one's public self-presentation. On a social scale, the result is interpersonal and intergroup win-lose conflicts, based on unwillingness and inability to reexamine premises, explore possible mutual aims, and develop trusting interdependence.

Taken together, these three conclusions imply that inquiry in action, as opposed to reflective inquiry, is a rare and undeveloped yet desperately needed personal and social art.

The first conclusion—that I was acting all the time— confronted me most dramatically during a series of events that followed my introduction to the twin ideas of authentic behavior (doing what one says and saying what one means) and trustful relationships by Chris Argyris, then a professor at Yale. His willingness to focus on individuals' actual behavior to see whether it matched such abstractions as freedom, concern, and trust seemed to me a tremendously potent method of learning about oneself and improving social interaction. So, when I was invited to join a Yale senior society (an institution bringing together fifteen seniors for two evenings a week), I suggested to the other fourteen prospective members that we invite Argyris to help us develop authentic behavior and trusting relationships. In fact, I added that I felt so strongly about the value of working with Argyris that I would not join the society if others did not wish to work with him. My enthusiasm seemed convincing, and the others appeared to agree. He would join us for the second part of the year.

During the first part of the year the fifteen members encountered the typical difficulties that most groups experience. Some members were more committed to talking together than were others; some felt closed out of conversations by more aggressive speakers; some felt coerced by group decisions; personal antagonisms developed. None of these issues surfaced very often in formal meetings. Instead, they tended to reveal themselves in two-person conversations or sarcastic comments. I was unsure how to repair these difficulties, but assumed that they would reinforce for all the members the relevance of Argyris' concern for authentic, trusting, noncoercive relationships.

As the second term approached, there seemed to be an undertone of interest in exploring other alternatives besides working with Argyris. Surprised at this development and a little scared that we might be deterred by inertia from working with Argyris, I made a careful argument about his relevance to the problems we seemed to be having as a group. We asked him to join us for an evening to give all members an opportunity to meet him.

The meeting with Argyris was exceedingly tense. At first, conversation seemed forced. Gradually antagonism towards Argyris began to emerge. Finally it became clear that a number of members felt antagonistic towards *me* for forcing Argyris on them. "Antagonistic" may be too strong and clear a term, for they liked and respected me, but at the same time they felt manipulated by my enthusiasm, logic, and rhetorical ability. Argyris decided not to meet with the group during the spring, and it became clear that there was no consensus within the group to meet with him. I felt defeated, rejected, uncertain about my continuing commitment to the group, and embarrassed.

I felt embarrassed because I'd been caught in the act, so to speak. In the very process of advocating noncoercive relationships, I had in fact been coercing my friends. In the process of attempting to learn about action, I had been acting in a way that prevented learning. The event was over before I had thought it would begin. With Argyris' help, I had already learned about the relation of my behavior to abstractions during the fall, rather than having to wait for the spring (although it took a while for this "positive" perspective to occur to me).

This experience dramatically exemplified my conclusion that I was acting all the time. It also showed me how unaware I was of the effects of my behavior. For six months I had thought I was accomplishing one thing and then, almost after the fact, I discovered that I had not only *not* accomplished that thing but had set up the principal barriers to accomplishing it.

Some time after this event, I began experimenting with inquiry as a mode of behavior, a process that led to my second conclusion—that inquiry could represent active social commitment. My first extended experiment was aimed at developing an antidote for my tendency to overwhelm others with *my* enthusiasm, *my* interests, *my* ideas, and *my* rhetoric. I decided to turn all my initiative in conversations to exploring *the other's* experience. Although my unaccustomed role exposed me to new discomforts at first—such as awkward pauses or uncertainty about how to show interest without intruding—this experiment turned out to be immensely rewarding. I found that exploration revealed every person with whom I talked to be fascinating in some respect and to be struggling with some of the same questions I was. Also, there came a point in many conversations where the other person would begin to take the initiative to explore my experience. When I responded to such initiatives, I could feel that what I was saying was being heard, comprehended, and valued by the other to a degree new to me. I gradually inferred that people shield themselves from rhetoric that is too glib and that never bothers to connect itself to their concerns, whereas they actively work to integrate what they hear when it responds to *their* question (a question of which they may not have been aware, or which they may not have been secure about asking, before the conversation began).

At this time, close to the end of my senior year, I first began to sense an inwardly evolving life-aim—a sense of how inquiry in action could become a socially relevant career as well as a personally necessary search. Previously, when I thought about possible careers, all choices felt relatively arbitrary. I had many competences, so they did not dictate narrowly what I could and could not do. Moreover, to base a career decision on an acquired competence seemed highly arbitrary to me. I began to realize that my enthusiasm for various jobs flagged after a time because I did not know why I was there, why *I* was doing *that* job.

My planning for the future had been highly tentative. I had won fellowships to divinity school and to teach and study in India, both attractive alternatives for a variety of reasons, but neither compelling. Only weeks before graduation, I was asked whether I would like to become associate director of the Yale Summer High School, a socially experimental residential program for bright but often unmotivated students from backgrounds of poverty. The position sounded as though it had been created with my needs in mind. I would have some opportunity to teach, giving me a first chance to experiment with creating a learning environment where experiential as well as cognitive learning could occur. Moreover, as the only fulltime staff member during the winter months, I would coordinate design of the school's curriculum and the organizational structure and also would visit schools around the country to contact past and future students. Then during the summer I would have primary responsibility for day-to-day internal operations of the school (while the director focused on long-range planning and relations to other institutions). The combination of opportunities—to observe schools, to design one, to take operational responsibility, and to work with students whose past schools had often *not* served them well and who would therefore be more likely to challenge our efforts than to be docilely subservient—this combination would require inquiry in action to a degree unmatched by any other job I had ever held or envisioned.

Never since accepting that job have I lost interest in the work I've been doing. I discovered that, for me, long-term concern depends on testing my deepest questions in my daily work as well as in my friendships. I've become increasingly confident in making my questions rather than my answers the basis of my work and relationships (not that the conclusions I have reached have no place; they become the ground upon which further questioning occurs).

Later I became director of another, similar program, Upward Bound. My work at Yale Upward Bound illustrates in a number of ways the relationship between genuine scientific inquiry and social change toward justice, fulfillment, and reconciliation. I was testing the obverse of my third conclusion—that lack of inquiry in action engendered social conflict and personal anguish.

I began the program because as a scientist of human events I found myself in the apparently anomalous position of having to create actively the environments I intended to study. For I discovered that a prime characteristic of existing social systems is that they suppress and distort information; consequently, they also suppress experiential learning. Since I wanted to gain information about experiential learning, existing systems were not, in general, promising sources of data. For example, most schools not only do not determine what their students learn experientially by attending them, but also do not teach the students the language, concepts, or skills for understanding what they are learning from their own experience. Consequently, the most one could possibly gain by studying already existing schools is knowledge of how persons individually and collectively distort experience. Such knowledge is useful but does not illuminate the process of valid experiential learning. In short, social activism is an unavoidable concomitant of a genuine search for truth, given the current relationship between truth and society.

In addition, I found that the scientist of human events must show a commitment to the people he hopes to understand and must develop a trusting relationship with them, rather than remain neutral and detached, if he is to gain deeply valid data from them (that is, data concerning not just their public rhetoric, but also their thoughts, feelings, intuitions, and intimate behavior). This truism remains shrouded as long as social scientists' subject populations either are drawn primarily from docile college students participating in experiments in order to earn a grade in a course, or are confronted by questionnaires whose very format prohibits intimate self-disclosure. The difficulties of gaining any data whatsoever become highly tangible the moment one's population includes poor, black teenagers who have been exiled, or have exiled themselves, from the schools they nominally attend. And when the data go beyond responses to cards flashed on a screen, to deep feelings of hatred for whites, and the researcher is himself white, he will have to find some way of dealing with hatred directed towards him without breaking the relationship. What is the true, objective action to take under these circumstances? I have found no manuals of social science methodology that attempt to respond to this question. Under such circumstances the scientist must be intuitively committed to the search for truth, centrally committed to it as a person, and able to transform that central, intuitive commitment into behavior appropriate for the moment. No preordained, "role-consistent," "neutral" behavior will earn him anything but mistrust from the person he wishes to understand. (Not that my role as program director in any sense automatically exempted me from mistrust as a person who was uncaringly using students for his own ends. In some ways, the combined roles of researcher and director doubled the mistrust, and sometimes my actual behavior tripled it.)

Thus, scientifically as well as personally, inquiry in action rather than reflective inquiry came to seem to me a critically important ability.

Yale Upward Bound was structured on the premise that we did not know how to solve the problem of schooling for alienated students from poverty-stricken backgrounds. The students collaborated in designing all elements of the program, making it an example of inquiry in action. Although virtually every one of the sixty students our first summer could have been expected to drop out of school the following year, only two did. Such a brief summary hardly proves anything, but it does suggest a link between inquiry in action and positive social change.

Later, several staff members travelled to a national meeting of Upward Bound directors to hear "nonstructured" programs condemned as ineffective and a plea made to directors to be more cautious in selecting students and dealing with political issues. These messages elicited severe protests, particularly from our small contingent, which regarded them as both betrayals of the ideals of the War on Poverty and contradictory to the facts about the relative effectiveness of programs with which we were familiar. Only months later did we hear from a central Upward Bound figure that the real concern of the main office was to dissuade *incompetent* Upward Bound staffs from attempting collaboratively structured programs. The indirect and general policy had been formulated to avoid alienating the local staffs by confronting openly their alleged incompetence.

This final episode illustrates several administrative characteristics all too common in contemporary schools: (1) the tendency to suppress and distort information; (2) the resulting tendency to undermine constructive social change and increase unnecessary conflict; and (3) the ultimate assumption that inquiry in action is an impossible ideal for most people rather than an exciting, demanding, inescapable common purpose.

The foregoing anecdotes sketch the personal background from which my effort to formalize an understanding of learning from experience emerged. They also suggest dramatic and historical qualities of inquiry in action that remain largely implicit in the rest of the book.

I hope that the formality of the model of learning from experience presented in the following pages does not obscure its demand of a growing commitment to inquiry in action from a person who aspires to become more than an automaton—who wishes to become conscious—who would realize his full humanity.

ACKNOWLEDGMENTS

As I leaf through this work, I see the influences of many individuals. Their influences have ranged from spiritual to operational, from intellectual to emotional, from supportive to confronting, from guiding to mutually exploring. I do not understand the forces that have brought me into contact with so many remarkable people, but I am profoundly grateful. I thank them all and wish to name a few who have influenced me directly rather than through the writings listed in the bibliography: Judy Torbert, Lord Pentland, J. Richard Hackman, Douglas T. Hall, Morris Kaplan, Michael Vozick, Patrick Canavan, James Carlisle, Richard and Mary Sharpe, William Coffin, Karl Deutsch, Craig Lundberg, Mick McGill, and the members of the two groups described in chapters five and eight.

One person has influenced me in all the ways mentioned above during the past eight difficult yet rewarding years. Chris Argyris has taken varied roles in relation to me—friend, advisor, dissertation chairman—all with startling virtuosity and unflagging discipline. To him I owe more than I can express adequately or even comprehend. Nevertheless, I make one small effort at expression by dedicating this book to him.

In all cases these influences opened paths that I then chose to take, sometimes to unanticipated destinations, so I feel full ownership of and responsibility for the final result.

In addition to thanking specific persons, I also wish to acknowledge both the spirit and the substance of the Danforth Foundation's support of my graduate years.

More recently, the editorial advice and encouragement offered me by John Moore of Columbia University Press and the care of Patricia Stauffer in typing the final manuscript have been most helpful. Finally, after I thought the manuscript complete, Maria Caliandro, in her role as manuscript editor, showed me that virtually every page could be improved. I am deeply moved by her carefulness.

CONTENTS

LEARNING FROM EXPERIENCE

INTRODUCTION

This book addresses the question of how people learn from experience. The topic is unusually slippery and easily eludes one's grasp just when one feels one has it defined and placed. For example, scientific investigation seeks objective knowledge, yet experience is unmistakably subjective; therefore, must not the essential nature of experience be distorted when rendered as objective knowledge? Or, to take another tack, is not scientific investigation itself merely one way of learning from experience, along with other ways such as dramatic or political action and poetic or religious illumination? If so, how can a scientific investigation hope to elucidate "how one learns from experience" generally?

These questions suggest that the topic of learning from experience challenges the very framework of scientific methodology, language, and results. For this reason, the book places an unusually heavy emphasis, compared to most studies in behavioral science, on developing frameworks for study and a comparatively light emphasis on developing theoretical propositions and empirical data, though these are by no means absent.

Just what is a "framework"? At some points in the following pages I follow Kaplan (1964) in referring to a framework as a model, which he defines as the most abstract and systematic level of knowledge. Particular theories are elaborations of aspects of models (although the models may not be explicitly formulated). I regard what has heretofore been named general systems "theory" as a model and attempt in chapter 1 to examine, amend, and apply the systems model to the process of personal learning.

In terms of observational methods, one can follow Husserl (1962) and regard intuitive or phenomenological observation as framing or bracketing empirical observation. Intuitive awareness involves direct consciousness of oneself or of how one is seeing whatever one sees in the outside world. By contrast, external awareness of empirical facts is mediated by senses and is "contained within" direct consciousness.

Phenomenological observation plays several roles in the book. In its most obvious form, it is developed in chapters 4 and 5 as a means of gathering data to assess the validity of the model of learning presented in chapter 1. In this sense, phenomenological data are viewed as confirming or disconfirming an abstract model in a manner analogous to the way empirical data confirm or disconfirm a theoretical proposition. Intuitive self-observation-while-in-action also plays a role in the book, in that self-observation over a number of years led me toward the theoretical categories of verbal behavior introduced in chapter 6.

Still another way in which the book emphasizes framework is in terms of scientific method and presuppositions. Kuhn (1962) has argued that science ordinarily operates within unexamined frameworks or, as he names them, paradigms. The discussion of the term framework in this introduction began with the assertion that "learning from experience challenges the very framework of scientific methodology." It is appropriate that the nature of this challenge be investigated in this book since I wish to be scientific. Chapter 3 develops a new paradigm or framework for science that is consistent with the model of learning presented in chapter 1.

Despite the emphasis on the development of frameworks in this book, particularly in part I ("A Model of Experiential Learning"), the various kinds of theory and data presented in parts II ("Approaches to the Phenomenon of Experiential Learning") and III ("Measurements of Experiential Learning") play equally important roles in the complete work. One of the aims of this book is to begin to explore how to be systematic across the three levels of scientific model, theory, and datum, (or, stated actively, across the three levels of scientific paradigm, strategy, and execution), rather than simply being systematic within one of those levels or across two. The span from intuitive model to empirical data is also critical because it will, I hope, contribute to reconciling the epistemological, conceptual, and experiential polarities which make learning from experience so difficult today: the polarities between subject and object, between action and reflection, between humanist and technologist.

Such reconciliations are as difficult to achieve as they are easy to talk about. In entering the mysterious territory of "frameworks," "paradigms," "self-observations," "presuppositions," "intuitions," and "models"—even if at first only intellectually—one quickly experiences one's own life-frame (more popularly rendered as "life-style") to be in question. The political, dramatic, poetic, and religious implications of scientific investigation begin to intrude more regularly into one's awareness, introducing new, more intense, more precise clarifications and confusions, joys and sufferings. Each act becomes more problematic, more significant, more powerful, more costly, more lonely, more dependent upon the support of friends.

I have found it especially difficult to achieve a reconciliation between my personal aspirations and my personal limits. This book is one effort to create such a reconciliation. I will consider it successful if it spans three levels for the reader as it has for me —if it puts not only his thought into question, but also his daily behavior and his overall life-style. Otherwise the reader will not truly have learned from the experience of reading this work.

Almost all who have read this book prior to publication have found some chapters accessible and motivating but others at first difficult. The trouble is that the various readers did not agree about which chapters initially provide access to the ideas and thus can serve as introductions to further chapters.

Scholars familiar with systems theory found chapter 1 ("The Interplay of Feedback, Attention, and Consciousness") a good beginning; psychologists familiar with other learning theories found that chapter 2 ("Experiential Learning Compared to Previous Learning Theories") provided the best angle from which to approach the rest of the material; those with a bent toward philosophy of science found that chapter 3 ("Science As Experiential

Learning") posed the critical challenge motivating them to proceed. These first three chapters have in common a high level of abstraction and thereby provide the framework for the later chapters.

Chapter 4 ("The Phenomenological versus the Empirical Approach") attracted readers with a bent towards methodological questions. Chapter 5 ("Attempts at Inner Self-Observation") initially engaged persons with some established concern in meditation. Chapter 6 ("Categories for Observing Verbal Behavior") appealed particularly to those with active, clinical interests in therapy or group dynamics. These three chapters share a quality of reflection about how to do something, whether it be research, meditation, or everyday conversation.

The final three chapters are the most concrete, focusing on empirical results. Chapter 7 ("Achieving Intersubjective Agreement in Scoring Learning") presents the final, operationally reliable definitions of the behavior-scoring categories introduced in chapter 6. It will be of critical importance to anyone interested in using the behavior-scoring procedure to analyze his own or others' activities, but may seem tedious to other readers. For some readers the credibility of all the ideas offered will depend on the explorations of the validity of the behavior-scoring procedure, in chapters 8 and 9—the former discussing correlations and the latter deviations between learning scores and other criteria of learning.

I

A MODEL OF EXPERIENTIAL
LEARNING

The following three chapters posit four different but related levels of human experience: (1) the world outside; (2) one's own behavior; (3) one's internal cognitive-emotional-sensory structure; and (4) consciousness.

In chapter 1 the quality of human attention and interchange (feedback) is shown to depend upon the relationships among these four levels of experience. In chapter 2 the quality of human environments and thought is shown to depend upon the relationships among the levels. In chapter 3 the quality of human science is shown to depend upon the relationships among them. Together, the three chapters provide a framework for how to study man and learning.

It may be helpful to provide a brief overview of the argument in part I. Examination of theory and data will indicate that people are generally *not* in contact with all four levels of experience simultaneously. Instead, people tend to be aware only of what they are focusing upon at any given time. If they are focusing on the outside world, for example, they tend to be unaware of their behavior that mediates this focusing (such as looking, moving, hearing, bodily posture); they also tend to be unaware of the particular cognitive-emotional-sensory framework that is focusing or defining the focus; furthermore, they tend to be immersed in the given cognitive-emotional-sensory framework rather than operating through it while maintaining an inner sense of alternative frameworks. That is, they are not conscious. Consciousness is thus defined as a transcognitive phenomenon.

As long as human experience occurs within the severely limited context of mere focal awareness, this model indicates that experiential learning *cannot* occur. One way of explaining this proposition is to say that all of a person's experience under such circumstances is defined by the particular cognitive-emotional-sensory structure he applies but does not have access to in terms of his immediate awareness. Thus, all of his perceptions of the world and himself, all of his "learning," and all of his experience are conditional upon the validity of these frameworks. But since he is limited to focal awareness, he has no means for assessing the validity of his frameworks and consequently no way of determining the final validity of his focal experience. In short, he has no way of being scientific. What he calls his experiences, his perceptions, his learnings may all be illusory.

Chapter One

THE INTERPLAY OF FEEDBACK, ATTENTION, AND CONSCIOUSNESS

How does one learn from experience? Why do some people appear to learn from experience—increasing the effectiveness of their action, increasing the accuracy of their beliefs about patterns in experience, and increasingly accepting their emotions as significantly related to situations—while others repeat habitual patterns without learning? What kinds of speaking encourage or discourage learning from experience? This book moves from a general model of learning, to be developed in this chapter, to the testing of a procedure of scoring verbal behavior (chapters 7, 8, and 9), in an effort to respond to such questions.

In this chapter I will attempt to describe the process of experiential learning by using systems theory and phenomenology to conceptualize it, focusing particularly on the notions of feedback, attention, and consciousness.

Rather than beginning with definitions of the various terms, I will discuss them naively and allow the initial, implicit meanings of the terms to prove themselves inadequate to the complexity of the phenomena requiring elucidation. Only as such inadequacies reveal themselves will the key concepts be elaborated and reformulated. In this way, the reader will share, and be able to evaluate, the sense of reality upon which the emergent model of experiential learning rests.

By way of an initial overview, we can say that experiential learning involves becoming aware of the qualities, patterns, and consequences of one's own experience as one experiences it. How basic such learning is can be indicated by the fact that to be out of contact with, and unaware of, one's immediate experiencing has been conceptualized as psychological illness (Rogers, 1961a). Experiential learning has also been viewed as a means of increasing one's competence to deal with other persons even if one is already healthy by clinical standards (Argyris, 1968a). It has also been viewed as a means of developing a growth-oriented, autonomous, self-correcting group of persons (Mills, 1965). It is my purpose in this chapter to arrive at a model of learning which underlies and supports the view that experiential learning is central to fully human being and doing.

FEEDBACK

The connection between experiential learning and systems theory lies in the concept of feedback, a term already much used by therapists, group trainers, and organizational consultants oriented towards experiential learning. In the vocabulary of systems theory, feedback is information from the environment which tells a system whether it is moving towards its goal effectively or not. If a system receives no feedback from its environment, or blocks or distorts what feedback it does receive, it will not be able to adjust its behavior to achieve its goals. Under such conditions, whether it achieves its goals will tend to become a matter of chance. Clearly, a system utilizing feedback is more likely to be able to diagnose and correct its behavior and thus achieve its goals than one that operates blindly.

The application of the feedback concept to experiential learning has occurred as follows: A person's senses and feelings have been conceived of as *receptors* of feedback about the state of his own organism and his relationship to the environment. If he blocks or distorts the information these receptors take in from his awareness, he is viewed as rigid, insensitive, closed, sick. Other persons in the individual's environment have been conceived of as *sources* of feedback. They can inform him about the impact of his behavior on them and whether, from their perspective, it appears as though he is acting effectively to accomplish his goal. It is possible to imagine a situation in which a person is receptive to feedback but other persons do not provide it. In such a case, the structure of the social situation, rather than the person himself, is viewed as closed (Argyris, 1968a). Of course, personal and social closedness in relation to receiving and sending feedback are related, for personal behavior patterns and personal values or assumptions about proper social behavior create social closedness, and social closedness can be internalized as personal closedness (Freud's description of the formation of the superego in the child would be an example of this process [Freud, 1933]).

In any event, experiential learning in groups has been conceived of as a process of opening feedback channels, so that people begin to become aware of their impact on one another, begin to become aware of, and learn the meaning of, their feelings as they relate to their own and others' behavior, and begin to learn how to achieve goals that are personally meaningful to them through the use of intra- and inter-personal feedback. For example, one theory sees learning as commencing with a dilemma or disconfirming feedback; this leads to attitude change, which leads to new behavior, then new information from others, and a new cycle of change if it is warranted (Schein and Bennis, 1965).

This exposition of experiential learning emphasizes the benefits it confers to any person who engages in it, both in terms of long-range efforts to orient himself towards meaningful goals and in terms of day-to-day efforts to achieve more immediate goals and subgoals. The benefits of feedback are so straightforward, not only to overt learning situations, but also to any goal-oriented enterprise, that one would expect to find feedback a common personal and interpersonal process, a process eagerly adopted by persons or organizations when they become familiar with it. However, this expectation is highly inaccurate. Empirical investigation indicates that feedback processes within persons, among persons, and within organizations are often so muted and distorted as to be unintelligible and consequently of little or no help, or even a hindrance in guiding the system in question.

Several short examples can illustrate muted or distorted feedback. On the personal scale, a person will sometimes become red in the face, bang his fist on the table, and shout at someone else, yet, when asked a moment later if he is angry, will insist that he is not. On the interpersonal scale, a person who is viewed as being too enthusiastic about his own action-suggestions may receive as feedback only that others seem to ignore him. He may not take this reaction as feedback at all, or he may interpret it to mean that he needs to be *more* enthusiastic and persuasive in the future. On the organizational scale, knowledge about an organizational problem may get severely distorted, as it travels up the hierarchy, by subordinates who do not wish to appear incompetent to their bosses; the problem may immediately be blamed on another department, its upward communication thereby creating a new problem of interdepartmental rivalry rather than resolving the first problem. Such examples of distorted feedback must be common, for a series of studies of many kinds of natural groups in schools and businesses has found that the verbal transmission, reception, and encouragement of direct, clear, personally relevant, new feedback is virtually nonexistent (Argyris, 1969).

Not only is personally informative and enhancing feedback a rare process, but therapists, group leaders, and organizational consultants invariably encounter resistances to opening feedback channels, and in some theories the diagnosis of these resistances becomes the major concern (e.g., Perls, Hefferline, and Goodman, 1965). These resistances (ranging from acquiescence to social norms which hold that expressing feelings causes trouble and is immature, to inner fears of discovering something unacceptable about oneself) and means of reducing them (from social isolation of learners during their learning experience, to focusing on specific incidents rather than on overall impressions in speaking to others) have been listed and discussed (Schein and Bennis, 1965). Unfortunately, there is no single model that links their existence to the process of experiential learning.

AGAIN, WHAT IS FEEDBACK?

In order to probe more deeply into the resistances to feedback, we must redefine the very concept of feedback as it operates in human systems. Other terms central to experiential learning, such as consciousness, will also have to be redefined as I introduce successive considerations influencing the elaboration of the model of learning.

The short examples of distorted feedback that I have offered, plus qualifying phrases such as "personally informative and enhancing" feedback, indicate that it is not obvious what defines feedback as useful and how it can be transmitted. T-group educators have described and limited what they mean by useful feedback in the following ways:

Laboratory training is experience-based learning which besets us with the problem of matching symbols with experience. . . . We attempt to learn from an analysis of our own experiences in groups rather than from what some expert tells us. Thus, the term laboratory implies that the delegate has an opportunity to become a researcher of his own and others' group behavior; he becomes both the subject and the experimenter-observer. . . . In other words, here-and-now learning is based on *experiences which are shared, public, immediate, first-hand, unconceptualized, and self-acknowledged* (Schein and Bennis, 1965, pp. 5, 13, 39, emphasis added).

Information in a laboratory will tend to be collected and used in such a way that it tends to increase the feelings of self-responsibility, self-commitment, and authenticity. Such information should be, as much as possible, non-evaluative and descriptive; and gathering of data should be under the control of, and for the use of, the participants. Under these conditions the message is "owned" by the sender and sent in such a way that it does not imply that the receiver must accept it or that the sender is correct. Also, information would not tend to be collected to control human behavior. Information collected would tend to be returned immediately to the relevant individuals to help them control or modify their behavior if they wished to do so (Argyris, 1962, p. 143).

At first encounter, the specifications that feedback be shared, public, immediate, first-hand, unconceptualized, self-acknowledged, authenticity-enhancing, nonevaluative, descriptive, and noncontrolling may appear both incredibly demanding and incredibly restricting. Why only these kinds of feedback, one wonders. I will try to show in the following pages that from the viewpoint of systems theory these specifications define all feedback rather than some special kind of feedback and that they appear demanding simply because we are not accustomed to talking in a way that produces feedback.

We are not accustomed to feedback-producing conversation because, in general, social processes seem to operate within the framework of what Bakan (1967) has critically named the "mystery-mastery" complex. The mystery-mastery social process discourages 'sharing of feelings, motives, and goals with others (the element of mystery). Also, it encourages people to behave so as to gain control over a situation in order to influence others if necessary without themselves being influenced (the mastery element). (This definition of mastery can include a nonparticipative member of a group or a jokester as well as the overt leader.) The mystery-mastery process tends to be somewhat self-defeating, because the lack of sharing leads to lack of clarity about one's own goals, feelings, and motives, and because each person's efforts to gain control over others mean that whatever control is established tends to be conformity-producing and thus reduces everybody's autonomy. Nonetheless, so common is this pattern of social interaction (see Argyris, 1969) that a number of theories treat the resulting pressures towards conformity rather than enhanced individual awareness as the *only* kind of social process that exists (Festinger, 1950; Freud, 1930; Hobbes, 1651; Skinner, 1960).

Systems theory has only recently begun to have a conceptual framework that is sufficiently elaborated that I can refer to it in order to conceptualize the alternative social process which experiential learning seems to involve, given the specifications for feedback that I quoted from Schein and Bennis and from Argyris.

A social process that does not produce new information and increased awareness in new situations, but instead distorts the new information to fit old categories, can be said, in terms of information theory, to produce "noise." Because systems theory was derived in large part from cybernetics, the study of how machines operate, and because when a machine is built the kinds of information (feedback) it can handle are specified by the construction, the problem of how to distinguish feedback from noise was at first little considered. However, a major problem for human and social systems, unlike machines, is what in their blooming, buzzing environment they are to define, identify, and accept as feedback and what they will reject as mere noise (von Bertalanffy, 1968). An early cyberneticist overlooks this distinction and its potential importance:

> When I give an order to a machine, the situation is not essentially different from that which arises when I give an order to a person. In other words, as far as my consciousness goes I am aware of the order that has gone out and of the signal of compliance that has come back. To me, personally, the fact that the signal in its intermediate stages has gone through a machine rather than through a person is irrelevant and does not in any case greatly change my relation to the signal (Wiener, 1954, p. 16).

If a signal is not coded properly, a machine will automatically reject it. A person, however, may obey my signal to him but at the same time feel resentful, leading him in the long run to disobey me and cease responding to me altogether. A human being may also cease to obey signals because his goals change and the signals are not relevant to his new goals.

It would seem logical that a system must somehow be unambiguously programmed with, or else discover or create, its identity and goals and its boundary receptors, in order to know what is informative and enhancing feedback from its environment. If this is not the case, there is doubt whether the system will accept and use effectively the potential feedback. If a system has no defined goal, no information can tell it whether it is reaching its goal. And without defined boundaries the system will be unable to distinguish between its own behavior and the feedback from the environment (consider the problem, for example, of disentangling feedback from behavior in the case of a puppy chasing his own tail).

Nor are these the only reasons why determining what is feedback can be problematic for human systems. As their environmental conditions and subgoals change, individuals must be able to redefine what they will accept as information, if they are not to become ineffective, neurotic, or dead. Thus, for human systems, whether a potential communication is feedback or noise is a complex issue related to boundaries, internal structure, and purpose and thus answerable only for one person at a time. What is feedback for one may not be for another.

Recognition of these problems has led social systems theorists to attempt to deal with them by postulating two orders of feedback over and above goal-directed feedback (Deutsch, 1966; Mills, 1965). Goal-directed feedback is referred to as first-order feedback. Its function is to redirect a system as it negotiates its outer environment towards a specific goal. The goals and boundaries of the system are assumed to be defined, so feedback is also defined. These assumptions underlie the definition of feedback on page 8. The two higher orders of feedback can be viewed as explaining how goals and boundaries come to be defined. Second-order feedback has been named "learning" by Deutsch. Its function is to alert the system to changes it needs to make within its own structure to achieve its goal. The change in structure may lead to a redefinition of what the goal is and always leads to a redefinition of the units of feedback (Buckley, 1967). Third-order feedback is called "consciousness" by Deutsch. Its function is to scan all system-environment interactions immediately in order to maintain a sense of the overall, lifetime, autonomous purpose and integrity of the system.

The terms "purpose" and "integrity," critical to the meaning of "consciousness," can be elaborated as follows: The "inner" conscious purpose can be contrasted to the "external" behavioral goal. Goals are subordinate to one's purpose. Goals are related to particular times and places, whereas purpose relates to one's life as a whole, one's life as act. Purpose has also been termed "intention" (Husserl, 1962; Miller, Galanter, and Pribram, 1960) and can be related to the literary term "personal destiny."

The concept of integrity can be related to Erikson's (1959) life-stage that has the same name. A sense of integrity embraces all aspects of a person, whereas the earlier life-stage in Erikson's sequence, named "identity," represents the glorification of certain elements of the personality and the repudiation of others (Erikson, 1958, p. 54). The distinction between a system's identity and a system's integrity can be sharpened by regarding identity as the particular quality of a system's structure, whereas integrity reflects the operation of consciousness. In this sense, consciousness provides a system with "ultrastability" (Cadwallader, 1968). Ultrastability gives the system the possibility of making changes in its structure because the system's essential coherence and integrity are not dependent upon any given structure.

These concepts require further consideration and amendment before they become clear and can help us to elucidate both what feedback is for human systems and why empirically we find that people resist feedback.

The difficulty with following Deutsch in his division of feedback into three orders is that it implies three different types of feedback with special facilities for each. But a system's consciousness and structure are both crucial for defining what its goals are and what it will define as feedback. That is, in a conscious system a behavioral goal depends for its formulation upon the conscious sense of autonomous purpose and momentary action-orientation. Moreover, units of feedback do not exist apart from structural definitions of feedback: "To be defined as a quantity of information a signal must be selected from a set or matched with an element of a set" (Rapaport, 1968) and to become feedback from environment to system, a signal must be both selected from *and* matched with a set or structure (Buckley, 1967). Consequently, so-called first-order, goal-directed feedback only becomes informative, enhancing feedback by virtue of its congruence with conscious purposes and structural definitions of what feedback is.

Moreover, second-order, structure-maintaining-or-changing feedback only becomes operative by the person's choice when third-order feedback is operative. For if consciousness is not operative, the system does not possess the ultrastability necessary to give up a given structure and make the transition to another structure without losing its sense of identity, which is its sole source of cohesion. Structure-changing feedback is further dependent upon the operation of consciousness in that the system's structural organization must be congruent with its conscious sense of integrity and action-purpose. Thus, second-order feedback only becomes enhancing and informative (i.e., true feedback) by virtue of the simultaneous operation of third-order feedback, or consciousness.

These considerations indicate that it is more helpful to view feedback as unitary but necessarily congruent with the three systems levels of behavioral goal-seeking, conceptual-emotional-sensory structure, and consciousness, if it is to be unambiguously informative and enhancing. According to this model, the structural level can be conceptualized as somehow framing, bounding, defining, organizing, or interpenetrating the behavioral level, with consciousness bounding, defining, organizing, or interpenetrating both of the other two levels.

CONDITIONS OF EFFECTIVE FEEDBACK

Feedback will not be maximally effective when the sending or receiving system is unformed at any of the three levels, when the system blocks and distorts transformations among the levels, or when the system has not defined what another system offers as feedback. These formulations are different ways of saying the same thing: the effectiveness and the existence of feedback are finally indistinguishable issues, just as the effectiveness and the existence of a system are finally indistinguishable, since a system is defined by, and organized for, its operations in the environment. To say, accurately, that feedback exists is to say that it is effective.

If we look at feedback from this perspective, we can immediately formulate the circumstances in which human systems will resist, reject, distort, not attend to, or not even define a potential communication as feedback. A human system will not utilize potential feedback when:

1) it is irrelevant to the system's conscious purpose and thus incongruent with any particular structure the system may adopt for defining feedback;

2) it is incongruent with maintenance of the system's consciousness;

3) it is relevant to the system's purported goals but incongruent with its structure, and the system's sense of coherence and identity are tied to a particular structure that blocks or distorts contact with consciousness.

Moreover, it is always problematic whether and how a human system will define a potential communication as feedback when the system is not fully formed in terms of goal, boundary, or identity.

Feedback among conscious, autonomous systems would involve:

1) a mutual sharing of experience at the levels of behavior, structure, and consciousness;

2) a formulation of that experience which encourages the other's efforts to specify and pursue behavioral goals that authentically transform conscious purposes; and

3) a consequent predisposition to mutual self-control rather than to external control.

These conditions are not utopian, but rather follow logically and pragmatically from the concept of feedback. Conscious systems, recognizing their need for feedback to operate effectively, will adhere to these conditions. Argyris (1965a) has reached the same conclusion, based on a slightly different theoretical terminology. As he puts it, only individuals with high self-esteem will transmit undistorted feedback that is useful to other people in achieving their goals. Consequently, a person aware of his need for undistorted feedback will seek to operate so as to enhance others' self-esteem.

We can now relate the perspective on feedback given by systems theory to the specifications for feedback developed by T-group educators (p. 11). For example, sensitivity to another's conscious autonomy would lead one to make one's feedback non-evaluative and noncontrolling because one would recognize the other person as the proper evaluator of feedback to him and as the proper controller of his own behavior, since both evaluation and control depend upon his autonomous purpose. It will be obvious to the reader that this kind of behavior——in its focus upon others as autonomous goal-setters and sources of feedback and its consequent emphasis on sharing and mutual self-control—is directly contradictory to the patterns of behavior resulting from the mystery-mastery social process.

WHY MYSTERY-MASTERY?

We have yet to explain why the mystery-mastery process is socially so common. Indeed, this more extensive application of systems theory to experiential learning seems to emphasize all the more clearly the *benefits* of feedback. Moreover, it shows that the resulting atmosphere, which enhances the effective autonomy of persons, corresponds directly with the major value that American society places upon freedom, dignity, and self-determination by the individual. How are we to reconcile this theory and this social value with the fact that empirical social behavior seems to demonstrate their very antitheses?

To answer this question, I will return to one of the conditions in which a system will not use potential feedback: when the potential feedback is relevant to the system's purported goals but incongruent with its structure, and the system's sense of coherence and identity are tied to a particular structure that blocks or distorts contact with consciousness. The possibility that a human or social system can be nonconscious has been suggested by a number of theorists in different but related terms. I have already cited Cadwallader's (1968) view that ultrastability may or may not characterize a complex social system. Mills (1965) has proposed a model of group functioning in which he places autonomous, growth-oriented goal-setting by a group at levels above those at which he has observed natural groups to operate. Allport (1967) has proposed a similar model of functioning on the personal scale, according to which the development of system-environment transactional consciousness requires that a person become increasingly complex and differentiated and achieve a higher level of integration over the course of his life. The person is not born with such consciousness and does not necessarily develop it. Jung (1962) has called such an increase in integration the process of individuation, involving a shift from ego-identification to self-consciousness, which, he says, few people achieve. From the phenomenological perspective, Merleau-Ponty has arrived at a very similar view, concluding that most persons do not achieve transcendental consciousness but, rather, understand their lived states "only through an idea which is not adequate to them" (1963, p. 221).

If man is not born conscious and if the predominant social processes do not encourage feedback consonant with the possibility of conscious, autonomous goal-setting, it seems likely that relatively few human beings develop consciousness. This proposition may at first appear highly unlikely because we tend to think of ourselves as conscious—perhaps not conscious of everything inside us, as Freud has shown, but certainly conscious of many things. The proposition becomes less unlikely if we treat consciousness as the integration of thought, feeling, and sensation and therefore as different from them. To be able to say "I think, therefore I am" may prove that I am, but it does not show that I am conscious. To be conscious of something according to this formulation, would be not merely to see it or touch it and think about it but to see it in the light of one's life-aim in relation to the world. Although some people have ideas or feelings about their life-aims in relation to the world, probably few of them actively experience their life-aims as organizing the way they see the world—organizing not in the sense of directing some of their daily activities but in the sense of bringing energy, coherence, and significance to every moment of their lives. Thus, we must distinguish between thought at the structural level—intellectual awareness—and consciousness. A person can think he is conscious without in fact being conscious; or, to reverse the statement, he can be unaware that he is nonconscious.

THE PROCESS OF ATTENTION

The entire argument presented up to this point has been based upon terms from systems theory, such as feedback and consciousness. The distinction just made between intellectual awareness and consciousness can also be demonstrated by reference to the process of attention. When we introduce the phrase "life-aim organizing the way one sees the world," we are talking about a process of attention and perception. The relation of feedback to attention is obviously crucial. A system only receives the feedback it pays attention to. ("My experience is what I agree to attend

to." William James, in P. Bakan [1966].) When we speak of feedback in man as necessarily congruent with the three levels of behavior, structure, and consciousness if it is to be unambiguously
informative and enhancing, we are also talking about the quality
of attention necessary to receive feedback at all three levels simultaneously; we are talking about a kind of perception that
breathes energy, coherence, and significance into what we see. Describing this quality of attention can help to clarify the concept
of three interpenetrating levels in man and the concept of his
typical nonconscious state.

Perceiving something is not a simple matter of attending to
what is there. The "I agree" in William James's well-known
aphorism cannot be divided from the attending. It is common-
place in perceptual research that subjects see what they expect to
see.

In fact, "perception" is at least fifty percent *assumptions,* and these assumptions depend on the total circumstances in which the perception
takes place. For example, if I am sitting in the station master's office
looking out of the window and I see a train start up, I do not have a
moment of doubt about whether I am moving because I am not *ex-
pecting* to move (Wilson, 1967b, p. 66).

In schizophrenics such expectations become elaborated and rig-
idly applied across all situations as an "ideational gating" to
filter out "disturbing connotative environmental inputs" (Silverman, 1966). These considerations have led theorists to conclude
that the decision whether to attend to something can occur, on
the basis of its meaning, after it is physiologically discriminated
(J. Deutsch and D. Deutsch, 1969). Thus an object (or word) may
be seen or heard, and yet the person may not "agree to attend
to" it because of its meaning.

This treatment of attention accords closely with that of phenomenology.

We are mistaken to think that we possess only one mode of perception
—our "immediacy perception" of things. I certainly possess this mode
of perception—which can be described as a kind of feeler reaching out
from my eyes, and feeling its way over the surface of the things around
me. But I possess a *second* mode of perception, which can hardly be

described by a simile, except perhaps to say that it is like switching on an electric light in a dark room and suddenly revealing a whole situation that it would have taken hours to assess by "feeling" around the room in the dark. In other words, we possess *meaning perception,* and the two modes of perception have to work together (Wilson, 1967b, p. 72).

Even though the study of attention reveals it to be highly intentional (Husserl, 1962) both in selection of a focus and in terms of the meaning-framework that defines an object as a "this" or a "that," we tend to experience ourselves as passively "seeing what's there." We are not in contact with our own action in perceiving. "The whole point of phenomenology is that there is no sharp dividing line between perception and imagination. The dividing line only applies when we think of perception as passive and imagination as active. As soon as we realize that perception is active, the old dichotomy vanishes" (Wilson, 1967b, p. 108). But if we remain out of contact with our activity of choosing what we attend to, we fall into patterns of choice (values) determined by external pressures of which we are unaware. Our actions become more and more alienated both from our inner responses and from new situational characteristics. Our perceptions and behavior become more and more stereotyped.

The assumption we tend to make in daily life, that things, events, or words are preconstituted entities which we passively perceive, is similar to the assumption that feedback exists whenever somebody speaks to someone else, or that it can be limited to issues of behavioral goal-achievement. In both cases, the world out there is assumed to be separated from the world in here. Yet we have already introduced the argument that feedback must be simultaneously congruent across three levels: behavioral manifestation (which to another person appears as an event in the outside world), structure, and consciousness (which appear as aspects of the inner world. Polanyi (1958) suggests a similar inseparability of outer and inner worlds when he speaks of the influence of subsidiary awareness on focal awareness. Holmer (1970), in reviewing Polanyi's work, has insisted that although our bodies may logically be subsidiary to all the objects of our focus in the world out there (since we invariably see them from our body), we

Table 1. "Levels" of experience

As denoted by systems theory	In terms of human attention	In the human system	In science	In organization	In society
goal-directed input-output	focal awareness	perception, behavior	empirical fact	raw materials, plant	distribution and exchange of tokens of value, symbols
structure	subsidiary presence	cognition, emotion, inner sensation	logical theory	formal structure and informal processes	norms, values
consciousness	thread of intentionality	life-aim intuition, conscience, will	intuitive model	abstract purpose	myths

do not ordinarily feel our bodies at all. We are not in active contact with the subsidiary element of our awareness.

Thus, attention as well as feedback seems to be best regarded as involving three simultaneous levels of experience. Focal attention, subsidiary awareness of bodily presence, and a thread of intentional meaning are all involved in each perception, yet the latter two elements are not present in our awareness from moment to moment. Rather, we tend to distinguish merely between two alternative modes of focusing, one on the world out there, the other on imagination in here. This distinction leads us to posit imagination or intellectual awareness as self-consciousness. Yet from the perspective of three levels of attention, such awareness is severely limited. Only ongoing appropriation, recognition, and awareness of our bodily presence and of the thread of intentional meaning corresponds to full consciousness. In the same way, only ongoing appropriation, recognition, and awareness of the levels of structure and consciousness on the part of both sender and receiver correspond to full feedback. (It should be noted that consciousness is used to denote a level when we are speaking statically and a process when we are speaking dynamically; neither perspective alone adequately defines consciousness.)

Consideration of the phenomenon of attention provides us with a dynamic sense of consciousness, complementing the static sense provided by the earlier discussion of feedback. Table 1 illustrates the interaction of the three levels of experience throughout human life. The critical twin claims advanced here are that these levels represent more than a conceptual hierarchy but that their experiential referents are obscured by the limits of our active awareness.

MAN AS NONCONSCIOUS—THE COGNITIVE DISSONANCE ARGUMENT

By the following analysis I hope to establish a further logical, empirical, and intuitive context for the proposition that men are for the most part nonconscious, and also to elucidate the link between their nonconscious state and the predominance of the mystery-mastery social process.

If man is not conscious, he is not in touch with his unique identity and goals (which would stem from the experienced inter-actions among his levels of awareness). Therefore, his image of himself is comprised of certain of his thoughts which he believes accurately reflect and integrate the totality of his intuitions, thoughts, feelings, and behaviors, thus describing his self-structure. However, if at the center of his self-image is a belief that he is a conscious, autonomous goal-setter (as American values teach us to believe), then his self-image must be fundamentally inaccurate. But even if he does not hold this particular belief, the very assumption that thought can integrate itself, feelings, and sensations must be inaccurate, according to the proposed model. A higher level than thought—consciousness—is necessary to integrate the elements at the level of thought.

Thought could reflect given feelings and sensations in integrating behavior, but it could not even integrate behavior adequately if it were isolated from feelings and sensations. Since either isolation of thought, feeling, and sensation or else nonconscious combinations of the three (as in attitudes) must be the case in the absence of the conscious level of integration, thought must be inadequate to integrate even behavior in nonconscious man. This deduction leads in turn to the deduction that a person's pattern of behavior will tend to be incongruent with his thoughts about his values (i.e., his preferred behavior patterns) and his beliefs about himself. But, since such incongruities indicate the need for structural level adjustments, and since the nonconscious person is not able to make structural changes because he is not integrated by the ultrastability of consciousness, and since to recognize either his incongruities or his lack of consciousness would threaten his structural-level self-image (assuming now that part of his self-image is that he is conscious), it follows that *the person will strive to remain unaware of incongruities between his values and his behavior and between his self-image and his behavior.* Since most people are nonconscious, the foregoing characterization should apply to a large majority.

The entire foregoing analysis is a series of deductions based on the particular formulation of systems theory that I have developed. It is borne out empirically by inferences which can be drawn from cognitive dissonance experiments. In a typical example of these experiments, subjects were instructed to perform a task which they afterwards reported to be very dull (Festinger and Carlsmith, 1959). Then they were offered either one or twenty dollars to tell other (supposed) subjects that the same task would be very interesting. The one-dollar amount was fairly low for such help, especially since it involved lying. On the other hand, the twenty-dollar sum was a windfall for relatively little work. The experimenters reasoned that the subjects offered one dollar would experience cognitive dissonance about telling the lie, which they would reduce by persuading themselves that the task had in fact been interesting. By contrast, the subjects paid twenty dollars were expected to justify their lie to themselves quite easily on the basis of its insignificance in comparison to their monetary gain. This prediction was borne out: when asked again, after lying to the (supposed) subjects, whether the task in question was dull or interesting, the subjects paid one dollar tended to report it as having been interesting, whereas those who had been paid twenty dollars continued to report it as having been dull. Those paid one dollar attempted to bring what they believed into line with what they had said to avoid the incongruity between their thought and behavior. The others could avoid the incongruity (in terms of making any effort to resolve it) simply by justifying it on the basis of their twenty dollars.

The experiments concluded their analysis at this point. But several inferential steps are still needed to show how the material confirms the model of man that I have presented. The first step is to recognize that to lie was dissonant to subjects only because of an unexpressed premise they made about themselves: that they were people who said what they felt or believed. Roger Brown (1965), who points out this unexpressed premise, reflects upon it as follows:

Probably this premise is one that almost everybody holds and so the Festinger and Carlsmith manipulation can safely be assumed to be a cause of dissonance. However, to eliminate the dissonance it is only necessary to hold the premise: I am a liar and habitually say what I do not believe. Ergo, I have said that the experiment was interesting. For very many experiments on dissonance the underlying premise is complimentary to the self. . . . Here are some of them: (1) I say what I believe; (2) I do what I want to do; (3) If I willingly endure something unpleasant it always turns out to have been worth it; (4) What I choose is always better than anything I reject (p. 597).

If we compare these premises to the characteristics of a conscious, autonomous system, we find that they match very closely. That is, these unexpressed premises indicate that persons commonly view themselves as congruent in expressing (behaving) their values (beliefs). They view themselves as autonomous ("I do what I want to do"). And they view themselves as conscious (and therefore maximally effective) goal-setters and achievers ("What I choose is always better than anything I reject").

The subjects' efforts to rationalize incongruities away rather than use them as feedback indicates, however, that they are nonconscious systems that are unaware that they are nonconscious. Which are we to believe, their behavior or their unexpressed self-images? Are they nonconscious or conscious? If the model I have developed is correct, then their self-images must be false. Indirectly, one might be led to question the validity of their self-images, given the prevalence of the mystery-mastery social process. Since this process directly discourages congruence and autonomy, it seems highly unlikely that "almost everyone" could be correct in their images of themselves as congruent and autonomous. But we do not have to adduce indirect evidence of the inaccuracy of these persons' self-images. The very structure of the experiments proves the subjects' self-images to be inaccurate. By becoming consistent with their actual behavior (telling the supposed subjects that the experimental task was interesting) when they report their belief in the final report, the subjects who were paid one dollar thereby became inconsistent with what they said in their first report (that the task was dull). And, in any event, the inconsistency between their original report and what they said to the (supposed) subjects remains. Their effort to diminish their inconsistency and to avoid lying only served to increase their inconsistency and their lying while simultaneously reducing their awareness of their incongruity. The fact that subjects forget their first report in their futile efforts to achieve a semblance of congruence after the fact indicates the lengths to which most of us go, no doubt ordinarily, to avoid awareness of our incongruities.

We can carry this analysis still further and ask ourselves, Why is it that these obviously ingenious psychologists, who created and carried out these experiments, never carried their thinking beyond the concept of dissonance to the unexpressed premises it implies and to the evidence of the inaccuracy of these premises which their own experiments provide? Not only why, but how? How could they, each time, hit upon a major inaccurate aspect of most persons' self-images without ever, evidently, consciously conceiving of their efforts in this light at all? In reply we can at least say that the organizing intuition upon which these experiments are based and which is here exposed was, for some reason, inaccessible to the thoughts of the very men who had the intuition. This inference provides further evidence of the inability of thought to organize and account for one's behavior (in this case the scientists' theory was unable to account fully for their actual experiment), when the thought is incongruent with conscious intuition. The fascinating aspect of this particular example is that the intuition succeeded in organizing the scientists' behavior even while failing to organize their thought. Their thought distorted the intuition but did not block its further transformation into behavior consonant with the intuition.

INTERNALIZING THE MYSTERY-MASTERY PROCESS

Through the analysis of cognitive dissonance, the personal function of the mystery-mastery process becomes clear. Once internalized in us, the mystery-mastery process perpetuates itself through us. We tend to avoid sharing feedback, not only because such avoidance concurs with social norms, but also in order to avoid facing up to our own incongruities and our fundamentally inaccurate self-images. Hence the attempt to mystify others and ourselves is redoubled. We also wish to control situations, not only because we are taught that this is the way to get ahead or stay safe, but also so that they do not reveal the at-least-occasional inadequacy of our structural configurations and our lack of conscious ultrastability. Hence the attempt to master others is redoubled. The mystery-mastery process cannot be dealt with simply by changing society in some external way, for it is deeply internalized in us, leading us to resist its exposure and change.

For any communication whatsoever to occur in these conditions, there must be a strong analogy between social structures and internalized psychic structures (since these structures mutually define information). Without going into detail, we can note that several recent theories of psychological and social structure indicate such analogies at comparable historical periods. Sigmund Freud's work can be viewed as one description of how the mystery-mastery process may be internalized by a child as he interacts with society (especially with his parents as he grows up). Freud regarded this internalization as resulting in three structural components—superego, ego, and id. From the perspective of the theory here presented, these components or institutions are separated conglomerations of thought, feeling, and sensation. Freud (1933) focused considerable attention on the role of the superego in controlling the personality and repressing the contents and "perverse" energies of the id. The ego or self-image served as a passive observer of this struggle, both mastered by the superego and kept out of touch with the mystery of the id. This picture seems to correspond in considerable measure to Riesman's (1950) analysis of the individual's passive acceptance of a role into which he is born or inducted in a tradition-bound society. Tradition masters the society and keeps it out of touch with the mystery of its developmental potential. Socially, central Europe at the turn of the twentieth century, when Freud was formulating his view of personality on the basis of his patients, was probably still close to Riesman's view of a traditional society. Hence, there appears to have been a correspondence between psychic and social structure at that time.

More recently, psychoanalytic theorists have focused more on the active, mastering function of the ego in relation to the total personality and on the mystifying function of the ego-defenses (A. Freud, 1946; Hartmann, 1958). The ego-defenses protect the ego from seeing aspects of one's interactions with the environment which violate the ego's perspective. This change in emphasis in regard to the dynamics of personal structure seems to correspond to an analogous change in the structure of society. Mastery no longer derives from tradition and deference to tradition, but increasingly from the raw ability to organize people, whatever the end. Such organized power can be thought of as analogous to ego-strength within an individual.

THE DISTINCTION BETWEEN INTERNALIZATION AND LEARNING

It is important to note explicitly that what I have called "internalization" is not equivalent to "learning." Internalization involves a diminution of contact with one's conscious action-orientation. "The hateful environment is both annihilated and accepted by swallowing it whole and blotting it out. . . . The social environment [thus comes to contain] all the reality there is, and he [who has internalized it] constitutes himself by identifying with its standards, and alienating what are potentially his own standards" (Perls, Hefferline, and Goodman, 1965, pp. 452–53). Internalization will make a person less aware of his action-aim, less aware of the character of his interaction with the environment, less aware of potential feedback that might question the validity of his internalized structure, and, therefore, a less effective actor, even though his behavior may accord with mystery-mastery norms and thus tend to be rewarded socially as successful. A great deal of what we conventionally call learning may in fact be internalization, or, to use the term from information theory, noise. The common absence of a distinction between internalization and learning has led me to call "experiential learning" what I am discussing in this book; the distinctive name corresponds to the common perception that I am talking about a special kind of learning. Strictly speaking, however, all learning is experiential, and the diminution of contact with consciousness inherent in the mystery-mastery process of internalization is the converse of learning rather than a kind of learning.

The human paradox is that the personal internalization of the mystery-mastery process appears to be necessary for a person to deal with society (to exchange information with it at all), yet at the same time this process operates in ways that actively resist and distort feedback. The optimal solution might be for a person to be able to use different structural arrangements at different times, using the mystery-mastery structure only to interpret social information in that mode. But how does one achieve this state in the first place, if one's internalized mystery-mastery structure obstructs the development of consciousness and thus of the ultrastability necessary for a system to change at the structural level?

To state this problem in another way, the obvious symbols of success in a mystery-mastery process will seem to be threatened by experiential learning. And, at the same time, the potential benefits of such learning will appear abstract, overly subtle, and unconvincing. For example, one person in a learning group in which I was designated as educator received feedback from others that he was viewed as a strong but cold and distant personality, so that others felt uncertainty about his motives and some distrust of his leadership. This person had expressed two goals: to find someone whom he could love and to be a good leader. But rather than perceiving the feedback as useful to him in reorganizing his behavior so as to progress toward these goals, and rather than feeling valued by others as a result of their concern to give him this information, he rebutted the feedback by answering:

I see myself on a pedestal. I'm proud of myself and I think pride is important for a person. Wouldn't it be better for a person to strive to attain his image of himself as a leader than to discover that he was actually a runt?

This person saw the feedback not as helpful but as destructive of a self-image of himself as a success. His self-image was static, statuesque, inflexible. Hence, he felt that his self-image, his pride, his value would shatter rather than adjust if he took the feedback seriously and thus acknowledged a discrepancy—a crack—between his thought-image of himself and his behavior as experienced by others. His sense of stability was entirely invested in this statuesque self-image, this single structure. His lack of conscious ultrastability prevented him from increasing the effectiveness, accuracy, and flexibility of his behavior and of his self-image.

The metaphor of one's self as a statue on a pedestal captures precisely the essential quality of a self-image for a nonconscious person. Some people may try out a number of different statues on the pedestal from time to time. Such a process might permit a person to substitute one self-image for another if the first were disconfirmed by feedback; the person would not really be learning anything, however, since each self-image would be equally immobile, equally unchanging.

Another adjustment that would fall short of experiential learning would be to attach a "feedback and change mechanism" to one's self-image. This mechanism would collect feedback, and the statuesque self-image would occasionally be shrouded for repairs and alterations. The statue would thus become a public and changeable self-image, whereas the repairman would become increasingly central but also increasingly mysterious because never examined. This solution to dealing with experiential learning is ingenious but dangerous. It is ingenious because it permits one to change and thus to appear to learn consciously, and to use the rhetoric of experiential learning without anxiety or obvious defensiveness. It is dangerous because one does not thereby come into contact with the conscious level and is unlikely to encourage others to do so; because one will therefore actually be able to operate effectively only in certain restricted environments, despite one's belief that one is flexible; and because one will believe one has mastered the process of experiential learning before truly recognizing it.

By this time, the process of experiential learning may begin to appear more impossible than self-evident. If persons tend to distort or reject any feedback that is not isomorphic with mystery-mastery categories, if social and psychological structures tend to reinforce one another's interpretations of the world, if the mystery-mastery categories discourage the development of consciousness, and if consciousness is necessary to begin with for the nondistorted reception and transmission of feedback, how then can experiential learning occur at all?

THE PROCESS OF "GROWING DOWN"

If consciousness were utterly alien to humans at birth and if society operated only according to the mystery-mastery process, experiential learning as I have formulated it could *not* occur. Alternatively, if consciousness were accessible to the child but not yet formulable at the structural level nor expressible at the behavioral level because the child had not yet grown "down" into his thought and body, and if there were adults whose education had somehow facilitated the interaction among their conscious, structural, and behavioral levels and who were therefore both behaviorally formed and in touch with consciousness, then the exchange between the child and such an adult would be characterized by experiential learning on both their parts. In the adult, experiential learning would be a regular aspect of his action. In the child, experiential learning would be more irregular, since it would not only involve the transformation of feedback among the three levels, but also the very forming of the lower levels.

If the child were initially educated in the mystery-mastery process and had come to internalize it to some extent, consequently ceasing to be aware of the organizing function of his consciousness, then the educational task of such an adult might be formulated as reawakening the child's consciousness, or as helping him to recognize its manifestations anew. The child, under these conditions, would be called to an effort beyond the boundaries of the mystery-mastery process, an effort to break through his internalized image of himself as a separate and integumented ego and into the life of consciousness which interpenetrates bodies and thoughts. And the motivation for such an effort, initially often distorted and blocked by the insensitivity of the mystery-mastery process to consciousness, would itself derive from this consciousness, which would already be informing him, even though unappropriated, blocked, and distorted.

This revision of the proposed model of human functioning would still leave us in agreement with those theoretical views and empirical inferences which suggest that adult human beings are for the most part not conscious. But it would lead us to conceptualize the process of becoming conscious—of experiential learning—not so much as the development of a higher level of integration on the basis of already existing lower levels in man, but rather as a rediscovery and disciplining of a life-source which leads to the formation or reorganization of the lower levels. The reader may have noted that my earlier references to experiential learning have hinted at this perspective in characterizing consciousness as the prime organizer of a total autonomous system and therefore as rediscovered, more than created, through experiential learning.

Is there, however, any evidence or conceptual support for this model of human growth, which figuratively holds that children rightly grow down rather than up?

Schachtel (1959b) has noted that the adult categories for memory and experience that are prevalent in Western culture are unable to accommodate the complexity and immediacy of a child's perceptions. As a result, these childhood perceptions find no place in the adult's memory, thus accounting for the common tendency to "forget" much of one's childhood experiences. In a similar vein, Fahey (1942a,b) and Flanders (1959) have shown that children's school experience systematically discourages them from asking the profound questions which parents find them to be concerned with in earlier years and which they initially bring to school with them. Together these studies suggest that children lose touch with a complex, profound, and immediate stratum of experience as they are educated into the mystery-mastery process.

Moreover, when we think in dynamic terms about the process of attention, we recognize that children are forever reading their own meanings, fantasies, and bodies into what they see. They have yet to develop the experience, discipline, and language to recognize which aspects of this interpenetration are common to all persons, which are unique to them, and which reflect specific space-time configurations. But rather than helping them develop such experience, discipline, and language, their families and schools commonly insist that meanings are predetermined, singular, external, and limited to what can be grasped in the focal element of attention alone (Roszak, 1969, on the myth of objective consciousness).

In terms of conceptual support for the model of persons (systems) growing down, we find an analogous model being developed to deal with the development of the human species as a whole. Theoreticians concerned with biological and psychological evolution have argued that the Darwinian theory of evolution cannot account for the differential levels of organization that characterize life, since these levels are not randomly accretive but rather reflect constant, intrinsic, analogous principles in their organization and interrelationships (von Bertalanffy, 1967; Koestler, 1964; Teilhard de Chardin, 1959). Not only are such organizational principles not accounted for in the Darwinian theory of evolution, but they dispute to some degree its dynamic postulate that beings of lesser complexity gradually evolved towards man. Even though Darwin's theory may be *historically* accurate, it may not be *ontologically* correct. In some sense, organizational principles must operate from high degrees of integrated complexity toward lower degrees, since the unity of any whole defines the functions of the parts at lower levels, as we have seen that a man's conscious life-goal is necessary to organize his thought and behavioral levels. Rightly understood, the human species as a whole may be (ought to be, but isn't?) growing down rather than (as well as?) up.

Still another source of support derives from the work of certain scholars who are concerned with the development of full human health. They have supported the notion that socialized humans need to break through internalized (mystery-mastery) habits to consciousness if they are to function cohesively (N. Brown, 1966; Jung, 1964; Laing, 1967; Watts, 1963). In their research and writing they have attempted to reconnect daily life with the mystical concepts of initiation or rebirth into higher consciousness. These attempts, in turn, remind us of the long-standing conceptual support for the idea of growing "down" that is inherent in the philosophical, religious, and mystical doctrines holding that organization, or grace, or consciousness grows "down" into a child as his body grows "up." I am referring here to the New Testament and to Platonic philosophy, as well as to traditions which are more esoteric (e.g., Evans-Wentz, 1960; Franck, 1967; Ouspensky, 1949; Schuon, 1963).

In the foregoing pages I have posited consciousness, structure, and goal-oriented behavior as distinct but interpenetrating levels of organization in human beings, rather than as different and discrete kinds of feedback. Second, I have interpreted certain general characteristics of human behavior as reflecting the internalization of what I have called the mystery-mastery process. Third, I have viewed the mystery-mastery process as blocking, distorting, and not appropriating consciousness—as limiting attention to its focal element. And fourth, I have defined experiential learning as involving three rather distinct aspects, depending upon the state of a system: in a child in whom experiential learning is encouraged from the outset, feedback is used partly to form the levels of structure and behavior and to distinguish among qualities of attention; in a person who has internalized the mystery-mastery process, experiential learning will have a quality of breaking through into higher consciousness as well as of reorganizing the lower levels—a quality of sensualizing and spiritualizing his moment-to-moment perceptions; in a person fully formed at all three levels and in touch with consciousness, experiential learning will be a regular aspect of his action in the environment in fulfillment of his ultimate concern.

Chapter Two

EXPERIENTIAL LEARNING COMPARED TO PREVIOUS LEARNING THEORIES

In formulating a new model of learning in chapter 1, I appealed for conceptual support to previous work in a variety of fields. Conspicuous by its absence, however, has been any extended reference to learning theory. This significant omission results from the simple fact that existing learning theories do not provide support for the model of learning here introduced. Nevertheless, a criticism of two existing theories of learning (and the models upon which they are implicitly based) will show that the model presented here permits us to identify unexamined assumptions and logical gaps in the existing theories. Moreover, such a criticism leads, toward the end of this chapter, to an elaboration of the model of learning presented in chapter 1, in directions and terms that are less scholarly and more personal in quality.

Mowrer (1960) has developed a two-factor theory of learning, including learning through external conditioning and learning through cognitive problem-solving. Other learning theorists have stressed the continuum between conditioning and problem-solving, seeing the former as a simpler precursor to the latter (Gagne, 1965). Still others have stressed the fundamental discrepancy between the kind of environment necessary for external conditioning and the kind necessary for effective, long-term, human problem-solving (Argyris, 1967). This last group holds that the learner (subject) not the teacher (experimenter) must control his own learning if he is to experience psychological success, increased competence, and permanent solution of problems. This position emphasizes the differences between Mowrer's two factors of learning. For the purpose of clearly distinguishing between two models of learning I will accept this position on the long-term problem-solving process, naming the kind of learning which involves subjective control *learning through goal-setting-and-achievement,* and the kind of learning which involves control of the subject by another person *learning through external conditioning.*

Beyond these two kinds of learning, which will be detailed below, Kobler (1965) has argued that a third factor or kind of learning should be added to Mowrer's two. A third factor is necessary, he argues, to account for life-integration through the development of a basis for meaning and a personal conscience in a person. I want to explicate the relation of this third kind of learning to the other two. This third kind of learning can be named *learning through self-recognition* and will be shown to be based on the model of learning introduced in chapter 1.

We must differentiate the kinds of thought, awareness, and environment that tend to be associated with, or conducive to, each of the three kinds of learning. Table 2 presents the distinctions and relations pursued in the following pages. The meanings of the various terms in this table will become clearer as the reader proceeds.

Table 2. Three kinds of learning

Kind of learning	Kind of environment	Kind of thought	Kind of awareness
I. external conditioning	unilateral inculcation	associative	diffuse
II. problem-solving through goal-setting-and-achievement	collaborative interdependence	logical, verbal	cognitive, absorbed
III. self-recognition	existential variety	intuitive, analogical	alert, relaxed intentional attention

EXTERNAL CONDITIONING

All forms of stimulus-response conditioning or learning (whether classical or operant) involve complete control of the environment, instruments, and goals by the experimenter or teacher. The learner is treated as a manipulable black box whose external behavior is to be changed. Phenomena such as "attitudes," "values," and "insight," referring to events within the black box, are irrelevant. Only behavior (verbal and other) is at issue. This total control conforms closely enough to social learning situations in schools (except that schools tend to use their control in inconsistent, ineffective ways, partly because their rhetoric tends to disown such control) to make research results about learning through external conditioning potentially applicable to them—at least, so the researchers commenting on the following research designs believe:

The social rewards and punishments applied to human beings may be treated as the equivalent to the food pellets and electric shocks used with rats. Similarly, social roles are the equivalents to the mazes which must be learned in order to obtain the rewards and avoid punishment. Human beings of course constitute a far more variable environment than laboratory hardware, and one on which S can exercise greater influence. However, since most of the theory in this area [learning and acquisition of values] is concerned with *the adaptation of S to a relatively constant human environment* (whether it be called culture, social system, or the personalities of the parents), this should not prove a serious stumbling block (Hill, 1952, p. 93, emphasis added).

Design 4 [one of a number of research designs] in the social attitudes realm is so demanding of cooperation on the part of respondents or subjects as to end up with research done only on captive audiences rather than the general citizen of whom one would wish to speak. For such a setting, Design 4 would rate a minus for selection. Yet *for research on teaching our universe of interest is a captive population,* and for this, highly representative Design 4s can be done (Campbell and Stanley, 1963, p. 190, emphasis added).

Many theories of learning assume from the outset that *all* learning is controlled by someone besides the learner. For example, in *The Conditions of Learning* (1965) Gagne does not examine different environments, as one might imagine by the title. On the contrary, all eight kinds of learning he describes, ranging from the simplest kind of sign learning to the most complex problem-solving, assume that the teacher (or experimenter) controls the learning goals and environment. The "conditions" of learning are essentially that simpler forms of learning must precede more complex forms if the more complex forms are to be successfully negotiated. Likewise, McGehee (1967) in an article on learning theory which integrates stimulus-response factors with cognitive (goal-setting-and-achievement) factors makes no distinction among environments. His principles could presumably all be used in situations of external control.

External control of a person leads to dependency by that person on the controller and to conformity to the ends of control, especially as the person values the rewards and is not aware of other sources of satisfaction for his needs. Such control can be internalized within the subject as superego, in Freudian terms, as an introjection, in Gestalt terms, or as an automatic habit, in Deweyan terms. Cultural values can exert the third kind of control by becoming the assumed ground or framework for the person's thought or behavior. He may conform to them and be dependent upon them without even realizing his dependence, being cognitively and emotionally unable to imagine alternatives. He may take the units, standards, and goals of his perceptions or actions as "natural," "necessary," as "reality itself," without recognizing his intentional appropriation of them for himself. In short, the dependency and conformity which result from external control can be unnoticed consequences to the extent that the culture as a whole operates on the basis of external control.

In this respect, too, laboratory experiments on learning tend to operate uniformly within the assumption of external control. Only recently has the underlying effect of the total laboratory environment on the quality of learning been investigated (Argyris, 1968b). In general, however, as Hilgard and Bower (1966) have noted, there has been little study of how subjects come to discriminate stimuli or how they go about setting their own goals. Instead, experimental stimuli are chosen on the basis of being clearly discriminable to subjects, given their cultural background, and the laboratory surroundings and interactions also accord with what will seem "natural" to subjects. "In the human laboratory, we tend to use stimulus variations that the culture has trained our subjects to notice and label. . . . The coding response is presumably conditioned to those background or situational cues which prevail despite changes in the proximal stimulus from trial to trial" (Hilgard and Bower, 1966, p. 530).

Although researchers may be correct in believing that laboratory control of subjects is analogous to social control of students in school (a belief less viable in times of turmoil and change such as the present), there are nevertheless two serious costs endemic to this kind of learning. One is that learners tend, unaware, to become adapted to and dependent upon a given environment and unable to orient themselves (to learn) under conditions when the environment is ambiguous or changing. The other is that there is no way of determining whether external conditioning is the *best* way to learn: its proponents claim it is the only way, and, since it is basically congruent with attempted forms of social control through education, the circle is closed, the argument over, before the issue has been joined. Recently, however, several fundamental theoretical attacks have been launched upon the entire stimulus-response perspective (Merleau-Ponty, 1963; Miller, Galanter, and Pribram, 1960). Basically, these attacks hold that *stimuli* are intentionally discriminated by persons (one may recall James's dictum, "My experience is what I choose to attend to") and consequently are theoretically indistinguishable from *responses* by those persons. From this perspective the whole stimulus-response framework becomes a somewhat confused description of what happens in the special situation in which educator and learner agree (1) what to classify as stimuli, (2) that the educator controls the learner, and (3) that the learner will not consciously appropriate his control over his attention (the agreements themselves necessarily remain covert). Apparently this special learning situation is empirically the common one. And since its basic processes are covert precisely to itself, they are, not surprisingly, presented in a confused way by those who regard it as the only possible learning situation.

What we have here is essentially another description of the mystery-mastery process.

PROBLEM-SOLVING

The second kind of learning is described by cognitive theories although, like the behaviorists, many cognitive theorists have not clearly described the fundamental environmental conditions of learning. As the name suggests, cognitive models of learning have focused on intraorganismic variables that are hypothesized to affect learning. In some cases, particular emphasis has been placed on the learner's setting of his own goals and/or on the effect of a collaborative, interdependent environment that facilitates setting one's own goals (Argyris, 1967; Dewey, 1922; Schroder and Harvey, 1963). It has been found that *whether* an individual sets a goal for himself and *what* he sets as his goal can greatly influence his learning and achievement (Locke, Cartledge, and Koeppel, 1968; McGehee, 1967). This factor is not apparent in "conditioning" experiments because of the covert agreements between the subject (if he is human) and the experimenter. In such situations the subjects tend to accept temporarily the experimenters' goals for them. Or, in any event, they are given no opportunity within the framework of the experiment to formulate or express any goals they have for themselves.

Since I have already noted the congruence between education as a process of cultural transmission and the controlled experiment as a setting for unilateral inculcation by the experimenter, it follows that social environments in which learners can overtly set and achieve their own goals are empirically rare. So-called T-groups were developed in an attempt to provide such an environment. Their initial emphasis was on studying social norms and creating norms conducive to individual goal-setting (Argyris, 1967; Bradford, Benne, and Gibb, 1964; Schein and Bennis, 1965). Recent research has verified differences in individual behavior, group norms, and cognitive processes depending upon whether a person's training or a group's leadership emphasizes unilateral inculcation or interdependent goal-setting (Argyris, 1969; Schroder and Harvey, 1963).

As noted earlier, unilateral inculcation tends to be associated with conformity to norms of, and dependence upon rewards and direction from, an authority viewed as external to the person who is instructed. The dependence can become an underlying preconscious framework for all of a person's thinking. Under different environmental conditions, the learner can think and behave within other sensory-emotional frameworks than dependence. Counterdependence, competitiveness, collaboration, and situational experimentation are distinct sensory-emotional frameworks, each of which defines the units, processes, boundaries, and aims of relational exchange differently (Harrison, 1965; Shepard, 1965). They will receive further discussion momentarily.

Another characteristic of the dependent framework, also noted earlier, is its lack of appropriation of one's dependence, conformity, and purposive attention. Consequently, to the degree that a person is dependent, he will tend to lack awareness of his sensory-emotional framework; units, processes, boundaries, and aims are all taken for granted as externally determined.

As one moves from dependence to situational experimentation, each sensory-emotional framework involves a greater awareness of itself as framework, and a clearer sense, therefore, of the limitations of thought and behavior within that framework, and an increased feeling of personal control of the framework. But the later frameworks are by no means necessarily developed. Persons, groups, organizations, and societies can remain framed within the dependent mode.

The thesis or initial interpersonal hypothesis of our [dependent-counterdependent] dialectic is "I need what the authority gives me; I cannot get it myself; therefore I must do whatever is necessary to get the authority to give me what I need." . . . There can develop very elaborate cognitive systems around this basic thesis. Indeed, whole lives and organizations and societies are complexly and intricately organized without ever exploring beyond this stage of development (Harrison, 1965, p. 39).

One phenomenon that T groups have always had to deal with is that persons seem to need to *learn how to learn* according to the goal-setting-and-achieving model. This fact in itself indicates the extent to which the general culture generates unappropriated dependency and conformity. Persons must develop new sensory-emotional frameworks for thought in order to become capable of learning through goal-setting-and-achievement. Although members may say they would like the freedom to set their own goals, an environment conducive to this process is so different from the conformity-producing, dependency-oriented environments to which they are accustomed that they tend initially to resist it and the educator's role in it. Consequently, an unlearning process must commonly occur along with the beginnings of this different learning process.

In the transition between external conditioning and collaborative goal-setting, the issue for the learner can perhaps be phrased most generally, "Why am I doing these various tasks? Who and what am I doing them for?" The answers to these questions may take various twists and turns in a person's experience, corresponding to the changes in his sensory-emotional framework. We have already seen the answer of the dependent perspective: "I am doing these tasks for somebody else as he defines them in order to get something I need or want," or, more simply, "I am doing these tasks because that's the way the world is."

In the counterdependent mode the answer might be phrased, "I will *not* do tasks for somebody else. I'll prove my independence by always doing the reverse of what the authority wishes and thus avoiding his influence." Of course, as critics of counterdependent behavior are fond of reminding us, consistent hostility to authority leaves the actor just as much determined by the authority as does consistent obedience. Often, however, a person does not become totally counterdependent, but rather alternates between dependence and counterdependence during early stages of a search for independence. In such cases, counterdependence can be seen as a step closer to independence because it no longer takes for granted that the external standards are necessarily valid.

In the competitive mode the answer becomes, "I'd better do things for myself and myself only because otherwise somebody else will beat me to the good things in life." Here the emotional emphasis switches from the external authority to oneself. In this sense, it is another step closer to independence. At the same time, however, the competitive mode assumes that the basic properties of life—"myself," "somebody else," and "the good things"—are preestablished, limited, and mutually exclusive of one another. The person acting in this mode does not verify these propositions for himself. In fact, if challenged, he will tend to maintain that they are self-evidently true (or, in a slightly subtler argument, that since most persons act as if they were true, they become true for all practical purposes). Such a person remains dependent upon broad cultural definitions for his basic world view.

In the collaborative mode the answer might be, "The good things in life include friendship with others and can be increased by working with others; also, we influence one another's view of what is good in life, so we might as well help each other to be aware and consistent and effective in defining what is good." This kind of answer is different from the previous ones because it provides a framework for *questioning* what is good rather than *assuming* what is good. Consequently, it encourages the questioner to develop a personally valid criterion of what is good for him.

These twists and turns tend to be negotiated in successful T-group settings (Bennis, 1964; Harrison, 1965; Mann, 1966; Mills, 1964, 1965). However, the final framework, which I call situational experimentation, cannot be fully negotiated in a T-group (unless someone takes the role of educator during the early stages, before collaboration has been attained) because it involves an effort to learn through full experiential awareness in all situations, not just in those collaborative groups which share a commitment to learn through setting and achieving people's own goals. Moreover, goal-setting-and-achievement becomes subordinate to learning, in the mode of situational experimentation, rather than learning being a by-product of goal-achievement.

Learning theorists focusing on problem-solving acknowledge only goal-achievement, not learning itself, as a motivating state; for example:

A specific resolve [to learn] needs to be carefully distinguished from motivation to *achieve,* which, as later discussion will show, is of tremendous importance to successful learning. If the student's "motivation to learn" means that he resolves *to be able to do something,* a something that can be achieved as a *result* of learning, then this is positive motivation of a substantial character (Gagne, 1965, p. 209).

LEARNING THROUGH SELF-RECOGNITION

To transcend the achievement motivation one must see one's life as a whole. This whole is the broader context within which specific events of goal-setting-and-achievement occur. But how can one become fully and rightly aware of the meaning, essence, and value of one's life as a whole? Such learning, however it occurs, involves *recognition of what one is* rather than *achievement of some goal* (although a certain kind of achievement may become recognized as that which characterizes one). Self-recognition requires an awareness of oneself which spans all social environments. It is not restricted to apparently collaborative situations, for one's life among others is not thus restricted. To put it another way, insofar as one is *dependent* upon a collaborative social environment for setting and achieving one's own goals, one has yet to achieve full independence.

In the mode of situational experimentation the question "Why am I doing these various tasks?" receives an answer something like "Because of all the reasons I usually give and think about, and no doubt also because of others of which I'm unaware. I wish to be as aware as possible of my living of this, my one and only life, but usually I find myself totally absorbed by whatever task I am working on. In some situations people will help me increase my awareness, but often increased awareness is threatening to others and to me. I wish to investigate my life-process as it manifests itself in all situations, and to understand especially, however it can be understood, my reluctance to investigate it." This answer is circular because it seeks to propel the person beyond mere thought about awareness to full experiential awareness. No longer will the person identify himself and the world through thought within some sensory-emotional framework. Rather, cognition will be recognized as capable of various modes in relation to emotion and sensation, within a wider framework of experiential self-awareness.

The preceding two paragraphs introduce many new terms in

an effort to make qualitative distinctions between kinds of learning, kinds of awareness, and kinds of thinking. The remainder of this chapter will be devoted to explicating these distinctions more carefully and fully, presenting a more complete picture of this third kind of learning—learning through self-recognition.

First, I will explore in somewhat greater depth the question why learning through self-recognition cannot simply be included within learning through goal-setting-and-achievement. It may appear that the basic issue in learning through self-recognition, "Who is it that is setting and achieving these goals?" can be restated in goal-achievement terms, such as, "My goal is to discover who I am." Such a statement would make learning through self-recognition one aspect of learning through goal-setting-and-achievement. True, such a goal would be different from goals that direct me into the external environment. This goal would appear reflexive if diagrammed as an arrow, the head of the arrow circling back upon its tail. Could not this diagram represent a feedback loop whose function is to regulate the relationship between inputs and outputs of a system? Am I not the system which wishes to learn about itself? Cannot the setting and achievement of the goal of discovering who I am be conceived reasonably as the development of such a feedback loop? The answer to all these questions must be no, for each assumes at the outset something about who I am, a something that cannot be examined in the learning process because it forms the framework of the process. Who posits the goal "to discover who I am"? How are my boundaries determined that it is possible from the outset to distinguish "inputs" from "system" from "outputs"?

Looked at another way, goal-setting-and-achievement presumes a process of discrimination (choosing this goal, not that) and a process of time (from goal-setting to goal-achievement). However correct and serviceable these presumptions may be in daily life, learning through self-recognition must come to include them as known rather than as assumed. But, you may reply, learning through self-recognition is itself some kind of process, and all processes occur within some framework which in bounding the process is not completely accessible to it, as the river bank is inaccessible to the water except as boundary, or as the axiology of a logical system is inaccessible to its propositions and proofs except as boundary. Skipping down a level, you continue, the process of a conversation is likewise inaccessible to its content (when people speak of "talking about process," they mean talking about *past* process, since even the previous comment is now a past process; there is always an unspeakable present process bounding the present content). Analogously, in psychological terms, Polanyi has pointed out that "we cannot look at our standards in the process of using them, for we cannot attend focally to elements that are used subsidiarily for the purpose of shaping the present focus of our attention" (Polanyi, 1958, p. 183). The various terms may be confusing, but the different examples do seem to have in common a reference to two "levels" of a given event, whether they be called water and stream bed, theorem and axiom, content and process of a conversation, or focal and subsidiary attention. The two levels in each case seem somehow to be of different qualities, and one level acts as a boundary or organizing structure for the other.

To pursue this problem further, we can turn it upside down. So far, we have been attacking it "from the bottom up," that is, from something called theorem to something called axiom, from the focal to the subsidiary, from cognition (goal-setting) to self (who I am). And in each case we find the "higher" inaccessible to the "lower." How about the other way around: is the lower accessible to the higher? What "accessible" means is suggested by the concept of the higher providing the organizing structure for the lower. MacIntyre (1962) and Merleau-Ponty (1963) have argued that thought causes, reveals the structure of, or makes intelligible, physical action. The verb is uncertain. They do not mean "causes" in a forced sequential sense. Rather they mean that thought names, weighs, and selects among a range of behaviors (the units themselves being determined by thought). The correct verb for the relationship between thought and action will transcend the active-passive dichotomy between the subject (initiator) and the object (result) of a forceful causation. The type of causation is closer to Aquinas's differentiation between principal and instrumental causes operating simultaneously. Thought becomes a principal cause in relation to behavior, which becomes an instrumental cause in relation to its intended effects. Thought bounds and interpenetrates behavior, organizes and observes relations within behavior.

Given this relation between the higher and the lower, my proposition is that the self stands in relation to one's thought as one's thought does to one's behavior. Thus, if cognitive goal-setting-and-achievement is a process for organizing or learning about relationships within behavior, learning through self-recognition may act similarly in relation to thought (as well as feeling and sensation).

If this is the case, the term "self-recognition" is, in a way, a paradox. The self can organize or learn about relationships within cognition-emotion-sensation but is itself presumably bounded and interpenetrated by a still higher level. This model seems to accord with D. H. Lawrence's more poetic rendering:

We are only actors, we are never wholly the authors of our deeds or works. . . . Gods, strange gods, come forth from the forest into the clearing of [the] known self, and then go back. . . . Know that you are responsible to the gods inside you and to the men in whom the gods are manifest. Recognize your superiors and your inferiors, according to the gods. This is the root of all order (Lawrence, 1923, pp. 16, 17, 20).

Or, in Maritain's and Melville's words:

The substance of man is obscure to himself. . . . If he knows it, it is formlessly, by feeling it as a kind of propitious and enveloping night. Melville, I think, was aware of that when he observed that "no man can ever feel his own identity aright except his eyes be closed"; as if darkness were indeed the proper element of our essences (Maritain, 1954, p. 82).

Most of us, however, are deaf and blind (in the Biblical sense) to these gods, to this enveloping darkness. We are totally absorbed in our thoughts or the behavior that seems to be required of us, defining ourselves as a more or less distinct ego about which we have some ideas. Jung has described the difficult process of individuation through which some men and women pass in their later life when they attempt to accept their unconscious as well as their heretofore conscious experiencing as a genuine aspect of themselves. That is, these people attempt to recognize their given selves under the cultural encrustations of their egoic self-concepts. He also uses the image of contact with a higher level or upper story:

If life can be lived in such a way that conscious and unconscious demands are accepted as far as possible, the centre of gravity of the total personality shifts its position. . . . The new centre might be called the self (distinguishing it from the ego). . . . If such a transposition succeeds . . . there develops a personality who, so to speak, suffers only in the lower story of himself, but in the upper story . . . is singularly detached from painful as well as from joyful events (Jung, 1962).

So, self-recognition involves recognition of both the conscious and unconscious at the cognitive-emotional-sensory level, the level at which ego operates, from a "higher" level which, again, is not fully visible to itself. The Greek *ek-stasis* meant to stand outside oneself, or in my terms to stand outside one's ego experience, one's total cognitive-emotional-sensory process, observing it from the self level. To attain permanent ecstasy would be to attain the ultimate in lucidity, not, as Webster's dictionary now maintains, to be "beside oneself, crazy." From this perspective, Camus's goal, "to remain lucid in ecstasy," (Camus, 1955) appears almost tautologous rather than unlikely.

Learning through self-recognition does not, however, merely bring one in touch with an additional level of awareness. This learning can bring one closer to the recognition of the very basis of awareness, the basis of the exchange among all "levels" of life. I have already noted that a "higher level" observes, interpenetrates, organizes, learns about relationships within a "lower level." The mysterious action for which I've offered several verbs in the previous sentence can be appropriated by learning through self-recognition because one can begin to compare two occasions of interaction between levels (between the behavioral and the cognitive-emotional-sensory level and between the latter and the self level). Moreover, the full action of the cognitive-emotional-sensory level on the behavioral level is visible from the self level. Finally, all the organizing forces from "below," "above," and within the cognitive-emotional-sensory level become visible.

A full knowledge, a direct experiencing, of the organizing action of consciousness becomes possible. In this sense, the term "self-recognition" is not paradoxical, for it tokens a self-knowledge so grounded, so alive, that further search becomes the equivalent of further life.

These considerations provide, in a somewhat *structural* way, in terms of a logic of life, a basic sense of the relation of the results of learning through self-recognition to personality. But they provide little sense of the *dynamics* of personality, such as learning or motivation, the processes that might lead one to verify this structure within one's own experience. Since this is an expository discussion and the reader tends to "rest" in its/his thought as he reads, the best entry into the actual process of learning through self-recognition may be through distinctions among the qualities of thought characteristic of each of the three kinds of learning described. So long as the reader remains "in" his thought—the second kind of thought shortly to be described—learning through self-recognition will remain a foreign and unknown process.

THREE KINDS OF THOUGHT

The first kind of thought can be associated with learning through external conditioning. The reader will remember that learning through conditioning treats only a subject's behavior. His "inner" cognitive state is considered irrelevant. Likewise, or in parallel, the first kind of thought is altogether out of contact with and irrelevant to one's behavior. Behavior is organized by external pressures in the case of a man working on an assembly line, for example, so thought is unnecessary to his behavior. At least, this is how the assembly-line worker conceives of the situation. Thought is characterized by a flow of fantasies, daydreams, disconnected association, commentaries on external events, memories. Almost everyone has experienced this kind of thought when driving a car along a turnpike on a long trip, or when typing something one has previously handwritten. In these cases, the goal may have been self-set, but continued thought is unnecessary to accomplish the activity. Instead, the mind functions in preconscious, robot fashion to discriminate traffic patterns, words, or new paragraphs, while awareness is absorbed in a flow of associations wholly unrelated to the present activity (Wilson, 1967a). Secretaries and assembly-line workers with whom I have talked report that this kind of thought predominates during their workdays, often volunteering comments like "I'd go crazy if I had to concentrate on the work." My description of this kind of thinking largely corresponds to the Freudian concept of primary-process thinking, which is also characterized by the absence of any negatives, conditionals, or other qualifying conjunctions and by the lack of a sense of past, present, and future temporal relations (Brenner, 1957).

The second kind of thought is a more continuous, more mathematical, linguistic, or logical sequence that is connected to other thought or to behavior. This corresponds to Freud's secondary-process thinking, which is described as "ordinary, conscious thinking as we know it from introspection, that is, primarily verbal and following the usual laws of syntax and logic" (Brenner, 1957). This kind of thought is essentially goal or task oriented and can therefore be associated with learning through goal-setting-and-achieving.

The third kind of thought is a window to the nonconceptual and the transconceptual. But "window" is too passive an image, for this third kind of thought turns toward and focuses upon emotional and sensory experience. It is simply the appropriated intentional attention. Its appropriation requires a new, experiential language that mediates among the languages of our senses and our emotions and our verbal language—the language of the second kind of thought. This language is eidic, intuitive, directly experiential, fundamentally conscious—not merely a formal metalanguage, which careful logical analysis has shown to be necessary to logic itself, semantics, and action (Watzlawick, Beavin, and Jackson, 1967). That is, one cannot program oneself with a metalanguage in the same arbitrary way as one can a computer. The metalanguage already sounds within us if we but develop the ears to hear it. Maritain speaks of a "spiritual pre-conscious" in which the key to this metalanguage is to be found:

There is still for the intellect another kind of life, which makes use of other resources and another reserve of vitality, and which is free, I mean free from the engendering of abstract concepts and ideas, free from the workings of rational knowledge and the disciplines of logical thought, free from the human actions to regulate and the human life to guide, and free from the laws of objective reality as to be known and acknowledged by science and discursive reason. But as it appears, at least in certain privileged or ill-fated people, this freedom is not freedom at random, this free life of the intellect is also cognitive and productive, it obeys an inner law of expansion and generosity, which carries it along toward the manifestation of the creativity of the spirit; and it is shaped and quickened by creative intuition (Maritain, 1954, p. 79).

In a further description of this kind of thought, Maritain evokes qualities introduced earlier in this chapter:

Man perceives himself only through a repercussion of his knowledge of the world of things. . . . The poet knows himself only on the condition that things resound in him, and that in him, at a single awakening, they and he come forth together out of sleep. In other words, the primary requirement of poetry, which is the obscure knowing, by the poet, of his own subjectivity, is inseparable from, is one with another requirement—the grasping, by the poet, of the objective reality of the outer and inner world: not by means of concepts and conceptual knowledge, but by means of an obscure knowledge which I shall describe in a moment as knowledge through affective union (p. 83).

The patterns of the language of the second kind of thought must be subtly and cunningly violated, as in poetry, to be opened to sensation and emotion and to the living order that informs both them and cognition. The poet must mold this language from a stance beyond it, an order above it and within it, if it is to reveal the thread of immediate experience.

An awareness limited to the second kind of thought alone is opaque to emotion or sensation. When a feeling or sensation becomes strong enough to intrude upon one's awareness, it tends to displace thought altogether for the moment. (I might add here that some persons tend to be absorbed ordinarily in their feeling or sensation rather than their thought, but the quality of awareness is similar.) The second kind of thought cannot know sensation and feeling except from the outside. It cannot interpenetrate them. At best, it can reflect about them. The extent to which our verbal training in this culture limits our awareness to the second kind of thought and consequently distances us from a knowledge of emotional experience is provocatively suggested by a study which has found that therapists' ability to be accurately empathetic with clients, to know, relive, and express their clients' feelings, is negatively related to the therapists' verbal ability as measured by a standard test (Bergin and Solomon, 1967).

Another study has distinguished between digital, logical thought and analogical, experiential thought in a way that generally corresponds to my distinction between the second and third kinds of thought, except that analogical thought (like the analogue computer) is viewed as the more primitive of the two (Watzlawick, Beavin, and Jackson, 1967). The model of learning presented here, on the contrary, views analogical thought as more complex (in touch with more aspects and levels of reality) and more conscious than logical thought; a person unlike a computer, is not preprogrammed with parameters and primary functions that infallibly guide his activities. He may be preprogrammed in some sense, or he may be an aspect of a developing universal program, but in either case he must do his own work of linking his behavior to his life-parameters, of consciously identifying and translating the higher order that informs him into behavior that accurately expresses it.

Even in realms considered to be purely cognitive, the need for the third kind of thought in interplay with the second kind can be seen. This is especially obvious in the case of discoveries, be they inventions or new theories. In invention, straightforward thought which proceeds circularly on one level within a given set of assumptions tends to be ineffective, since the given assumptions are often precisely the barrier to the invention of the required product. "Synectics," a procedure to encourage inventive thought, emphasizes the hindering effect of verbal thought, and instead trains people to think analogically (Gordon, 1961). Similarly, in the development of scientific theory, a number of writers have emphasized the need to break through purely conceptual thought to an intuitive level which reorganizes previous knowledge in a more satisfactory and inclusive way (Koestler, 1964; Murphy, 1958). Like Maritain, they allude to aspects of this kind of thinking that are alien to progressive, goal-oriented thought —for example, a passive receptivity to an order within things and experiences rather than an imposition of order upon them; also, the role of sudden insight or inspiration rather than empirical induction or logical deduction.

This third kind of thought provides an exit from the paradox of conceptualization. Kaplan's formulation of this paradox is that "the proper concepts are needed to formulate a good theory, but we need a good theory to arrive at the proper concepts" (1964, p. 53). Haley (1967) formulates it as "What we know about human beings depends upon our *method* of examining them, and our method of examination depends upon what we think human beings are" (p. 139). The paradox arises from thought caught within itself, unable to gain access to its own assumptions, axioms, and boundaries, disconnected from experiential awareness. All these conditions tend to characterize the second kind of thought when learning through self-recognition is absent.

We search in the second kind of thought for "the right way of looking at things," "the right way of thinking about things," all the while looking and thinking in a variety of attentional modes (or being distracted to other matters) without appropriating the action of our looking and thinking. We consider thought to be passive in relation to action; we are looking for the total picture —the still life that is perfectly "objective." Artists in this century have announced through their painting that a still life seen from only one perspective is a fiction, but we have not incorporated this insight into our daily thought.

Experiential awareness of the intentional quality of one's attention would immediately convince one (though one would forget it upon reimmersion in the second kind of thought) that unity, lucidity, and objectivity are not to be found in some abstraction, some theory, some method, but rather in one's one and only life in the world. Each abstraction, method, or theory is suited to some attentional perspective but distorts phenomena if "held" and applied to other attentional perspectives. The constants of the action of evolving consciousness are not abstractable from experiential awareness itself. There is nothing to hold onto, yet there is order; but the belief that order is "that which can be held onto" can obscure one's view of living order; thus the struggle.

**SOME DISCIPLINES LEADING TO
SELF-RECOGNITION**

The model of learning through self-recognition rests uncomfortably in one's cognitive awareness for the reasons just discussed. Is it the right framework, we ask? It can never be the right framework in the abstract. It itches to be experientially verified. At the outset, only its itchiness, its action towards experiential awareness, suggests its rightness for one. Only the effort of learning through self-recognition can continue the verifying process. What are the disciplines through which this learning, this verification, can occur? Again, a full exposition of methodology is impossible at the outset, since the very terms will require matching with experience. The scope and quality of the problems encountered in connecting this theory to personal experience will be illustrated in chapter 5, when a group of people attempt to do just that. Some initial comments on method are, however, offered below.

A basic mode of learning through self-recognition is simple self-observation. Unfortunately self-observation is made difficult by the tendency of the second kind of thought to absorb our attention entirely. Self-observation involves taking a picture of one's inner state at a given moment, not introspective, cognitive reflection. This "picture" is not an imaginative picture, just as the "language" of the third kind of thought is not verbal language. The difference between self-observation and introspection (which, I agree with Hebb [1969], is actually hallucination rather than vision) must be discovered through continued attempts at self-observation, with some guide to help one to make the distinction at the outset. If we try out self-observation, we quickly begin to encounter major facts about our ordinary cognitive-sensory-emotional states: we see how infrequently we observe ourselves, how much resistance our cognitive awareness puts up, how blatant, empty, or dull we often seem within, how disconnected our thoughts about ourselves are from this "dull" actuality, how difficult it is to observe ourselves while thinking or acting, how quickly self-observation ceases and passes into a combination of pictorial and verbal associations (perhaps about what was so fleetingly observed). In short, we begin to see many things that we will tend to evaluate as negative initially (when we pass into associating and imagining about what we see), compared to our more positive self-concepts that tend to stress our unity, awareness, authenticity, and ability to make good, free choices (see chapter 1, p. 25 ff).

Through continued attempts at self-observation, we begin to see increasingly that at any moment we are in touch with only a very limited number of our thoughts, feelings, and movements, and that most of the time our awareness is immersed in one or at most two of these. The rest never even appear as possibilities, are not even remembered, until another moment, situation, or person provokes them. But we ordinarily think and act as though we were altogether present each moment. We think, "*I* am here; what shall *I* do? *I* will do such-and-such." This tendency can be seen in regard to small plans or promises. I decide to wake myself early tomorrow morning by the alarm clock; I really wish to work. When the alarm clock rings, I turn it off and return to sleep because I wish to sleep. Last night's I should have known better than to think I would get up. But last night's I knew only that it really would get up if the alarm clock awakened it, because it really wished to work.

A second mode of learning through self-recognition is to investigate incongruencies, resistances, and distortions in transformations among levels (self, cognitive-emotional-sensory, and behavior). For example, I intend to work now, but when I come to myself I realize I have been daydreaming. Somehow, I "forgot" my intent. But if it was a self-intention, then I became disconnected from the self level of awareness when I "forgot." Identified with the daydream, I am a different I than at the previous moment. And what is the second shift in "I," the "coming to myself" "out of" the daydream? Is it possible to see, feel, taste these differences? Or, perhaps the "intent" was no self-intent in the first place, but merely a disconnected cognitive association formulated as a goal. Then the disjunction between intent and daydream suggests a disjunction in cognitive structure, or a lack of integration between linguistic awareness and the phenomenon which prompted the association, or perhaps the interference of the emotions. Do I really want to work? Could I develop a taste for an intentional impulse within me that I could trust more than the cognitive associations? When I do follow through on things, what intentional impulse am I trusting? Or, still another line of investigation from this experience of disjunction, what is the process of coming to myself? Is there a moment when, as the phrase suggests, I remember my total self? These questions are possible experiential questions, possible intentions in learning through self-recognition. How long can I pursue such questions before becoming caught up in a daydream? How strong, clear, and centered is their intentionality? The strength of my inner self-questioning in this experiential manner—this third kind of thought —rather than in a purely cognitive, introspective manner can itself be a primary datum for the extent of my contact with centered intentionality. But what I know irreducibly as a dilemma at the outset of such questioning is the disjunction in me and the intention or lack of intention to investigate it. I experience the passivity inherent in ordinary thought (whether it be the first or second kind of thought) and its resistance to active questioning. I can begin to experience questioning as an active illumination of processes—as the functioning of appropriated intentional attention—rather than as an intellective verbalization.

A third mode of learning through self-recognition is to block off the cognitive-emotional-sensory processes or cease to attend to them waiting for the appearance of centered intent and awareness. What "block off," "cease to attend," "waiting," and "centered intent" mean is directly in question. I do what I think this means, attempting to observe myself as I do so. The attempt to resist the "temptations" to reidentify with cognitive-emotional-sensory contents leads either to contact with a finer attention that can interpenetrate these contents without being absorbed by them, or to reabsorption.

A fourth mode is to try to develop a given thought, feeling, or sensation "in a straight line," rather than diverted by other associations or by situational pressures. This discipline, if successful, inevitably leads one into touch with the total cognitive-emotional-sensory structure and breaks the identification with the single element. Examples of this process occur in cross-country running, mathematical discovery, and certain forms of psychotherapy (starting from sensory, cognitive, and emotional elements, respectively). If one begins any of these processes in habitual rhythms, one quickly nears exhaustion, frustration, or fruitless cycling (respectively) because habit is inadequate for the present test. One must remember, establish contact with, and be reorganized by one's centered intentions, by conscious thought-feeling-sensation dealing directly with present experience, in order to break through the inadequate chrysalis of habit to new learning.

A fifth mode of learning through self-recognition can be to "play off" the conflict between two elements of the cognitive-emotional-sensory structure without iduntifying with either. In this case, "waiting" for intentional resolution may be easier than the "waiting" initiated by one element as described above.

A sixth mode is to observe and distinguish among different qualities of attention, depending upon whether one is identified totally with a single level, or in contact with two levels at the initiative of one or the other, or with the three levels of self, cognitive-emotional-sensory structure, and behavior.

A seventh mode of learning would be to identify the presence or absence of the intentional level in one's awareness according to the motivating force of the goal one sets oneself. This process uses the goal-setting-and-achievement model of learning as a passive input, with observation of how the goal is set (externally? cognitively? intentionally?) as the active learning process. This mode of learning was implicit in the first two examples, since the different I's encountered are distinguished in part by the presence or absence of intentional awareness.

These descriptions of modes of learning may help the reader to make them operational, i.e., to attempt them in relation to his own experience. Based on the earlier theoretical discussion, they are not very surprising, and in fact have a circular quality—

"Intention is intention; you will recognize it when you see it."
This circularity derives from the linguistic problem inherent in
translating learning through self-recognition into the second kind
of thought. The translation is merely verbal, yet learning
through self-recognition is consciously experiential. No one can
supply another person with self-recognition. Each must appropriate his self at his own initiative. One's self is the fount of one's
initiative. Learning through self-recognition is indissolubly tied
to the development or realization of the organizing motivation of
one's self: centered internal motivation (the self-actualization mo-
tive referred to by Goldstein [1939], Maslow [1954], and Rogers [1963]; not the lower, partial, cognitive-emotional-sensory
drives).

Also, this third kind of learning is indissolubly connected to
full personal growth. It represents the reconciliation of mind and
body, of the psychological, the biological, and the cosmic. Some
theorists have asserted that learning and maturation are mutually
exclusive processes, but this assertion is based on a view of
growth as purely biological and genetic. This book represents
conscious self-recognition as biologically possible but also as, of
necessity, voluntarily, individually developed. The individual
can be the growing tip of the universal evolution of consciousness. These are high-sounding words; whether they are meaningful must be left to individual verification.

Maslow (1968) speaks of learning through self-recognition as
introspective biology and biological phenomenology, "implying
that one of the necessary methods in the search for identity, the
search for self, the search for spontaneity and for naturalness, is a
matter of closing your eyes, cutting down the noise, turning off
the thoughts, putting away all busyness, just relaxing in a kind
of Taoistic and receptive fashion." Such a meditative posture
may at first be a literal, behavioral necessity and later a cognitive-emotional-sensory possibility in the midst of outer noise and
turmoil. (It corresponds closely to the third mode of learning
through self-recognition.)

From everything that this chapter has proposed and exposed,
we would expect the motivation to learn through self-recognition
to be less recognized the less one appropriates one's self level,

one's intentional attention. Thus, paradoxically, at the outset when there would appear to be the most learning to do, there is the least motivation to do it. This paradox results from immersion in the second kind of thought. In fact, experientially, one is least in touch with one's experience at the outset and therefore has least material for learning. Moreover, internal motivation derives from experience of lack of integration, an experience we shield ourselves from in the second kind of thought. Consequently, to argue that initial lack of internal motivation to learn is reason to discount internal motivation in strategies for motivating learning is to discount the very possibility of learning through self-recognition—as the following learning theorist does, no doubt without awareness of this consequence:

Some discussions of the problems of motivation speak of "motivation to learn" as if this were a specific kind of resolve by means of which the student could say to himself, "I must learn this," and learning would then follow. But if there is this kind of specific motivation, it does not appear to be very effective. A number of studies have shown that under many circumstances learning occurs about as well when such resolve is absent as when it is present: this has been the general finding in investigations of "incidental learning" (Gagne, 1965, p. 209).

In conclusion, the reader may note that although learning through self-recognition has been introduced in this chapter as one of three factors in a general learning theory, it can also be conceived as the gateway to a satisfactory unitary model of learning, the model explicated in chapter 1. In terms of learning through goal-setting-and-achievement, learning through self-recognition is necessary for setting one's own goals, for it informs and interrelates them in the context of one's one and only life in the world. In terms of stimulus-response learning, learning through self-recognition is necessary to reveal the function of the learner as discriminator and organizer of both his responses *and the stimuli* to which he responds.

To return to the language of the first chapter, learning through self-recognition is the kind of learning necessary for a nonconscious person to become conscious. And this is not merely one among many kinds of learning, for consciousness is a condition for all genuine learning.

Chapter Three

SCIENCE AS EXPERIENTIAL LEARNING

The discussion in chapter 1 of problems surrounding the unambiguous definition of feedback, or information, has implications not only for human learning but also for accurate scientific knowledge, especially when that knowledge is achieved by human beings studying human beings, as in the social sciences. For science is concerned with developing unambiguous, shared information.

In particular, the contingency of unambiguous feedback upon the conscious, autonomous purpose of a human system, as shown in chapter 1, suggests that science is not a neutral, value-free process for accumulating nonpersonal facts that will be instrumental to whatever ends they are applied. Rather, science must be viewed, from the systems perspective, as itself a valued action-project chosen by the scientist and dependent for its accuracy upon his development of contact with consciousness and his resultant sensitivity to his own and others' structuring of the world.

Let us approach this proposition more carefully, however, turning first to a brief characterization of contemporary science and then to a fuller characterization of the systems model of science.

THE FRAMEWORK OF CONTEMPORARY SCIENCE

A prominent learning theorist relates knowledge to action-values as follows: "Knowledge . . . is *instrumental to values. . . .*

The possession of certain bodies of knowledge does not in itself predispose one to either decency or its opposite" (Bruner, 1966, p. 204). Thus knowledge is viewed as neutral and passive in relation to action; yet "instruction in the values of a society or in the values of a profession or group or family is based upon the *acceptance and/or rejection of axiomatic or unprovable propositions about preference*" (ibid.). Taken together, these propositions hold, on the one hand, that knowledge is divorced from action and from valuation and, on the other hand, that knowledge is rational while action-values are somehow irrational or ungrounded (unprovable). If the latter is true, then the action of gathering rigorous knowledge—science as a profession—is not itself a rational enterprise but is based rather on unprovable preference.

This perspective on knowledge and action seems to accord with Kuhn's (1962) description of the process of ordinary scientific inquiry as occurring within the bounds of a paradigm, a set of axioms, that remains unexamined by the science. The limiting paradigm is internalized by young scientists during their professional education, and their subsequent research becomes "a strenuous and devoted attempt to force nature into the conceptual boxes supplied by professional education" (p. 5). The resulting knowledge will be rational within the limits of the paradigm or axioms, but the paradigm itself will remain ungrounded.

In this description the mysterious, unexamined axioms seem to be associated with an effort at conceptual mastery over nature. That conceptual mastery of nature is the object of contemporary science is suggested by von Weizsacker in describing atomic physics: "In atomic physics, matter is defined by its possible reactions to human experiments, and by the mathematical—that is, intellectual—laws it obeys. We are defining matter as the possible object of man's manipulation" (1957, p. 71).

Science in its present formulation thus appears to be an example of the mystery-mastery process described in chapter 1 (in fact, D. Bakan [1967], from whom I have taken the term mystery-mastery, uses it to describe science). Of the three levels which affect contemporary science (the axiomatic, the conceptual, and the empirical), science examines only two—the conceptual and the empirical. Of course, the very term "axiomatic" encourages lack of rigorous examination when we take it to mean "assumptions taken for granted." But the original meaning of axiom is "self-evident truth," and it is conscious intuition which illuminates self-evident truths when we learn to discriminate it (Husserl, 1962; Jung, 1964). As we saw in the cognitive dissonance experiments in chapter 1, when a scientist's theory is out of contact with his intuition, his theoretical extrapolations from his empirical data will tend to be distorted (a danger that Kubie [1960] sees as general for scientific theory and of which I will provide further examples).

The foregoing characterization of contemporary science suggests that it is not so much the particular scientific paradigm now ascendant that is challenged by the three-level systems model presented in chapter 1, but rather the whole concept of a science based on unexamined paradigms, out of contact with conscious intuition, and operating in the mystery-mastery mode.

AXIOMS OF A NEW MODEL OF SCIENCE

Let us now portray more fully the systems model of science. Having introduced the model in chapter 1, I will continue with a series of axioms about science that are inherent in the model of multilevel experiencing.

Axiom one: Science is an action-project requiring the development of consciousness by individual scientists for success and thus if truly pursued, is in conflict with the mystery-mastery process.

To accord with this perspective, scientific knowledge would be introduced to the nonconscious apprentice scientist in a manner elucidating the interrelation of increasing knowledge about the world out there and increasingly accurate self-awareness (requiring contact with consciousness and the ability to translate its intuitions into analogical thoughts). An impressionistic measure of how distant contemporary science is from this model of science is how unclear this interrelation is in most disciplines and methodologies. The succeeding axioms describe further implications of this concept of science.

Axiom two: There is no such thing as an empirical fact apart from a structural (theoretical) organization which defines it as such.

This proposition derives from the view that analogous structures in system and environment are required for information to be defined as such and transferred (see chapter 1). It shows that the project of verifying theories through their ability to predict empirical facts is partial at best, since theory (and, more generally, the whole way the scientist structures his studies) ultimately defines the facts. Empirical testing may be able to eliminate incoherent theories but cannot alone verify the perspectives of those which are predictive (e.g., cognitive dissonance). Such theories must also be tested against conscious intuitions. Otherwise, the theory, out of touch with consciousness, cannot possibly account for the structural organization of the empirical facts. Conflicts between different predictive theories will be irresolvable under these conditions, as Russell amusingly documents in the clash between behaviorist and Gestalt learning theories:

One may say broadly that all the animals that have been carefully observed have behaved so as to confirm the philosophy in which the observer believed before his observations began. Nay, more, they have all displayed the national characteristics of the observer. Animals studied by Americans rush about frantically, with an incredible display of hustle and pep, and at last achieve the desired result by chance. Animals observed by Germans sit still and think, and at last evolve the situation out of their inner consciousness. . . . I observe, however, that the type of problem which a man naturally sets to an animal depends upon his own philosophy, and that this probably accounts for the differences in the results (1927, pp. 32–33).

Axiom three: Scientific information is not a passive, neutral phenomenon that is instrumental to any kind of action, but rather directly derives from and sustains a given action-orientation.

This proposition derives from the function of information in orienting a system's operations in the environment, requiring a concomitant sense of conscious purpose and behavioral goal on the part of the system. A number of other writers, not using the systems model, have regarded knowledge as fundamentally for action (MacMurray, 1953; Polanyi, 1958). The validity of any supposed piece of scientific information depends upon its being an authentic transformation of a conscious purpose through a theory. From this perspective the validity of all current scientific facts is highly questionable, since their properties as transformations of conscious purposes are not only not specified but actually denied (e.g., Bruner, as quoted).

Axiom four: Knowledge cannot characterize self and world separately, but rather characterizes self in relation to world.

This proposition follows from the second and third because knowledge is defined by the analogy between system and environmental structures and because a system itself is defined in part by its boundary and exchange with the environment. The proposition must be recognized not merely as a formal one to be taken into account in theoretical models of knowledge, but also as an existential one whenever a person is engaged in studying something or attempting to relate what he has learned to others. Because of its personal quality, knowledge must be formulated so as to adhere to the conditions of enhancing, unambiguous feedback developed in chapter 1 and so as to disclose the relationship between investigator and investigated.

Axiom five: The distinction between the inner, subjective world and the outer, objective world is relative, at most. It holds at the bodily (behavioral) level. One's conscious and structural levels, however, are not integumented; rather, they interpenetrate behavioral-level boundaries (e.g., thoughts interpenetrate bodies).

This proposition derives from my particular formulation of the interrelation of systems levels (chapter 1). The concept of interpenetration of levels (suggested in such works as Fink, 1966; Ouspensky, 1949; White, 1940; Yogananda, 1968) is not familiar to social science, which, with its heavy emphasis on empirical measurement, has paid little attention to the qualitative difference between thought and behavior, not to mention the difference between consciousness and thought. However, some such concept is needed to begin to account systematically for what has variously been called empathic cognizance (Carson, 1969), intuitive knowledge (Cohn, 1968; Suzuki, 1955), knowledge by "indwelling" (Polanyi, 1958), recognition of I through Thou (Buber, 1965), extrasensory perception (Rhine, 1947; Jung, 1961), or precognition (Priestley, 1964). All of these terms signify a type of knowledge that exceeds behavioral cues and hence is regarded with suspicion by many behavioral scientists. But, as Northrop has argued (1959, p. 126), even the most rigorously controlled physical experiment involves this kind of knowledge, since its formulation is guided by concepts which, by virtue of being concepts, are not empirical operations but rather defined by their relation to other concepts, and are crucial to the conclusions scientists draw from their empirical data (see also Blalock and Blalock, 1968).

Northrop and Blalock and Blalock conclude that there is, in the nature of things, an inevitable gap between concept and datum. The systems model adds that there is also an interaction between the two (and all) levels—the tracing of which would reveal the organizing dynamics of the universe. The difference between concept and datum appears to be a bothersome gap because the hypothetico-deductive model used by contemporary science cannot gain access to the dynamics of interlevel transformations. The hypothetico-deductive model involves focusing from theory (and other aspects of a study's structure that usually remain implicit) to datum (behavioral level) without reference to intuitive consciousness. The datum is the object of attention for the nonconscious scientist and his structural organization shapes the datum subsidiarily, distinguishing it from the ground or field. The interaction between the structural and behavioral levels cannot be appropriated at those two levels because "we cannot look at our standards in the process of using them, for we cannot attend focally to elements that are used subsidiarily for the purpose of shaping the present focus" (Polanyi, 1958, p. 183). Consequently, the world is viewed as out there at the end of one's perceptual focus, as accessible only on the behavioral level.

The implicit organizing work of the structural, subsidiary attention is represented, partially at most, through theory. And the conscious intuition or intentional awareness, which, being a different kind of sight from focal attention, can interpenetrate the levels of structure and behavior and thus see their interaction, is left out of account altogether. As a result, the nonconscious scientist overlooks and does not report such intuitive facts as the interaction between his structural and behavioral levels, or his interaction at the behavioral level with what he sees (Argyris, 1967; Friedman, 1967; Rosenthal, 1966), or his and his subjects' mutual interpenetration by language, in the case of social science (Langer, 1967).

Consciousness that is impartially interpenetrating different men is their only basis for common, objective knowledge. Their bodies and behaviors are bound to be different, and men's structures will to some extent reflect these behavioral differences in their organization. Hence, structurally, others' behavior will be at least to some extent alien to one (that is, the other person's behavior will to some extent be incomprehensible, irrational, or distorted by one's own, different way of structuring behavior). Persons can therefore be genuinely and fully related only through conscious appropriation of their own and one another's interlevel dynamics that result in particular behaviors. Permanently conscious persons would agree about the objective meaning of one another's behavior, for consciousness is not committed to or biased by a given person's particular structure, but rather impartially interpenetrates his and others' structures and behaviors.

Paradoxically, from the point of view of our juxtaposition of the public and private realms of our lives, consciousness is simultaneously necessary for personal autonomy and common among persons. Its presence is thus crucial at one and the same time for attaining objectivity, intersubjectivity, and subjectivity. These three modes are not hostile but complementary. The supposed objectivity which the hypothetico-deductive model of science opposes to supposed subjectivity finds no epistemological or ontological grounding, since it takes the world of appearances for granted (Husserl, 1962), takes it as the only level of reality (limiting reality, in Heidegger's terms, to the ontic level), and does not account for the scientist's subjective commitment to the scientific project of objectivity (Polanyi, 1958).

> *Axiom six: Abstractions at the level of thought cannot encompass human activity because thought, feeling, and sensation together organize activity at the behavioral level, and their organization, in turn, is accessible only to a higher level of organization, that is, to consciousness.*

This proposition derives from the analysis in chapter 1 of the ineffectiveness of attempts by thought alone to create accurate images of oneself and the world. It has also been foreshadowed by the elaboration of the fifth axiom. But in focusing on the capacity of thought for reflecting reality, the sixth axiom permits us to identify a point at which Western psychologists and philosophers have bulwarked the hypothetico-deductive model of science and differed fundamentally from the implications of the model of science here introduced. They have tended to view logical abstraction as a higher stage of thought than immediate intuition. For example, Northrop (1959) has viewed the Eastern emphasis on immediate apprehension by intuition as equivalent to the Western positivist attempt to restrict the whole of reality to the behavioral level. Likewise, as already noted in chapter 2, Watzlawick, Beavin, and Jackson (1967) have viewed intuitive, "analogical" thought as more primitive than abstract, logical, "digital" thought. These perspectives are at variance both with the remarkable inner disciplines that seem to be necessary in Eastern schools to realize immediate consciousness (indicating that it is anything but primitive) and with the model of human systems here presented that suggests that analogical thought is the congruent transformation of conscious intuitions, whereas logic is the internal elaboration of thought. Thus, this model views analogical thought (the third kind of thought described in chapter 2) as requiring a higher level of systems evolution than logical thought (the second kind, in chapter 2).

> *Axiom seven: A primary characteristic of the mutual interaction of systems is their highest level of organization relative to*

one another, and this relativity determines the quality of data available to each regarding the other.

Boulding (1968), Koestler (1945), and Teilhard de Chardin (1959) have already advanced the proposition that different levels of organization characterize different phenomena and are crucial to understanding them. The methods of contact and exchange of information (and the nature of the information) between man and various systems of different levels of organization (e.g. galaxies, animals, molecules) presumably vary and would differentiate fields of inquiry.

This axiom opens the way to clarification of some perplexing epistemological problems in the competition between neurology and depth psychology for primacy in describing what goes on inside a man's brain-mind. Are brain and mind the same thing? How do they intersect? This axiom tells us that the answers to these questions will not be found by concentrating harder on neurological or psychological data, but rather by becoming aware of the effect of the system that perceives on the nature of the data perceived.

This axiom can also serve to dispel the notion that a model such as systems theory represents a single monolithic methodology, a notion that sometimes results from its superimposition upon existing bodies of knowledge in various fields to show that it can organize them more satisfactorily than the preexisting framework. This kind of superimposition is possible precisely because systems theory is really a meta-theory, a model, rather than a logical theory. Its axioms initially concern the intuitive unity of knowledge, but as they are elaborated they begin to point to different fields and methodologies, as this axiom does.

Having characterized the contemporary paradigm of science and the systems model of science, I shall now turn to a more specific discussion of their differences with respect to the social sciences. The discussion will, in turn, prepare the ground for the application to this study of still more specific guidelines for social scientific inquiry.

HOW CONTEMPORARY SCIENCE CONTRIBUTES
TO SOCIAL IRRATIONALITY

The discussion can begin with an example of the effects of treating social scientific knowledge as though it applied to a world out there that was essentially unrelated to the observer. Whenever knowledge is presented in this way, its accuracy about whatever it characterizes "out there in the world" only serves to contribute to the actor's blindness to the ways in which his own action also manifests the very problem he is setting about correcting out there. For example, Ichheiser (1968) has suggested that such social phenomena as stereotypes, prejudices, ideologies, and aggression result not only from projection, whereby we see and condemn in others what is actually in ourselves and not in them, but also from what he calls the "mote-beam mechanism," whereby what we see in others is actually valid but we overlook that it also exists concomitantly in ourselves. The problem is always felt to be out there, and more accurate, more scientific analysis of the world out there serves increasingly to confirm for the person who would act on this knowledge that the problem is indeed (wholly) out there. What the mote-beam mechanism protects the scientist (and others who use the knowledge) from seeing, in terms of the theory I have advanced, is the fact of his own nonconscious and therefore incomplete state (despite his knowledge) and its contribution to social irrationality.

One consequence of the underlying but false commonsense assumption that knowledge is about a world "out there" is that all action to correct social irrationality, based on the knowledge which is in turn based on these assumptions, *must* be ineffective. It will always be directed away from oneself and externalized. Technology—the essence of that which is directed away from oneself and externalized—thus becomes a prime instrument in the combat against social irrationality in the modern, scientific state. And, in keeping with his view of his instruments and methods as value-free and neutral, the scientist often proclaims technology to be value-free (McDermott, 1969), thus consistently obscuring its human function of concealing our nonconsciousness, which is in fact the source of social irrationality.

A more restricted example of current scientific thought will also show how its definition of rational social action actually feeds social irrationality. Bartos (1967) supposes that a piece of research, known to a negotiator, shows that socially mature negotiators will tend to make more concessions than immature negotiators. The negotiator also discovers that he will be facing another socially mature negotiator in an upcoming negotiation. He concludes that he will get a better bargain for his client in this case by *not* making concessions. If the other negotiator is also aware of this research and adopts the same strategy, several results follow: (1) it will no longer be empirically true that these socially mature negotiators make more concessions than immature negotiators; (2) both of their strategies will fail to yield the expected results; and (3) neither one is likely to end up with a better bargain for his client. This possible series of events seems to indicate that the application of scientific knowledge to action is directly dysfunctional and increases the irrationality of the resulting behavior.

Let us examine more carefully why this is the case. Bartos uses this hypothetical situation to argue that empirical knowledge based on descriptive theory indicates *constraints on persons' choices,* but not *criteria for making better choices.* Instead, normative theory, such as games theory, is offered as an analysis of rational social solutions in conflict situations. According to the scientific paradigm I have outlined, however, this distinction between descriptive and normative knowledge does not hold up because all knowledge is aimed toward increasing the probability of effective systems action. Let us return to the hypothetical example and to games theory to see why both their definitions of "rational" lead to irrational action.

We find that the negotiators' action-decisions in the hypothetical situation included characteristics not directly determined by the scientific knowledge, but nevertheless implied by omission. Each negotiator decided to *exploit the other* with his knowledge, rather than to *understand himself* better. In other words, each decided to view his self-interest as exclusive of the other's rather than as mutually interpenetrating, and each decided to apply the knowledge to the other rather than to himself. (Ironically, the piece of knowledge itself [which results from an actual study] indicates that the more mature negotiator intuitively recognizes that his self-interest *does* interpenetrate the other's.) These aspects of their decisions are to be expected of nonconscious systems, which appropriate their mutual interpenetration incompletely at best and which operate according to the mote-beam mechanism. Thus, the difficulties of the negotiators are created not by the content of the knowledge itself, but rather by the assumptions about its use which its formulation permits and which their cognitive-emotional-sensory structure leads them to make.

According to Bartos, the function of games theory, being a normative theory, is to specify rational action, so we would expect it to avoid the false assumptions inherent in the formulation and application of the descriptive knowledge in the hypothetical case just discussed. When we turn to games theory, however, we find that its basic theoretical structure accords with the social assumptions that led the hypothetical negotiators to attempt to exploit one another. Games theory defines each player's rational self-interest as exclusive of the other's and directs the player toward maximizing his self-interest as currently conceived, rather than toward possibly understanding himself better (Rapaport, 1966). Shepard (1965) has suggested that this concept of rationality is common to many current economic, political, psychological, and sociological theories. Thus, the use of games theory would tend to result in the same difficulties which the hypothetical negotiators experienced, the same social irrationality.

VERIFICATION OF AXIOMS AS A SCIENTIFIC TASK

Games theory can serve further as an example of how a theory derived from the hypothetico-deductive model can obscure the human potential for discovering, changing, or verifying axioms, treating them instead as elements to be taken for granted. I noted (first and fifth axioms) that because scientists do not now form a consciously intentional community, scientific knowledge is neither objectively nor intersubjectively grounded. Yet, by the rules of science as presently defined, current science is objective.

Only as scientists themselves develop consciousness will the meaning of objectivity change for them. Scientists will change their axioms defining social reality and objectivity from those inherent in the mystery-mastery structure to those which are grounded in consciousness. The structural "rules of the game" will thereby change. Such a change cannot occur within the framework of games theory as it is presently formulated. It does not allow for changes in the rules—game structures are defined as fixed and beyond the control of the players. Thus, the axioms upon which each game structure is based are unchallengeable and unverifiable within the context of the game. Again, by omission, a process critical to greater social rationality is discouraged by a current theoretical formulation. (Here I might remind the reader that it is in the study of experiential learning itself that the human potential for recognizing, verifying, and changing the rules of a game is increasingly being recognized, as described in chapter 2, pages 43–45.)

The verification of its axioms thus emerges as a major problem for science, particularly since this aspect of verification has not been attended to in the hypothetico-deductive model. That verification of its axioms is a problem for science has been recognized before, but no model of science has been presented wherein this problem can be formulated as a positive task. For example, Rogers (in Rogers and Skinner, 1956) has attempted a move similar to Bartos' division of normative and descriptive theory, in order to highlight the scientist's freedom of choice and action-orientation. He maintains that

In any scientific endeavor—whether "pure" or applied science—there is a prior subjective choice of the purpose or value which that scientific work is perceived as serving. This subjective value choice which brings the scientific endeavor into being must always lie outside of that endeavor and can never become a part of the science involved in that endeavor (p. 1062).

The difficulty with Rogers's formulation is that we have already shown in the preceding pages that the contemporary scientist begins with certain "prior, subjective," commonsense action-values and perceptual assumptions about the world that influence his theorizing but are false. If these values and assumptions are to be treated as the scientist's purely subjective attributes which "must always lie outside" scientific investigation, then there is no possibility of achieving an objective science. I would agree with Rogers, however, that these values and assumptions are not accessible to scientific method as it is currently formulated, since it divides the scientist in two—separating the subjective from the objective, the actor from the observer—and attends only to his characteristics as an objective observer in a scientific study. By contrast, the systems model I am proposing does not recognize this duality as final.

INTERNAL AND EXTERNAL VALIDITY

Verifying axioms corresponds to what is more commonly called establishing the external validity of a study, except that the term "external" aptly betrays the misapprehension of contemporary science about this process. External validity is conventionally contrasted to internal validity (Campbell and Stanley, 1963). Internal validity derives from designing, executing, and analyzing a study so as to avoid systematic distortion of empirical data. External validity, however, supposedly derives from studying a representative sample of people, so that the results of the study may be generalized across all persons. The trouble is that generalization from a particular sample to the population at large is *impossible in principle*. Thus, no study ever succeeds in achieving "external" validity.

There are two interconnected reasons why it is impossible to establish external validity by the hypothetico-deductive model of science. The first is that, "whereas the problems of internal validity are solvable within the limits of the logic of probability statistics, the problems of external validity are not logically solvable in any neat, conclusive way. Generalization always turns out to involve extrapolation into a realm not represented in one's sample" (Campbell and Stanley, 1963, p. 187). Thus, neither logic nor empirical support of a hypothesis by a given sample ever permits generalization beyond that sample on logical grounds.

The second reason for the inaccessibility of external validity to the hypothetico-deductive model of science is the misconception of what can be generalized. The generalizations that that model attempts are about reality at the behavioral level, at the level of manifestation, as though it were the single and inclusive reality. But the model of science here proposed suggests that empirical realities are unspecifiable apart from logical theories and intuitive models, which are not mere abstractions but represent levels of reality different from the empirical reality. Consequently, the essential, general characteristics of any one level cannot be determined apart from its interactions with the levels above and below it and its organizing characteristics in comparison with other levels. The inevitable contradictions which result from treating different levels of reality as one level have been recognized intellectually in the fields of symbolic logic, linguistics, and human action (Watzlawick, Beavin, and Jackson, 1967).

To put this point another way, I have shown in earlier examples (e.g., the negotiators, and games theory) that the very attempt to formulate theories on the basis of what statistically appears to be the case at the behavioral level, without reference to the intuitively verifiable fact of intentional consciousness, inevitably leads to partial and distorted theories rather than to theories of general validity. Or, in still another formulation, the generalizability of scientific findings depends not only on congruence between the surrounding empirical conditions of the sample tested and the conditions of the sample to which someone hopes to apply the knowledge, but also on the congruence between the intuitive action-aims in both cases and on the authenticity of the transformation between the intuitive and the empirical in the study.

In short, it is the introduction of the intuitive element of knowledge by the paradigm of science formulated here that gives this new paradigm access to the external validity of a study. At the same time, the task of establishing external validity becomes reformulated as the task of verifying intuitive axioms, for valid intuitions are precisely what are applicable to other moments and situations when they occur.

GUIDELINES FOR SCIENTIFIC
SOCIAL INQUIRY

A number of more specific guidelines for the researcher of human events can be constructed on the basis of the seven axioms and the foregoing discussion. As I present the guidelines, I shall also discuss how this work attempts to meet them. Some readers may prefer simply to glance over the underlined guidelines and examine them in greater detail after completing the book. Much of the discussion of how this work seeks to meet the guidelines refers to future chapters and may be more meaningful after the reader is familiar with them.

Guideline one: The researcher must apply all three elements of knowledge to the same action-study.

All three processes operate continuously. To take any of them for granted is necessarily to distort one's observation and conceptualization, to obscure the transformations among the three levels represented by the three terms of knowledge: intuition—consciousness; logic—structure; empirical evidence—behavior. I attempt to realize this guideline here by formulating an intuitive model of learning (chapters 1 and 2), a series of logically distinct theoretical categories (chapter 6), and an empirically reliable and valid behavior-scoring procedure (chapters 7, 8, and 9).

Guideline two: The methods themselves must be recognized as provisional and as mutually modifying insofar as the scientist has not yet achieved permanent consciousness.

The application of this guideline in this book is recognizable in two broad ways. First, the intuitive model of learning presented in chapter 1 is gradually derived by attempting to explain the *empirical* paradox that experiential learning is resisted by human beings even though it appears to be beneficial for them. The emergent model is partly elaborated, partly validated, by *logical* deductions from it, which help to reconcile inconsistencies in existing theories. Thus, the empirical and logical methods serve to modify the intuitive model.

In the second place, the empirical methodology of the scoring procedure (chapter 7) is quite obviously interpenetrated by logical and intuitive judgments by the scorers, based on the theory and model.

Guideline three: A methodology for a specific study is fully defined only when it is related to the researcher's action-aim, his degree of conscious development, and the topic in question.

My action-aim in this book derives from the interaction of three elements, as far as I am aware: (1) my understanding of my life-aim as reconciling man (myself) to his real possibilities, rather than leaving him (me) behind as I (that part of me with which I identify) explore ahead; (2) my sense of my current limits at the structural level that make me a more competent theorizer and observer of events and relations than actor with others; and (3) my behavioral goal of completing a limited Ph.D. dissertation that would be satisfactory to my faculty—the dissertation having formed the basis for this book.

These three elements derive, in turn, from my experiences and my efforts toward consciousness in recent years. Primarily motivated by the impulse to explore, four years ago I attempted to direct a school that encouraged experiential learning, at a time when I myself was searching for a personal sense of aim and limits. Consequently, both my limits and those of the school were unclear, and the resulting anxieties among the participants were often converted into acts framed by the mystery-mastery mode, rather than into acts authentically transforming a search for higher consciousness. As for myself, I found that I tended to use my own sense of inner search and incompleteness, my uncertainty about my limits, and my ability to empathize with others' feelings, as ways of avoiding conflict (retroflecting it on myself, to use a concept of Perls, Hefferline, and Goodman [1965]). Except at times when the school as a whole could agree on some limit, I tended to feel that any particular limit was arbitrary. In practice, this inability to reconcile my own and others' needs for limits with our inability to agree collaboratively on these limits often led to actions remaining incomplete. Lack of completion meant that the actions did not become clearly defined and that new actions (for which limits might be changed) could not be started, both results that diminished experiential learning.

It is still difficult for me to judge to what extent my retroflection of conflict and the incompleteness of many actions was a necessary and appropriate manifestation of the school's and my early strivings to grow down into a structural and behavioral form and to what extent they represented an active resistance to full learning. Whatever the judgment, it seems to me that, in the act of this study, setting, accepting, and working within limits has helped me to gain a more balanced perspective of human learning. (And if this discussion, by its logical mode and lack of mention of behavioral and emotional missteps, makes me appear extraordinarily rational and controlled, let me add that I struggled with bad feelings concerning the issue of working within limits for well over six months. I felt unwilling to accept my faculty's influence and to change my dissertation topic from a focus on my experience with the school.) The formulation and testing of a behavior-scoring procedure, which comprised the initial dissertation plan, was a limited act that reconciled my recent experience with current scholarly practice and emphasized my theoretical and observational abilities. Chapters such as this one, the previous one, and chapter 5 on meditation have slyly sneaked into the final study, despite the original, limited plan.

My past experiences have led not only to the task of this book, but also to its topic and theoretical emphases. For example, my interest in finding an intuitive model to account for the deeply internalized quality of the mystery-mastery process, although still pointing to the possibility of conscious learning, derives from my repeated experience at the school I directed of the opposition of two fundamental ways of viewing and acting in the world—which might be named "manipulation" and "exploration." I am hopeful that the model provides a conceptual resolution to this dichotomy, while my struggles with the logical limits of the book provide me with an experiential resolution to the dichotomy.

In chapter 6, to offer another but related example, the reader will find me heavily emphasizing the effectiveness of confrontation in interpersonal relations. This emphasis derives in large part from listening to tapes of my own behavior as director of the school and hearing what I did *not* do, time after time, when there were differences within a group. My inability to confront others at appropriate moments, rather than always being supportive or self-disclosing, helped make it inevitable that manipulation would be used to set limits and reach conclusions at the school.

> *Guideline four: The intuitive, logical, and empirical elements of knowledge can be distinguished not only for the content of a particular scientific project, but also for the mode and intent of a project. The relative emphases of a given project must be made explicit if the extent and limits of its validity are to be appreciated.*

The distinctions and interpenetrations of the three terms of knowledge in the content of this book have already been traced in reference to the first two guidelines. In terms of mode, the overwhelming emphasis of this study falls upon the elaboration of *a way of thinking about* experiential learning and scientific inquiry. Its analysis of events focuses upon patterns of thought of other scientists (in chapter 1 and this chapter), patterns of thought about interlevel interactions (chapter 5), and patterns of thought about behavior (comparison of scoring procedure to members' perceptions, chapter 9). My own action is confined to the presentation of thought—to this writing. Thus, the logical element of knowledge dominates the mode of presentation, whereas the intuitive model and explorations and the empirical findings dominate the content of the study.

This emphasis on *a way of thinking about* behavior, relations, and intuitive axioms is close to current assumptions about what science is, but it is only one of several modes possible for conscious science. The two other primary modes of conscious science are touched upon in this study but are not fully developed because of my limited capabilities, the limits of my goal in writing the book, and the limits of what is currently recognized as science. One mode attempts to awaken the scientist and his colleagues to fuller experiential awareness. This mode is reported in chapter 5 in terms of the guided meditations and is actively attempted in the short reading experiments offered the reader on pages 106–7 of that chapter.

The other mode attempts to organize people to participate in the scientific search for truth. This mode is touched upon in chapter 7 and 8 in the discussion of training the other two scorers and in the allusion to the selection of members for the two groups studied. The exigencies of such organizing are also touched upon by the questions at the end of chapter 5.

The scientist retains a particular concern to make these two modes—awakening and organizing—comprehensible to, and verifiable by, others, but even this particular concern cannot be realized without extensive exploration of how to act in and describe events framed by the intuitive and practical modes.

In plain language, conscious scientific investigation requires religious experience and discipline, on the one hand, and political organizing, on the other. Contemporary science maintains the illusion of neutrality toward religion and politics only by refusing to recognize the challenge of verifying its intuitive axioms and by reducing politics to the routine administration of questionnaire-mailings and data computations (Laing, 1967; Mannheim, 1936).

The model presented here reopens the question of the active relationship of religion and politics to science. At the same time, the logical mode of the doctoral thesis has restricted the investigation of this relationship to currently acknowledged patterns of writing and procedure. Since the modes of intuitive awakening and political organizing consonant with the scientific process of verification of conclusions are little known, less reported, and still less recognized as relevant to the development of current science, it would be unfortunate if the congruence in mode of this particular example of the new paradigm of science with the mode of the currently predominant paradigm were interpreted as indicating the limits of the new paradigm as a whole. I hope the exposition in these pages will help to avert this result.

Guideline five: At the outset of exploration within the paradigm of conscious science, knowledge, to be accurate, must be formulated so as to indicate the mystery which yet surrounds it, in particular the complementarity between the growing self-awareness on the part of the scientist and the increasing accuracy of his knowledge.

This study attempts to fulfill this guideline by its formulation of the model from which the guideline derives, as well as by its discussion of the limits of the study in relation to the other guidelines.

Guideline six: The researcher must distinguish among three general topics of social scientific study, whether at the individual, group, organizational, or social scale: the mystery-mastery process, experiential learning, and conscious action.

Social science up to the present has focused predominantly upon study of the mystery-mastery process, inevitably somewhat misconceptualizing it within the total context of human possibilities, since social science has not recognized it as merely one of three general human possibilities and has therefore taken for granted certain distorting assumptions of the mystery-mastery process itself. The paradigm of science presented here indicates that the framework of the mystery-mastery process cannot be clarified except insofar as the investigator himself attains the perspective of contact with intuitive consciousness through experiential learning. On the other hand, the process of conscious action is unspecifiable except by a fully formed, permanently conscious scientist, so at present its methods and manifestations remain almost wholly shrouded. This overview indicates that the topic of experiential learning currently stands as the central challenge and most fruitful concern for the social scientist, both in terms of his personal professional development and in terms of the advancement of social science as an enterprise.

The foregoing discussion of the relationship of this study to the six guidelines attempts to provide a brief and impressionistic model of the kind of procedure necessary to establish the effectiveness and comprehensiveness—the external validity—of a study. The comments merely illustrate the guidelines and therefore only hint at how this study fits into a general framework of knowledge. But the general framework is itself no more than hinted at by the seven axioms at the outset of this chapter. Being by no means fully conscious (that is, in regular touch with intuition), I would be presumptuous to attempt to be precise about a framework that must, finally, be intuitive and intuitively verifiable.

In general terms, then, this study has a higher likelihood of presenting a valid way of thinking about learning and science than have studies within the hypothetico-deductive model, since this way of thinking is overtly connected to both the level above thought (intuition) and the level below thought (behavior). Given the derivation of a reliable and internally valid behavior-scoring procedure, this study can be said to present a generally valid way of thinking about intuition, thought, and behavior, since this way of thinking permits the study to reflect the transformation of an intuitive model into consistently discriminable patterns of behavior.

What is generalizable from this study is not a scientific way of intuiting or a scientific way of behaving, but only a scientific way of conceptualizing intuition and behavior.

II

APPROACHES TO THE PHENOMENON OF EXPERIENTIAL LEARNING

The following three chapters explore and develop two approaches to studying the phenomenon of learning from experience, the phenomenological approach and the empirical.

If learning from experience involves conscious appropriation of the interaction among one's structure, one's behavior, and the world outside, then to study only others' behavior as part of the world outside—that is, merely to adopt an empirical methodology—would be to distance oneself from the phenomenon in question. All interactions among consciousness, cognitive-emotional-sensory structure, and one's own behavior would have to be inferred rather than directly observed. By contrast, the phenomenological method of observing one's own inner process makes possible the direct observation of the phenomenon of learning from experience. Thus, in theory, the phenomenological method ought to be more potent and appropriate for this study. In practice, however, people's lack of training in self-observation while in action poses an obstacle to obtaining full and valid data by the phenomenological method. Consequently, I will use both approaches in this study.

Chapter 4 presents a more detailed comparison of the two methods, giving special consideration to the less familiar phenomenological method.

Chapter 5 describes the phenomenological process and findings of a group of my friends who attempted to identify the quality of consciousness in themselves and to observe the interaction among levels of their experience.

Chapter 6 develops a series of theoretical categories for interpreting verbal behavior, based on the model of learning. It then exemplifies the categories by clinical analyses of verbal behavior in different settings, in order to distinguish between verbal behavior conducive and not conducive to experiential learning. The theoretical categories, in turn, become the basis for a quantitative behavior-scoring procedure, the reliability and validity of which are established in chapters 7, 8, and 9. That is, the theoretical categories represent inferences about a person's inner processes as reflected by his various behaviors, which can be measured empirically.

Chapter Four

THE PHENOMENOLOGICAL VERSUS THE EMPIRICAL APPROACH

To set out to learn about learning from experience has so clearly a circular quality to it that the project poses the question, From what perspective shall we learn about learning? Merely to adopt a perspective without such questioning would be to presume that we know already (although we claim only to be learning) how to learn about learning.

The simplest resolution to this confusing circularity is to adopt two different perspectives of study. Then, if the results based on both perspectives confirm the model of learning presented here, our confidence in it can be infinitely greater than if we used but one approach.

The two most general, divergent perspectives that command respect as scientific approaches in the West are phenomenology and empiricism. Empiricism is by far the more familiar of the two to most social scientists; phenomenology is both more recent in origin (having been introduced by Husserl in the early years of this century) and more often considered part of the realm of philosophy. Approaches similar to or derived from phenomenology have marked four relatively limited strands of social science: (1) introspectionist psychology, which died a quick death before Husserl's efforts to describe subjective experience became widely known: (2) symbolic interactionism, a branch of sociology inspired in part by Alfred Schutz (1966, 1967), one of Husserl's students, and popularized by Herbert Blumer (1969); (3) ethnoscience, an anthropological approach that aims to describe the way a given culture typically organizes knowledge (Sturtevant, 1969); and (4) a phenomenological approach to organizational behavior, being advocated in certain California schools of public administration.

Despite its relatively limited impact on the social sciences, Husserl (1962, 1965) maintains that phenomenology is fundamentally more scientific than empiricism because it takes nothing for granted, whereas empiricism takes for granted both the world out there and the scientist's ability to perceive that world, exempting these assumptions from study.

Let us more carefully contrast the Husserlian phenomenological approach with the empirical approach.

CONTRASTS BETWEEN THE TWO APPROACHES

Whereas the empirical approach strives to determine patterns in the world outside, the phenomenological approach suggests that the world inside shapes the world outside and that a scientific study of phenomena must consequently begin with an analysis of the world inside, that is, with an analysis of subjective (personal or cultural) processes of patterning external phenomena.

From this common proposition the Husserlian and social scientific strands of phenomenology have tended to proceed in different directions. Whereas Husserl strives to attain and describe a pure consciousness which brackets one's everyday assumptions about phenomena in the world outside and thus gives access to the phenomena as they really are in themselves, the social scientific strands of phenomenology have tended more toward describing the assumptions made by different persons and cultures about the world outside. In other words, whereas Husserl strives toward a subjective, normative method for arriving at the objective, empirical world, social scientific phenomenologists tend to strive toward an objective, empirical method for arriving at the subjective, normative world.

I will attempt a third kind of project: to use a subjective method to study the world inside (thereby approximating Husserl's practice of phenomenology) and an empirical method to study the world outside, the aim being to verify as objective the normative model informing both methods.

The phenomenological approach demands of the scientist that he study his inner subjective experience directly. By contrast, the empirical approach studies externally observable behavior and infers subjective experience theoretically (if at all).

The empirical approach can be unobtrusive; that is, measurements of natural behavior can occur without subjects being aware that they are objects of study (e.g., a conversation preserved with a hidden tape recorder [Webb et al., 1966]). By contrast, in the phenomenological approach the observed party is necessarily aware of the observer, since they are one and the same. Thus, the extent to which the measurement itself influences the measured phenomenon always presents itself as a question. (This question also arises in the case of obtrusive empirical measures such as questionnaires and interviews.)

Another aspect of the difference between the two approaches is that the phenomenological approach is necessarily dependent for data upon the subjective report of the investigator, and such reports are liable to cognitive, emotional, or linguistic distortions of what he has actually observed. By contrast, empirical measures that are unobtrusive or that measure behavior directly are not liable to this kind of distortion.

Empirical measures are, however, liable to sensory distortions of various kinds (e.g., subjects misreading instructions, tape recorders malfunctioning, researchers miscounting results), whereas phenomenological investigation does not directly involve perceptions of the outside world.

Finally, by its direct access to intuitions the phenomenological approach makes second-order theories (e.g., models or axioms) capable of verification, whereas the empirical approach can verify only hypotheses concerning the world outside.

Several of the enumerated contrasts could be said to give the phenomenological approach an edge over the unobtrusive or behavioral, empirical approach: the lack of assumptions, the lack of possible sensory distortion, and the potential for verifying second-order theories. Other considerations favor an unobtrusive, behavioral, empirical approach: the lack of possible linguistic distortion, and the lack of possible distortion due to the research instrument itself. In general, however, the two approaches study different levels of experience, and their advantages and disadvantages derive from their distinct concerns. In this respect, it makes no sense to speak of one approach as more scientific than the other.

Husserl was never able to show satisfactorily that a state of awareness could be achieved wherein the world outside as seen by oneself becomes equivalent to the world outside as it really is. Thus, phenomenology must be described as concerning itself with direct observation of subjective experience—with the interaction of consciousness, cognitive-emotional-sensory structure, one's own behavior, and the world outside as seen by oneself. Consequently, it makes possible the direct verification of a model such as the one proposed here (i.e., the very concept of four levels of experience). The empirical approach concerns itself with reliable measurement of the world outside and of behavior as part of the world outside and, consequently, makes possible the verification of hypotheses about relationships among aspects of the world outside.

There is also an obvious potential overlap between the two approaches. One approach studies one's own behavior and the world as seen by oneself, whereas the other studies behavior as part of the world outside (or as part of the world seen by others), as well as the world outside in general. So long as there are discrepancies between one's own behavior as seen by oneself and the same behavior as seen by others or between the world as seen by oneself and the world outside, the genuine scientist will find it difficult to determine what is really true, and the authentic actor will find it difficult to be fully effective. Therefore, not just the use of the two approaches, but more particularly the development of a set of categories that can simultaneously guide both phenomenological observation and empirical measurement toward intersubjective reliability and validity, becomes a critical task. Only such a set of categories could aspire to adequacy for thinking about one's life in the world. The present model and the theoretical categories of verbal behavior to be presented in chapter 6, which rest within the model, address this task, as will be shown below.

COMBINING THE TWO APPROACHES

To study experiential learning phenomenologically and empirically required creating rather special social conditions. Since the model of learning presented in chapter 1 suggests that experiential learning is a socially rare process, it seemed necessary to create special social conditions to assure obtaining at least some empirically measurable behavior purportedly reflecting experiential learning to contrast to other behavior purportedly not reflecting experiential learning. Such a contrast was necessary to determine the validity of differentiations made by a behavior-scoring procedure. However, training persons to observe themselves also required special social conditions. Since I wished to combine the two approaches and since the training of phenomenological observers presumably involves experiential learning, the two distinct reasons for creating special social conditions merged into the following design: I asked two groups of persons to meet in a series of three sessions for the purpose of learning from our common experience. In both cases I tape-recorded and transcribed the members' verbal behavior for later scoring by two trained scorers and myself, using the behavior-scoring procedure presented in chapter 6. After an initial two hours of unstructured conversation in both groups, which served to establish base learning scores, I asked members of one group to participate in a series of guided meditations to explore their inner experiencing and see whether their observations confirmed categories of my model of learning (e.g., consciousness, different levels of experience, focal versus subsidiary awareness). In the next two meetings this group explored how to maintain an inner process of self-observation while behaving among others. Meanwhile, the other group was striving to learn with the help of some existing sensitivity-training techniques. Members of both groups were asked their perceptions of their own and others' learning after each session. An analysis of the data from these questionnaires was sent to the members of each group during the course of the meetings.

The design yielded five kinds of data that could be compared: (1) data on the process of training one group of people for phenomenological investigation; (2) subjective reports of their phenomenological observations; (3) data on the process of training scorers to use the behavior-scoring procedure reliably; (4) learning scores based on transcripts of members' behavior in each group at the beginning and end of the series of meetings; (5) perceptions by members of each group of one another's relative learning.

The two forms of "process" data (the training of phenomenological observers and the training of empirical scorers) are of special importance to this work. Whereas in most scientific studies the arduous task of developing valid measures remains in the background of the final report of results, in this case it belongs in the foreground since it involves human learning, the very process under study. Moreover, since the two forms of training both involve applying concepts of the model of learning to one's active observation of inner or outer phenomena, rather than merely reflecting about the concepts, they should both yield a valid sense of the scale of the task of using these ideas in one's daily life.

The first two kinds of data (the phenomenological) are presented and analyzed in chapter 5 as a direct test of this model of experiential learning. The other three (empirical) kinds of data are presented and analyzed in chapters 7, 8, and 9 as a direct test of the theoretical categories of verbal behavior in chapter 6 and, thereby, as an indirect test of the model, since the theoretical categories are nested within the model.

We can turn now to a closer look at each approach.

THE GUIDED MEDITATIONS

The reader may well wonder why he should trust the validity of phenomenological reports when those reports derive from investigators who are being guided and are not fully trained. Will the guidance and lack of training not distort the results? There are several answers to this question: (1) guidance and lack of training could well distort the results; (2) they will not necessarily distort the results; and (3) irrespective of whether they distort the results, guidance and lack of training are necessary attributes of phenomenological research at this point since it is at a primitive stage of development as a recognized science.

To determine whether the guidance creates conformity to my concepts rather than genuine investigation by the group members, we will remain alert for signs that they are parroting my categories rather than struggling for words appropriate to their own experience, for signs of unwillingness to disconfirm my descriptions when they appear not to fit a member's experience, and for inconsistencies within and among investigators' reports. Conversely, we can determine whether the guidance yields any signs of enhanced contact with subjective experience rather than mere conformity to prescribed categories. Since I believe that the model does accurately differentiate various qualities of experience, I expect that sharing its categories in a setting where others are actively exploring inwardly will enhance a sense of individual awareness rather than create external conformity.

The lack of training of the investigators, which makes the guidance necessary, may distort their reports, but it also provides another source of clinical data—the vicissitudes of their training. This process is of particular relevance to this model of learning, for the hypothesized, socially dominant, mystery-mastery process militates against inward exploration and against sharing the results of inward exploration. Therefore, if the process of training reveals that the investigators find it difficult to reconcile inner exploration and outer sharing, this result itself will serve as a source of confirmation for the model.

The more important question is, Why present data from untrained investigators in the first place? The answer is that because research at all like this has not been attempted in American academic psychology for the past half century, there is no accepted expert in this kind of introspection, nor even an accepted process for training such investigators. To have made various assumptions in training investigators and then to have presented sophisticated results of their investigations would have been to overleap the current frontier of scientific research. Colleagues might well disown such results because they disagree with the underlying assumptions. Consequently, the relative lack of training of the investigators is inevitable at this stage of the research.

PREVIOUS BLOCKS TO SCIENTIFIC
INTROSPECTIONISM

It will enhance our understanding of the phenomenological approach derived from this model of experiential learning if we ask why earlier efforts by academic psychologists to use introspection as a data-collection method ended abruptly in failure.

Three central problems in the academic introspectionist efforts of Titchener, Brentano, Wundt, and Kulpe around the turn of the century, appear to have led to the demise of introspectionism at that time (D. Bakan, 1967). One problem was that to focus on inner experience would seem to modify that experience to some indeterminable extent, thus restricting the validity of results to rare moments of direct introspection. A second problem was that significant emotional experiences could not be induced at will for study, while, at the same time, all efforts at introspection seemed to encounter resistances in the investigators. The third problem was that the different methods of training the investigators may have accounted for discrepancies in different scholars' results, and no criterion existed for determining the relative validity of the various training methods.

The guided meditations and subsequent group explorations to be described in the next chapter address these three problems. As to modifying experience by awareness, the model of attention introduced in chapter 1 holds that focal awareness, subsidiary awareness, and intentional awareness are distinct. To focus on one's inner process, when that is ordinarily subsidiary, would indeed change the way one experiences it. In fact, even raising one's subsidiary attention to recognition without focusing upon it would change the way one experiences it. Thus this model leads us to posit, not a method for tapping one's inner process without influencing it, but rather a prediction that there are distinguishable kinds of introspective influence. Moreover, if our models of attention, feedback, and science are at all valid, then, even though moments of full appropriation of consciousness may ordinarily be rare, they are essential to valid knowledge and effective action. In consequence, it is not as accurate to say that the validity of results is restricted to rare moments of introspection as it is to say that the validity of one's ordinary conclusions is extended or exceeded by the results of such introspection.

The argument becomes still more persuasive when we recognize that, according to the model of interacting levels of experience, awareness is an integral aspect of experience, not something superimposed upon a preexisting experience. Thus, the issue is not modified experience versus unmodified experience, but rather experience in which the role of subjective awareness is consciously appropriated versus experience in which the role of subjective awareness is not appropriated (which recalls chapter 2, page 41, where the same distinction between appropriated and unappropriated experience arises in another context).

Actually, further work may show that it is possible to appropriate intentional awareness without appropriating subsidiary bodily awareness, giving a person a kind of detached, bird's-eye view of his ordinary focusing process without directly influencing it. This possibility is suggested by the quality of heightened experience reported by alienated geniuses such as Dostoevski, Nijinsky, T. E. Lawrence, and Nietzsche (Wilson, 1956).

In regard to the second problem—that of inducing emotional experiences for observation while at the same time avoiding emotional resistance to self-observation—the model of feedback in chapter 1 specifically recognizes and explains resistance to experiential learning. Such resistance is intimately connected with significant emotional experiences, since the resistance protects assumptions about oneself in action with others from existential exposure, whereas significant emotional experiences are associated with exposing, risking, challenging, testing, and discovering authentic transformations or incongruities across levels of oneself in action. Thus, an introspective process must aim toward enlarging the investigator's awareness beyond the focal element if it is to begin to yield comparative data, and such an enlargement or deepening of awareness will in turn encounter resistance. Again, the model leads us, not to posit some means of avoiding the resistance, but rather to predict that resistance will be a central phenomenon in the process of introspection. (Here we should also recognize explicitly that "introspection" is a poor word for the process suggested by this model of attention, since introspection connotes focusing inwardly at the expense of involvement in, and emotion in relation to, the outside world. By contrast, this model maintains that one's focal choices in relation to the outside world are ultimately enhanced by raising to awareness the subsidiary and intentional elements of attention.)

In regard to the possibility that differences in training may have been responsible for different scholars' results, the method of training investigators is here presented rather than assumed. As with the other two problems, my concern is not to minimize the extent to which the method of training influences the results, but rather to assure that the influence is of a kind that enhances validity rather than conformity. I have already indicated some of the signs that may help us to determine which kind of influence the guidance or training actually has (p. 93).

A common theme of the previous blocks to scientific introspectionism seems to be the inadequacy of the implicit model of science guiding those efforts, which aimed at obtaining isolated, uninfluenced, sterilized data. By contrast, my response to these blocks strikes the theme that they represent legitimate and investigatable dilemmas, given a model of science that seeks data in the midst of action—that strives for objective observation in the midst of influences. The complement of this theme is that, unlike sterilized data, the resulting information is synchronous with and therefore applicable to action in everyday life.

THE BEHAVIOR-SCORING PROCEDURE

The model of learning and science presented in the first three chapters has the same effect on the empirical approach as on the phenomenological approach. That is, it influences me to choose a particular empirical method (the scoring of "natural" behavior by trained judges), and particular categories for the resulting scoring procedure. As is true for the phenomenological approach, the theoretical categories are synchronous with, and therefore applicable to, action in everyday life. Let us examine more closely what this synchrony means and how it comes about.

First, the process of observing others' behavior is common to everyone's daily life, unlike some empirical methods, such as administering questionnaires. Second, I derived the theoretical categories of the scoring procedure from my efforts to observe and respond effectively to others' behavior. (Later, within scholarly literature I found elucidation and confirmation of some of the categories.) Third, the analytical categories of the scoring procedure nest within the model of different levels of experience, making "empirical" observation of the world outside compatible and continuous with "phenomenological" observation of the world inside.

This nesting occurs as follows. The scoring procedure includes three distinct but interrelated levels of analysis, corresponding to the different levels of experience posited by the model of learning. The first level of analysis purports to describe the possible permutations of interaction between behavior and the world outside. These categories will be named "focal functions of behavior." The second level of analysis purports to describe the possible permutations of interaction between the structural or subsidiary level and the level of behavior. These categories will be named "structural modes of behavior." Finally, the third level of analysis purports to describe the variations in quality of behavior as it is or is not interpenetrated by immediate consciousness; the two poles of this dimension will be named "conscious appropriation of behavior" and "denial of responsibility for behavior."

The scoring procedure thus provides synchronous categories for thinking about one's inner experience, thinking about one's behavior in the world, and thinking about others' behavior in the world in a way that opens toward others' inner experience. It is not merely an analytic tool detached from action, but also a means of conceptualizing behavior that can aid an engaged person in acting effectively, if he can view his and others' behavior through this conceptual framework while in action. The important point here is that the usefulness of the theoretical categories in action is not for retiring into one's thought, reflecting about what is happening, and then returning to the engagement with some insightful comment. When thought is used analytically in alternation with behavior, the analytical categories of thought tend *not* to be the ones that actually frame the verbal behavior. The theoretical categories to be presented become useful in action only when they have been so integrated into a person's functioning that they actually frame his perceptions and behaviors when he is in action.

DIFFICULTIES IN TRAINING SCORERS

The previous comments, as well as the scale of the task of applying three levels of analysis to each unit of verbal behavior, indicate that training scorers to judge behavior reliably according to this scoring procedure represents a major investment necessitated by this approach. The scoring procedure is not operational in any simple, mechanical sense. It is not accessible to any normal person schooled in making ordinary discriminations among behavioral cues. Instead, it becomes operational only when individuals are motivated to stretch their intelligence and human sensitivity to the utmost, not only in the process of learning the scoring procedure, but also at each instance of applying it.

This demand upon the scorers is consonant with the model of science presented in chapter 2, which indicates that the scientist of human events must personally develop and sustain consciousness if he is to be objective. The demanding quality of the scoring procedure may appear, however, to contradict a dictum of the empirical approach, that the measurement process used in a given study be replicable by other scientists. Behavior-scoring procedures in general (Argyris, 1965b; Bales, 1951; Dollard and Auld, 1959; Dunphy, 1968; Mann, 1966; Mills, 1964;) are sometimes criticized because the difficulties of replication tend in practice to make them the "property" of their inventors and the inventors' immediate students.

I do not believe these are valid grounds for criticism. There is no reason why, in principle, scoring procedures cannot be replicated. However difficult further replication may be in practice, the very fact that a scoring procedure has been learned reliably by several scorers exemplifies the replicability of the measurement process. Further, although other empirical methods may make lower personal demands on the scientist interested in replication, they all assume extensive professional training of various kinds. No measurement process is in fact replicable by the ordinary, untrained citizen. In this light, objections to, and lack of replication of, studies using behavior-scoring procedures indicates resistance to personal (i.e., experiential) learning by scientists. Replicability can hardly be advanced as a major issue of practice in any event, since replication is exceedingly rare in practice throughout the social sciences. Moreover, in my opinion the direct access to behavior offered by scoring procedures, as contrasted to the indirect access offered by archives, questionnaires, interviews, or impressionistic observation, more than compensates in validity of the results for the possibly idiosyncratic categories of a particular scoring procedure. Finally, since the scoring procedure presented in this book is derived explicitly from a model of science considerably at variance with the contemporary model, we should expect it to be difficult to replicate. To dismiss the findings on the grounds of this difficulty would be tantamount to rejecting the exploration of alternative models of science in order to determine which is more valid.

In closing, we can see that, as they have previously been formulated, the two approaches I am adopting to study learning from experience have exemplified the polarizations in contemporary science between observation and action and between subject and object. Both approaches are modified by the model of learning and science presented here, so that they move toward integrating observation and action, subject and object.

Chapter Five

ATTEMPTS AT SELF-OBSERVATION: PROCESS AND FINDINGS

This chapter reports the events of a series of three meetings among a group of people willing to test with me whether my concepts of different levels of experiencing feedback and different elements of attention seemed valid inwardly and interpersonally in terms of their experiences. What the members said during the three meetings is treated, not as scientific data to be analyzed according to the research design, but as scientific interpretations by the members of the group, based on data about their internal experiencing and thus not accessible by any scientific method except introspection.

The composition of the group was homogeneous in some respects, heterogeneous in others. All members were friends of mine before the meetings, and most knew some of the others present. Half of the group was male, half female, and twelve of the fourteen members were married couples. All members were in their twenties, averaging late twenties. Twelve were college graduates and nine of those had done some graduate work. Fields of academic specialization ranged from mathematics to law to religious studies to psychology to biology. Jobs clustered around educational organizations, but ranged from elementary school to college teaching, from prep school administration to research assistantship. Half the group had fairly extensive previous experience with experiential learning, mainly in T-groups.

I had described my intentions and plans for the meetings to individual members when inviting them. The first meeting began with my simply encouraging the members to try to learn from their interaction with one another for the next two hours. This period provided a base against which to compare, in the empirical analysis, their behavior after the guided meditations.

The group was then introduced to my concepts of attention and interacting levels of experience through two guided meditations. The justification for the guided meditations was that if my concepts were accurate descriptions of actual experience, then using them in a setting where members were inwardly exploring should help them to become aware of more aspects of their experiencing.

First the words spoken in guidance are reported. Then members' experiences during the meditation are given. The reader is also offered the opportunity to verify some of the qualities of experience by experiments of his own. Thereafter, the events of the second and third meetings are reported.

THE GUIDANCE

What I'd like to do first is to begin by asking you to close your eyes, first giving you a sense of what you might be looking for when you close your eyes. And then after a minute or so of doing —wandering around inside—I'll say some things about the kinds of efforts that can go on inside—what you might be finding—and you might try to follow what I'm saying, but not get lost in my words. Try to keep your own inner questioning or inner exploration alive to see if my words are matching what you are finding. Don't just listen to me, but try to keep two things going at once, so to speak. So the initial thing that I'd like to suggest is that you try closing your eyes, letting whatever is going on inside happen—thoughts, images, feelings, pulse, breathing— you become aware of, but don't get lost in any of it. Don't get lost in it. And see what that involves doing. Whether that's possible.

(*Silence for about four minutes.*)
One thing you may notice is the sense of focusing on one thing and then on another, sort of not really knowing what to do besides focusing on this thought or that image or sensation. You follow one thing at a time, perhaps get lost in it, then remember that you're supposed to be doing something and search for something else to focus upon.

(*Silence for about half a minute.*)

There's a sort of something that is focusing on something else even when our eyes are closed.

(*Silence for about half a minute.*)

How could we get in touch with who is doing the focusing? If we try to focus on him, we find that we are focusing on something else, but there is still something focusing.

(*Silence for about half a minute.*)

We have to find some other effort besides changing the focus, besides looking somewhere else. We keep looking somewhere else; we don't stop doing that; we are still looking around.

(*Silence for about two minutes.*)

Okay, we might stop now.

Members of the group proceeded to discuss their experiences during this meditation and I interspersed my interpretations of their experiences. Then I led a second meditation as follows:

What I'd like to do now is create another exercise where it would be possible for us to try to be in touch with these four different aspects of experience at once—what's happening outside, our own behavior, our thought (which will be very transparent in this exercise—we may have the impression we're not thinking because we won't be absorbed in thought—the thought will be trying to keep touch with all these other things, it won't be doing its own thing, so to speak). And then in this particular exercise, consciousness—if we're lucky—I think will make itself felt physically as a presence. Now, we can talk afterwards whether any of that happens. Does—does that sort of an exercise seem right for now; I mean, have I laid a groundwork that makes that exercise seem like a meaningful one to try?

(*Short discussion reformulating the idea for one member.*)

Shall we try it now? Again you will need to be in a position where your back is somewhat free.

(*People shift positions so they are sitting straight on chairs or the rug, rather than reclining.*)

And if we begin by trying to get in touch with the weight of our body on the floor—how the floor is supporting our body. And, in particular, that it's holding our back up, our backbone, and our head on top of our back. Feeling the sense that without any effort the floor is supporting our head.

(*Silence—each silence between half a minute and a minute long.*)

And not so much weight on the floor as just a presence.

(Silence.)

And maintaining this awareness of our presence on the floor, we begin to notice our breathing, not influencing it, just noticing it.

(Silence.)

Our body is present and breathing.

(Silence.)

And maintaining that awareness, we notice the sounds around us.

(Silence.)

We are present, breathing, listening.

(Silence.)

And maintaining that awareness, we notice the feeling of other persons here. . . . Not an image of other persons, but a feeling; and we breathe and rest on the floor.

(Silence.)

And now, maintaining this awareness, we notice an energy in our stomachs.

(Silence.)

The energy connects us to everything: our sitting, the airplane [the sound of an airplane over the house is heard], the others.

(Silence.)

My thought tells me this is a difficult state to maintain; it keeps trying to draw me away from it.

(Silence.)

If you wish, we could stop.

THE PROCESS OF FOCUSING

A number of comments by members of the experimental group immediately after these two guided meditations and over the course of two more meetings indicated the varying effects induced by the exercises. Some were quickly able to confirm or disconfirm the author's statements relating to inner experiencing. A representative and almost complete selection of comments is offered below. They are not reported in the sequence in which they were spoken, however (except when that is specifically stated), but rather are arranged to permit generalizations based on and illuminating the models of feedback and attention. Thus, in relation to the process of focusing in the first exercise:

Member 1: I had a sensation . . . of looking down, of looking up, something focusing on something else; and then after you spoke I had the sensation of just being in here, but I felt the category was wrong when you said there's still something focusing. I didn't feel that was right. It felt like I was just there, as though the activity of looking had stopped. I wasn't focusing.

Member 2: I think I'm really unsure about whether I was focusing or things were focusing on me, things were drawing me to focus on them. I began by being mostly rooted in my body—in my back, feeling my back, and my head and my eyes—and I was just, involuntarily almost, drawn out by sounds. They were focusing on me; I didn't want them.

Member 3: I was responding to the soothing quality in your voice. And kind of tuning in to moving around and feeling my hands and my hair and the way my hands felt being on my head. And then a, you know, cognitive kind of trip I took with you. "Okay, I think I've just been thinking about the fact that it's focusing from one thing to the next. Okay, for a description." Okay, but then I got kind of disappointed; like you took me all around this thing: right, there's got to be somebody focusing, but maybe that's not the way to look at it. And uh, so you stopped. You didn't take me all the way. And I wasn't going to do it myself.

Member 4: I was very confused about whether I had any control over the sort of rapid exchange of images in my mind. . . . I would try to push my thoughts in a certain direction and sometimes I could and sometimes I couldn't.

Member 5: I kind of get the feeling, rather than of focusing on something, of flashing a lot rather than I was doing anything actively, like focusing, that's what that word means to me.

Member 6: At moments where I had the feeling that I was becoming in touch with more or less everything, I would focus on it and I would lose it and it would dart away. And it reminded me very much of—that I often push my eyes shut with my hand and try to focus on something I see in the black there. When I try to focus on it it darts away to some other area, or color just goes out of the line of vision type thing. I felt that same frustration, that the harder I tried the more impossible it was becoming.

These comments indicate early experiences with nonfocal qualities of awareness, and the perplexities which these experiences induce in our habitual conceptual categories. When persons are

not totally absorbed by their current focal awareness and notice
the changes in focus, as Members 2, 4, and 5 report, the quality
of their freedom and self control, which they ordinarily take for
granted, comes into question. Are they really in control? And do
their efforts to establish control work? Their sense of personal
will and control is associated with the ability to manipulate elements in their focal awareness, and they find that this kind of
control is not effective in regulating the still unknown relationships among focal, subsidiary, and intentional awareness.

The comment of Member 1 points to another element of experience with nonfocal qualities of awareness. When, by habit, one
is totally absorbed in the content of whatever one is focusing
upon, one retains no independent sense of awareness, as provided
by a subsidiary recognition that one is doing the focusing, during
experiences. If then, by contrast, one attains a "taste" of
awareness—a recognition of subsidiary awareness—such a taste
seems incompatible with focusing.

In Member 1's case, the exercise seems to have brought him in
touch with his focal mechanism at the structural level, the *"something* [*in here*] focusing on something else." This experience is
subtle, fragile, easily lost if one continues focusing, since there is
a strong habitual tendency not to maintain a dual awareness of
the subsidiary focusing process and the object focused upon. This
can be illustrated for the reader by reminding him of his presence
as he reads. Ordinarily, he is so involved in the changing words
that he loses awareness of himself as focusing on the words.

*Now, if, instead, he makes an effort to maintain continuous
awareness of his own presence as breathing, sitting, looking,* the
reader may find it necessary to pause briefly or to cease paying
as much attention to the words, letting them go out of focus perhaps and returning to read them several times. However, experimenting back and forth between an unfocused sense of sensual
presence and his ordinary concentration on what he is reading,
the reader may find a kind of relaxed alertness in which his
"taste" of presence does not interfere with focusing on what he is
reading. This subsidiary taste of presence will not last long:
shortly the reader will encounter some sentence which fascinates
or irritates him and he will become reimmersed in what he is

reading. But in the meantime I suggest that his initial taste of presence, achieved at the temporary cost of stopping to focus, is comparable to Member 1's "sensation of just being in here."

The incompatibility felt between focusing on something and maintaining an independent subsidiary sense of awareness is again reflected by another comment after the first exercise:

Member 7: Before you started talking I was—the consciousness of my own body or my own presence was very minimal. And when you mentioned pulse it came as a great surprise to me. I was paying no attention to that. I was somewhere—I had this sense—not quite seeing, not quite feeling, not quite hearing, but somehow sensing around the street and the block—I didn't have a sense of it being cold but of just being there and very temperate, both in temperature and in impact on me. And the sound of the digging [of snow, going on outside the house] was just crystal clear, beautiful. Then, when you started talking though, I followed along and I think I began to think—I think I got seduced by your words and the concepts you were using. I did focus on things one by one. The problem I had in that was, yes, what you're saying makes sense now, but does it describe what was going on before you started to speak?

It seems that Member 7's independent sense of awareness was of the continuing presence of the outside world. Our usual focus upon one and then another discrete object in the outside world leaves us unaware of the continuing presence of the outside world amid these changes. This can be illustrated for the reader by reminding him of the page behind these words. Ordinarily, as he reads, he is so involved in the changing words that he loses awareness of their continuing existence here on the page.

Now, if, instead, the reader makes an effort to maintain continuous awareness of the page behind these words, he can do it most easily by ceasing to pay as much attention to the words—letting them go out of focus slightly and taking in the whole page. Experimenting back and forth, the reader may find a kind of relaxed alertness in which the words flow by recognizably as he reads, but without his losing contact with the page behind them. In this condition his focusing on the words loses any discrete, willed, wrenching quality it may have had and instead seems to

be attracted by the whole context. I suggest that this flowing, relaxed alertness is similar to the experience reported by Member
7.

The reader will have noted that there is considerable similarity
between the process and results of the two experiential exercises
just offered. They suggest that full subsidiary awareness includes,
both a recognition of one's own body and of the outside world as
background to whatever one is focusing upon. However, Member
7 reported a disjunction between the two and Member 1 showed
no evidence of being aware of an external background of sound
in his comment. We can only speculate that this difference in
ways of structuring experiences results from a habitual disjunction between "inner" and "outer" on the part of the two members.

CHANGING QUALITIES OF
AWARENESS

A number of other members reported changes in their quality
of awareness during the exercises:

Member 6 (first exercise): I found it very difficult to focus on my
breathing from the very beginning because my eyes were fluttering and my—until the halfway point when you began talking—
when they stopped fluttering as much. But while they were fluttering, I felt that my whole awareness fell from being sort of tipped
forward like in my eyes. And it gradually went down into my
upper shoulders and then into my chest and breathing and I was
still aware of my eyes fluttering somewhat and I felt as though I
was being drowned by every swallow I took. Unusual to hear it
the way I was hearing it. And as I fell deeper I found myself sitting up straighter. My head was settling in and was becoming
more comfortable. Becoming aware of different parts of me, and
then became aware of a tingling of my fingers—a pulse—you
know I hadn't been able to find the pulse at all at first, and that
made me scared.

Member 8 (first exercise): When it ended I was just getting into
it. In the beginning it was very difficult to, well first of all I started
thinking, "Who is speaking in me?" and all I could think of were
all the noises in the room and realized that my eyes were darting

around in their sockets. And then, you know, that just kept going for a while, and then I realized that I hadn't been thinking of anything and that was kind of nice. And then it stopped, and I was sorry it stopped because it was kind of nice not having anything in my head.

Member 8 (in reference to the second exercise): The first thing that I felt was when you said, put the body in a straight line with the floor, I began to feel ten feet tall, like I'd just stretched. And then the first thing that struck me was that I could feel my muscles relax. One of them gave this big jump and then my head sort of wobbled and wow it was clear. When you said the people around the room, it was like a flash of lightness and then a kind of buoyancy and I didn't see anyone there—just a kind of blankness and light.

Member 9 (second exercise): I thought it was a very exciting thing, really exciting. I think what started it was when you said, "Feel the other persons in the room." I didn't have images, and then my breathing seemed to become a part of it. I was breathing in a circle—right. . . . I really can't explain it—I don't know—I was very much *there* and I did feel energy coming from my stomach, I felt, "He didn't have to say that because I know. It's happening." And then when you said it's hard I thought, "No, it's not hard; it's very easy." I first thought that as long as I kept breathing—it was one of the first times in my life when my breathing was very deep and very flowing. I usually have a lot of trouble breathing, but it just seemed like the key was in breathing somehow. But then it, ah, started to go. . . .

Member 4 (second exercise): You know, when you said about the energy in the stomach, I thought, "Who's he trying to kid?" But then I looked, and there it was.

Member 10 (second exercise): I was in contact with the floor and breathing and listening. And as you asked us to go through all the stages, you were just describing things that were already happening. It wasn't—it was happening already. But there was a struggle going on; as you got closer to talking about consciousness, it got harder . . . War. Different kinds of consciousness. War. Being different people, wanting to reach out in different directions. . . . Sort of like contradictory patterns of organizing—contradictory images that couldn't comfortably flow into one another. . . . The thing that I was associating with consciousness is best expressed as rage.

On the basis of these comments it seems fair to conclude that the guided meditations provided access to rarely experienced qualities of awareness for a number of the members in the experimental group. Nor was the impact of the exercises necessarily immediate. One member reported at the beginning of the second week that the meditation had seemed unfruitful to him, confirming his previous sense about meditation. However, during an exercise in the second meeting, where the task was to conduct a group discussion while each individual member attempted to keep alive some sort of individual effort to maintain contact with several levels of experience, this member began speaking while looking into his lap. He reported that each time he looked into his lap his sense of awareness descended into his chest, an experience he had never had before, but that it was difficult to talk and maintain this sense of awareness, and that each time he permitted his glance to rise to the other persons present his awareness immediately leaped back into his head. He also reported that when looking at others he tended to be absorbed in presenting himself well to them, although he recognized from occasional tastes of this absorption that he was "highly self-conscious." It seems likely that the reports by others of their experiences the previous week, if not the meditations themselves, helped to prepare this member conceptually to make the sort of effort that resulted in his experience the second week.

That example provides a clue about the relationship between these experiences of different qualities of attention and the concept of feedback. If one tends to be absorbed in a process of presenting oneself favorably to others, one would tend to censor feedback insofar as it relates to other levels of experiencing besides the level of external appearances. The resulting concentration on others' apparent reactions would leave one unaware of one's immediate inner structuring of the situation and of alternative possible structurings. One's ability to understand, test, contribute to the development of, and act effectively in any situation would be reduced. (It should be noted, however, that one can be absorbed in one's inner imaginings as well as in external appearances. Several comments on pages 108 and 109 suggest a process of breaking out of such inner absorption. Member 8 speaks of her head becoming "clear"; Member 9 says, "I didn't have images"; Member 10 speaks of "contradictory images" simultaneously present.)

Several examples quoted earlier indicated that other members also tended to be absorbed at the level of external appearances, to the point that their eyes continued to "look about" after they were shut (Members 6 and 8). The following comments seem to indicate a similar process:

Member 5 (first exercise): I had such a hard time keeping my eyes closed when we started that I finally put my fingers over them because I was really struggling. It was detracting from anything else—you know, concentrating on keeping my eyes closed. And I've never had that feeling before.

Member 7 (second exercise): When you suggested that we stop whenever we wanted to I was enjoying it very much and I didn't want to stop until in listening I could hear people around me breathing differently or moving or straightening up the cups or whatever. But I knew they had stopped and then my interest in continuing sort of vanished. Maybe I was—maybe I was more aware of people than I thought.

One can hypothesize that the resistance to keeping one's eyes shut under such circumstances derives from one's habitual checking of external appearances to gauge the quality of one's performance.

There was some evidence that members were censoring their feelings about others, presumably in favor of the external cues others communicated or in favor of their own self-images (one's view of oneself as though from the outside), which do not admit of such feelings:

Member 11 (the member who found the meditation unfruitful): I had trouble in my thought with feeling other people. It didn't happen. I kept conceptualizing it. Having images.

Member 4: Earlier . . . I thought I could hear about six different people around breathing and usually I can't even hear myself breathing, so that was very exciting. But then when you said "feel the other people" later in the thing, maybe it was that I was hung up on wanting to feel warmth or a wave of warmth or something, but I kept getting sort of cold air. It may have been the wrong sort of way that I was looking for it, but I—it didn't seem to work for me.

The reference to cold air introduces another aspect of some members' relationship to their own feelings. Certain members seemed to be aware of something like feelings, but they tended to conceptualize them in terms of sensations (like cold air) or other visual images. The lack of particular terms to denote feelings suggests that these persons are not ordinarily aware of their feelings from moment to moment. This lack of familiarity is further illustrated by the following comment:

Member 7: I felt that [feeling the other people during the exercise] was different and I also felt that I wasn't quite prepared for it from what you had said before. Everything else you said was sort of expected. That was unexpected. . . . I felt a little dismayed in not immediately sensing that the way I'd sensed the other things you'd said. . . . Later on it seemed to come in, though in a very strange sort of, just sort of present way. No real contact with people, but just sort of a circle of presence. I think the most powerful feature of the experience for me was at the points where I felt I was integrating something—several things at once. Which occurred. I had this sense of whiteness almost. Maybe it was because I was dizzy. Powerful, energetic, bustling, whiteness. Not just in my head but all around. No images.

(See also the end of Member 8's comment, p. 109.) The words used to describe these experiences are vivid enough to seem admissible as evidence that something was going on inside these persons in response to the author's observation, "We notice the feeling of other persons here." Yet the meaning of these inner experiences—their informative value as feedback—is far from clear. The speakers do not seem to have concepts to fit these experiences into their ordinary thought processes as indices of relationships among levels of experience and persons.

BLOCKS AND DISCONFIRMATION

Given the conceptual confusion provoked by these exercises, and the difficulty of applying thought to the tracing of several, simultaneously interacting levels of experience rather than applying it simply to naming and analyzing the level of focal experience, we would not expect all members of the group to succeed in opening themselves to this kind of experience at first try. If such experience were so easy of access that everyone achieved it at the first attempt, then many of the statements about the strong mystery-mastery forces toward total absorption in focal experience would be suspect. In fact, however, not only did members report *various* experiences, with common themes emerging only through the analysis based on our model of feedback and attention, but some members also reported an *inability* to reach the kind of awareness indicated in the second exercise (the following comments are a direct sequence from the tape):

Member 1: I tried to watch my breathing and my weight, but after a while things became very unclear. And then when the next one came I would lose one. I couldn't believe that you could imagine that we could do five things at once. So then what happened was that I would start at the beginning again and with each breath I was adding one more thing [laughs] and then it would topple at the end—it never quite got to the energy in the stomach.

Member 4: I was doing it sort of check-list style: back still here, still breathing, still. . . .

Member 1: Yeah, each time I would add something I would have the sense that, well, I really didn't have to add that because that was already there in a subsidiary kind of way, but now I was focusing on it.

Member 2: Yeah, I [inaudible] like that too, except I was always able to kind of go back to the floor and I just felt suspended, I felt floating, I felt I was really integrated and everything: I was breathing and I was suspended on the floor, kind of above it, I was listening; and I really felt like I was doing all of them at the same time, but I didn't come to any energy. . . . The energy was where I really got lost.

The preceding comments indicate that the climate of this group session was such that members were not under social pressure from me or the rest of the group to report experiences in conformity with my verbal guidance (I had suggested in the second exercise that "we notice an energy in our stomachs"). The ability and willingness of members to react variously, sometimes in disconfirmation of my ideas and actions, is further demonstrated by their response to a questionnaire after the session. The following excerpts represent the range of responses to two different questions. The first series of responses was to the statement-question: The idea of a conscious level of experience which we rarely, if ever, open ourselves to suggests the possibility of some sort of personal inner effort towards consciousness. What aspects of this idea now appear valid or invalid to you?

Most Valid	**Least Valid**
Member 4: The reality and importance of inner experience.	Whether "personal inner effort" is the best way (even a possible way) to get at it.
Member 5: The fact that it [consciousness] actually exists (I had always considered my thought process as the integrative power) and that it can be achieved with effort.	I find it hard to practice this "conscious level" in normal, everyday life—must set aside time to "meditate."
Member 11: That there is a tension arising from the attempt of another "voice" to surface.	That an experience of this conscious level might be a basis for different interpersonal behavior.

Member 1: I agree with the statement, but the nature and scale of the effort seems difficult to understand.

Member 9: I'm convinced of the validity of the whole system as I see it, but the achieving of it seems very difficult without group support or direction.

Member 6: The fact that those "moments" of consciousness are not everyday occurrences, but in themselves make up for all the un-moments of my life.	Because of all the un-moments it is least valid for me to make a constant (in a total sense) effort.

It seems reasonable to interpret these responses as generally confirming the idea of a level of consciousness with which we are rarely in touch. Most members' reservations about the idea seemed to concern the possibility of consciousness in their day-to-day lives, that is, in conditions other than guided, group-supported meditation. These reservations actually serve to confirm the relative uniqueness of the effect of the experimental engagement and to dramatize, as one member put it, "the scale of the effort" necessary to expand one's everyday awareness to receive consciousness.

The second series of responses was to the question: What aspects of Bill Torbert's personal style and conduct of this session do you see as most and least conducive to communicating the concepts and creating opportunities for persons to test their validity and usefulness?

Member 4: Torbert good at accepting and assimilating new information from the group, but a bit condescending in implied assumption that "inner experience" was new and/or unusual for group member. Maybe . . . maybe not.

Member 11: Bill is willing to accept results which deviate from his theories, but offers perhaps insufficient metaphors to describe what kinds of consciousness I should be looking for.

Member 2: The supportive manner, soft, calm, smooth voice helped me in the meditation exercise. [Later] I felt he could have explained more clearly the idea of consciousness—he seemed so slow, talking with such difficulty, heavy.

Member 3: He was messin' too much with philosophy, but he really seemed to have selected states in the second exercise that tuned into where I was or could be with just a little suggestion.

These four comments touch upon all the perspectives mentioned by the other members and thus can serve to summarize their comments. They both directly express the feeling that the author could be disconfirmed and actually present disconfirming comments.

Several conclusions seem possible on the basis of this summary of the guided meditations and members' reactions to them:

1) The guided meditations did have the desired effect of encouraging contact with different qualities of awareness among most of the members of the group. There is some evidence that

these qualities are sensuous, structural, or background-like, corresponding to the notion of subsidiary attention.

2) The group environment was experienced by members as conducive—perhaps even necessary—to these qualities of awareness, but not as coercive of conformity in their reports of their own experience. Thus, members' reports of their inner experiencings can be trusted within the limits of their ability to conceptualize and verbalize them accurately.

3) There are, however, several strands of evidence that indicate that members were not familiar with the interrelations of these different qualities of awareness nor capable of integrating their appropriation of different elements of attention—that is, they could not fully conceptualize the contents revealed by the different qualities of attention-awareness.

These conclusions and the experiential dilemmas they point to open toward the concerns and efforts of the two meetings of the experimental group after the guided mediations.

LATER MEETINGS OF THE
EXPERIMENTAL GROUP

I had originally intended to include in the meetings with the experimental group some discussion of the categories of interpersonal feedback that will be proposed in chapter 6. In several exercises, members were to be given a chance to test the usefulness of the behavior categories for describing their own and others' behavior. My intention was to work with the group toward reconciling expanded subjective awareness with more effective interpersonal interaction by exploring how different contents of expanded awareness would influence the character of interpersonal feedback. I presented the categories of conscious appropriation (intentionality, relationality, momentary validity) and the structural modes (mystery-mastery, exploration of structure, support, self-disclosure, confrontation [all to be discussed in chapter 6]) at the second meeting, with discussion. Group members generally found it difficult to relate all these categories and levels of analysis to the levels of experiential awareness they had encountered

during the meditation exercises the previous week; they felt
flooded by the number of concepts; and they generally felt that I
spoke too much.

Consequently, I changed my strategy in the middle of the second meeting, leaving aside the categories of behavior, and sug-
gesting that members speak to one another while attempting the
same sort of inner effort as the previous week during the silent
meditations. That is, rather than move directly from the inner,
ineffable, sensual meditative experience to outer, empirical, cognitive behavior categories, I decided to attempt to help members
experience their behavior with others from the inside, hoping
that the behavior categories would eventually appear to flow
from directly distinguishable qualities of their experience rather
than to be alien, imposed categories. The lesson for me in this
change of strategy was that inner, sensual, transfocal awareness
and outer, interpersonal, focal awareness were indeed experienced by members as dichotomous, mutually exclusive kinds of
awareness. This lesson was repeatedly demonstrated during the
rest of the meetings, as the reader will see.

It was during this exercise of speaking to one another while attempting to recognize the subsidiary element of attention that
one person (Member 11) reported his sense of awareness as shift-
ing from his chest to his head, depending upon whether he spoke
and listened while looking into his lap or while looking at others
(see p. 110). From this perspective, the behavior categories could
be seen as involving head awareness and looking at others, since
they involve analysis of external manifestations, rather than involving chest awareness and inner sensation of oneself. Another
member supported this dichotomy among qualities of awareness,
reporting in the postmeeting questionnaire that "talking and
thinking about the concepts [have put me] so much in my head
right now that I can't possibly begin to get back to the integrating of feeling, thought, sensation" (Member 2).

There were also other indications that whatever inner efforts
members were making produced qualities of awareness considerably different from those they ordinarily experienced when concentrating focally in conversation with others. One member (11)
reported hearing his voice as though it were coming from a

phonograph machine, unpleasantly mechanical and automatic, continuing to operate even when he was not wholly immersed in what he was saying. Another member (9) reported a dense energy operating within her, quite distinct from her activity of listening and speaking to others, leading her to a disconcerting sense of duality between herself and the ongoing conversation. Still another member (6) reported that, contrary to her usual sense of passivity and peripheral participation in conversation, she found herself in touch with so many reactions to what was going on within and among other members and herself that she was confronted with the frustrating problem of how to choose what to say.

These comments all suggest that, in expanding one's awareness through one's own effort to include a taste of levels of reality other than the one being focused upon, one can experience the multiplicity of phenomena that reveal themselves as overwhelming and chaotic, and oneself as many-sided, unintegral, and "spaced-out" within oneself and in relation to others. Suddenly, instead of being aware of a single thing at a time, one becomes aware of many things at once without knowing how they relate to one another or are regulated. Whereas within the limits of focal awareness one can feel oneself to be free and in control of oneself (for one sees and acts as usual), when one attains a perspective from which one experiences one's seeing and acting going on as usual and is aware of more as well, what previously seemed free and self-controlled now appears automatic and arbitrary. We can understand why such experiences would feel "unpleasant," "disconcerting," and "frustrating" by contrast to the falsely positive self-concepts described in chapter 1. In short, such experiences directly contradict the socially and personally approved illusion that one is generally free and in control of situations.

On the other hand, these experiences also give opening indications of the inner states that would be associated with high degrees of intentional awareness. The ability to hear oneself talking, for example, would be crucial to maintaining an active sense of the moment-to-moment validity of what one was saying. A sense of duality between oneself and an ongoing conversation would be essential to a sense of relationality to others present, as opposed to undifferentiated fusion with them. And, finally, contact with many reactions to a situation and the need to choose among them in responding can be seen as contributing to one's sense of intentionality—one's sense of personally determining one's own behavior.

During the third meeting of the experimental group, two further exercises were undertaken in the effort to bridge the gap between meditative awareness and verbal awareness. In the first exercise, members closed their eyes and searched for the quality of consciousness in silence and after a few minutes reported their experience while continuing the inner effort. The second exercise was to assign members characteristics that were opposite to the way they had been manifesting themselves in the group and then to conduct a discussion together through these opposites, attempting to be genuine. In both cases, the aim of the exercise was to help members achieve a nonhabitual, transstructural, conscious awareness of themselves while in interaction.

The first exercise was oriented toward reporting present inner experience, as compared to the exercise at the second meeting that was oriented more toward interpersonal feedback with a background of inner effort. The distinction between this exercise and the guided meditations of the first meeting is that in the case of the guided meditations the members reported *past* experiences. It may be that members regarded themselves as being "carried through" the guided meditations (as suggested by the comment of Member 3, p. 105), whereas this exercise required them to initiate their own efforts. In any event, the sense of resistance and conflict that members felt was expressed openly.

RESISTANCE TO INTEGRATED AWARENESS

The felt conflict between transfocal awareness and ordinary focal awareness was immediately evident in members' expressions of inner resistance to the first exercise (the comments on the following pages are directly sequential except for occasional omissions of irrelevant comments).

Author: (Proposes the exercise.)

Member 3: Sounds harder to me to do. That's my own reaction if it entails communicating with other people and doing it. That's harder than looking inside myself.

Member 6: I guess I'm sort of opposite in feeling and that is that I'm having a very hard time coming into myself cause I've been going, going, going all day. Even the energy of listening to Bill was outward-type energy and when I tried to bring it in, you know, it would stay in a little bit and I would feel my body and try to think how I was reacting toward what he was saying, to how I was listening to what he was saying. And I feel if we were to do a meditation exercise, it would be helpful maybe after a couple of minutes of silence to hear in a sense other people's trips to see if I have anything similar, or if I haven't gotten going yet, to maybe help me get going.

Member 4: Right. I was almost, you know, resenting looking forward to the silence if it was going to be completely silent, hopin' it wouldn't last too long and thinking, "Will it last ten minutes? I hope not." 'Cause I really want to be with other people some, too. So I hope people will at some point talk.

Member 8: I like the idea of people talking because that's what I react to. Thinking for a few minutes by myself is okay, but from what you said before it's like this consciousness you're talking about is like the start of a reaction to something coming in. You know, at the point that you start to react. I'd like to have something to react to rather than just my own thoughts.

Members reported after the exercise as well that the two kinds of awareness seemed to conflict with one another and be mutually exclusive:

Member 9: I found it terribly hard to keep watching or keep tasting as other people were talking. It was very distracting to what was happening here and I sort of wanted to get into what they were saying. And I couldn't do either.

Member 8: I felt the same thing, that I was listening to them and giving up just listening to myself inside, like the words were just sort of coming in and I, all I was doing was listening and I wasn't thinking anymore.

Author: How did that compare to your expectation? You know, when you wanted the words to stimulate you.

Member 8: Well, it's funny, but it's the opposite .

Author: Yeah, that's what it sounds like.

Member 8: Yeah, it's . . . I guess I'll have to think about that.

Member 7: Some of the things that people said fit right in with what was going on very easily. Not that it was similar, similar feelings or images, but it just came in without distracting me. . . . But when you [author] started talking the last time, it didn't work that way. It was, it was something completely different from what was going on, not in terms of its content or image so much as in terms of the whole way of structuring you seem to have. And I can't fit words to it, but to force myself to: it seemed abstract and, you know, it just didn't come through.

Author: And it had a disturbing influence?

Member 7: Yeah, shortly after that I just quit. I don't know, maybe I was just getting tired, too.

Member 1: I was feeling—I don't know how to describe it—but it was really a shock to me when you first spoke and then when several other people spoke too, really a shock. And I tried to figure out what it was like and the best thing to say what it was like was when you begin to doze off and then you wake up suddenly. It was like that. But I didn't fall asleep. I was very aware of, you know, it felt like sort of cold water or cold wind flowing through me from your direction.

Member 7: Cold water?

Member 1: Yeah. You know the way your body shakes or does whatever it does when you just wake up?

Member 13: I think there really is a difference between doing it in yourself and doing it in front of somebody. Because when you first spoke it was like an interruption. But then I thought "everyone is going to be talking, so I've just got to listen." Everything that people said was very, very interesting; nothing that I was doing in myself. And I learned a lot from listening, but I couldn't really do what I was doing before. It was either-or. Either being very calm or letting what people said sink in and being sort of interested. But it was very hard—it took a very conscious effort to get back, and it was too bad I had to block everything out by trying to forget what I had heard.

Member 5: I feel like the difficulty I have is that I just concentrate so hard on focusing what I'm trying to focus on that I can't find time to be conscious of myself and my energy level. Somebody says something else and I can't . . . I either have to let something go and focus on that. I can't seem to make myself go both ways very well.

Member 12: I had, I had, it was almost like pain trying to say something. 'Cause I felt like it was sort of expected, and so I wanted to. But if I was going to say anything that was sort of coherent with what was going on, it wasn't going to be in whole sentences. I really had problems making, formulating a sentence. And then I would get one formulated and all ready to say it, and then I would realize I wasn't feeling it anymore. I was feeling something else. And then I would have to give up for a little while and kind of float.

THE "EFFORT TO RELAX"

I had spoken, before the exercise, of the subtle "effort to relax" involved in maintaining contact with several levels of reality simultaneously and continuing to perceive and behave focally. I said that one aspect of the "effort to relax" is an acceptance of what one experiences in oneself and others, rather than breaking contact with experiencing by evaluating the experience. Evaluation, I maintained, can play a constructive role in experiential learning when one is deciding what to focus on in perception and behavior, thus aiding contact with a level of experience. But evaluation merely obstructs experiential learning if applied in such a way as to break contact with other levels of experience. Thus, from the transcript:

Contact with consciousness . . . involves not reacting negatively to what's going on inside me, like ordinarily very often when I look inside and I see I'm in a certain condition, I'm very nervous or something, I say, "Oh, God, now stop being nervous." And the moment I begin reacting and say "Stop being nervous," I think I usually cut off any contact with consciousness of my condition, identifying instead with my control over the situation as represented by my statement "Stop being nervous." I go into a thought, my structural perspective, I'm judging myself very much at the thought and feeling level.

But just at the moment when I directly saw, tasted, experienced something there, when I saw how I was being, what my state was, that I was being nervous, that I was talking too quickly, just at that moment I think there's always a momentary contact with consciousness. But we very quickly throw a blanket over it by judging it at the lower level of thought: "it's bad" or "it's good," either one. We use the judgment to get away from whatever we were a moment ago, or to hold onto it if we think it was good.

Whereas thought can easily break contact with consciousness, it cannot so easily initiate contact with consciousness by deciding to make an effort to do so. I discussed this dilemma with the members before the exercise, as follows:

Author: One of the things I feel I've been working on . . . is what is the distinction between consciousness and thought and feeling. And very often I find myself, like I decide, "Okay, now I'm going to be conscious." I *think* to myself, and I start looking around and say, "Well, what's going on in your head, Bill?" And maybe I start getting a little tingling sensation in my hand, but what I feel after a few minutes of that is an enormous pressure in my body because my head is directing everything that is going on, my thought is attempting to look at itself and at everything else that is going on at that level. And I very often ask in that state, "what are your feelings now?" and I experience a great emptiness in myself or undifferentiated pressure. . . .

Member 6: I've been tuning in and out of what you've been saying and I can't listen anymore.

Member 9: Same here. I'm finding it very hard too.

Member 5: I have a question. Are you saying that we should try to postpone the evaluative part and sort of stretch the consciousness, or try to do that?

Author: No, not exactly. It's a good question—exactly what we have to do is the difficult question. I can't possibly give you the exact words for doing it because one of the things you'll find is that you do something. What I hope I'm doing is that the moment that evaluative mechanism goes into operation for you, you will have a little sort of memory of what's been said and you'll, you won't identify with the evaluation completely. You see, ordinarily I think we get totally absorbed by our evaluation. Our awareness narrows to include only the content of our evaluation, not even the fact that we are evaluating, much less our continuing behavior and the world outside. And now maybe as you see that beginning to happen, sometimes you'll, you won't go into it completely, you won't be totally absorbed by it—it'll keep going.

Member 5: Sort of seeing yourself being evaluative.

Author: Yeah, exactly, but the problem is, you might try to do that intentionally once, "Well, I'm just going to watch myself be evaluative." And if you're watching yourself just from your thought, you won't be able to continue the evaluation, you'll interrupt yourself, and you'll find that you have to force the words out like, "That's terrible," while hearing yourself think that, and you know that has nothing to do with the way you are usually evaluating. If you successfully get to this other viewpoint, the evaluation will just keep going, but you won't be totally absorbed by it. There'll sort of be a presence that's watching that in you.

Member 13: So it's sort of like being able to watch yourself do whatever you are doing.

Author: Right. I want to be careful about using the verb "watching" too much. Because for most of us I think that's associated with a sort of telescope in our heads. So another word that might be better might be "tasting." That we taste the evaluation going on. I just offer the other word because otherwise it might be harder to get a feel for it.

Member 13: So it's definitely not thinking about your own thinking.

Author: Right. Exactly, exactly. But this is what you'll see yourself trying to do, and once again you'll have another opportunity because once again the first move will be "Oh, that's bad, that's not what I'm supposed to be doing." And you'll go searching for something else. But if you do that, you've once again become absorbed in the evaluation and decision process at the level of thought. So at the moment when you say, "Oh, I'm just thinking about thinking," there's already something else there that's consciousness. You don't have to go searching for it at that moment. It's already there.

METAPHORS FOR RELEASE FROM THOUGHT

Now that I have sketched the context around the first exercise of the third meeting, both in terms of the kind of effort I suggested and the kinds of difficulties the members experienced, we can turn to some of the qualities of awareness reported by members during the course of the exercise itself.

(*Three minutes of silence, then the following comments with short silences in between.*)

Author: I have this thought in my head that something very different is going to happen. I keep looking around for that different thing. My mind is hypothesizing what it will look like. Sort of sweeping out the room to be sure nothing else gets in the way.

Member 4: I'm pretending about that right now, and I'm thinking about how, when you go outside at night and your eyes get used to the smaller amount of light, you can see the stars, and in the same way here it's as if, once the visual images begin to calm down, you begin to see all the other incredible levels of activity within the room, all the inward thoughts and flashes of communication between people. I mean, it's like a secret fireworks that's going on all the time.

Member 7: A great deal is going on and has been going on. It just occurs to me like that, sort of seeing a huge sky late at night with dusk colors and grey clouds, the landscape is black and somber. And then all of a sudden I'm seeing the same scene through a very constricted opening, and then my whole vision is engulfed with it again. It's just visually the same thing as the thought "everything and nothing." For a while I was marking things that I was going to mention, and now it doesn't seem important.

Member 6: I can't get away from seeing pink and orange and black, mostly diagonal lines but sometimes little points. My head is very full of thought, kind of as abrupt as the diagonal lines. My eye itches and I had to resist itching it. I can't get out of those two categories of thought and colors and sights in front of my eyes. I can't fall down and encompass anything else. . . . But as I just spoke it disappeared while I was speaking. I didn't see those colors, but only saw black.

Member 9: I keep telling thoughts to get out of there and then I sort of get drawn into them and wish I hadn't said that, that I could have just watched those thoughts instead of saying "get out."

Member 6: I just fell into my stomach by pretending I was Alice in Wonderland chewing on the cookie and falling, falling down the rabbit hole, and my head was spinning. And now I'm kind of located in my chest. I don't see much, I'm just more in touch with my body.

Member 13: Since the beginning, my head has felt really light, I think. Nothing really has been going through it. [Inaudible] no images. And it seemed especially like a contrast to all the effort I was making when I was listening to Bill in the beginning and what he was saying. It seemed like all that tension just went away and nothing else really came into its place.

Member 7: The thinking that I know I'm doing and that I'm aware of doing while not wanting to is very isolated, sort of a stream that I can see, feel going on, but it's not total. But it puzzles me because I feel that in the state I'm in now I could play chess very, very, very well, which one normally thinks of as totally thinking process. But I can see that my thinking is very small, very defined and separate from everything else.

Member 4: Sometimes it's better to just let the thoughts skim through lightly than to make the whole effort to block them.

Member 7: Yeah, if you try to block them it takes over everything else.

Member 4: Right.

Member 7: It's like the thoughts are a haze over a meadow. They're there and you can see them and they come and go, but the whole meadow is alive with other things.

Member 13: My feet are falling asleep, but they don't feel like my feet. They're outside of me completely. And, well, it's very strange.

Member 12: I feel like I'm floating in a dark ocean after swimming a long time, so that you're really tired. You kind of give up and let the waves carry you, tow you around. But you're really tired and don't really have thoughts, so it's hard to talk about.

Member 6: I feel very dissatisfied with words.

Member 7: I said meadow, but it was really more like a swamp. And when I try to say "Well, that's interesting. Why is it a swamp?" there's just confusion, blocking, clamor.

Member 4: No firm footing.

Author: So many things come through me. As each person speaks, whole different waves of feeling, images flying through, various sensations, and I keep wanting to say "This one is the right one." If I could just find a home in one of them, stay awhile. They're just all going through at such a tremendous rate. And as I speak, the words are so disconnected from everything that's happening inside really. It just keeps going. So that they don't provide any sort of final summation of what's happening either. Yet I right now do sort of feel at home in some way, but don't want to focus on that particularly. That would destroy it somehow.

Member 8: I'd like to take my ears off. All I can hear is words, and I don't want to hear them because they stop within the walls of my head. And they just sort of bounce around and I don't have time for anything else.

Perhaps the two most striking aspects of these reports are the emphasis on thought as only one aspect of all that occurs within persons, rather than as encompassing and framing, defining and directing all experience, and the amount of imagery and metaphor to which members resort in the effort to describe their experiences. These two aspects would seem both to complement and to counter each other. If thought is itself but an aspect of experience, then it could not hope to formulate experience accurately except by resort to word-combinations that point beyond themselves, as in metaphor. On the other hand, if with eyes closed I begin to describe a landscape or rabbit hole or swamp or sea, I can easily become totally absorbed in this description to the point of losing contact with the quality of experience which suggested it.

How then, the reader may ask, can we be sure that the images to which the group members treat us can make any claims to approaching truthful representations of what is happening within them? We can look more closely at the speakers' statements for clues as to whether they became absorbed in their descriptions or not. Examining the statements for such clues, we find several categories of images. My initial image of sweeping out the room is an attempt to describe a state of absorption in thought, a state which I acknowledge myself to be experiencing in the earlier part of my statement. The next image, of stars at night, is presented simply as an image ("I'm thinking about how . . .") and only retrospectively applied to what is happening within the speaker, so in this case we cannot be sure whether the speaker is simply trying to make a good thing out of his image. After the exercise, however, this speaker characterized his images as follows:

I felt like I was sending out messages to a lot of different people. . . . In fact, I was trying to make the sun come out on Susan's ocean for a while. [Laughter.] And they weren't really things I was working on. *They were more things I had done by the time I thought them.* (Emphasis added.)

The statement of the third speaker during the exercise most clearly indicates that he is not absorbed in his image of night sky and somber landscape, for he surrounds the image by indications that more is happening that he is aware of than merely the image ("A great deal is going on"; "and then all of a sudden"). Member 6 explicitly describes an image that she "can't get away from seeing" rather than a metaphor for some other inner experience. Yet her very ability to speak about it and then to note its disappearance indicates that she was not totally absorbed by it.

Thus we can begin to see more clearly that it is not by some abstract claim to represent the exact state of affairs within oneself that these statements may be said to gain credibility but rather by their concrete attention to the actual degree of absorption the speaker experiences. In other words, a number of the images and metaphors are not intended to represent the full truth about what is happening within the person at that time, but rather a limited truth about the quality of absorption he is experiencing, a limited truth about his limited awareness.

Only the image of thought as a haze about a meadow alive with other things as well makes direct claim to release from absorption in thought, to encompassing thought itself within a wider region of awareness. That the speaker in this case is not merely absorbed in some image of a meadow as he speaks is indicated by his later statement reformulating the image to that of a swamp in an attempt more closely to approximate his experiencing. Furthermore, the two following comments indicate that this image has meaning for others also, as Member 4 is able to identify a quality of the image that makes it accurate for his experience ("No firm footing") and I then translate this quality into the impossibility of finally summarizing what is happening. There is in a sense no home, only a path: "so many things come through me" and keep going.

THE FINAL EXERCISE

The final exercise of the third meeting contrasted strongly with the meditative exercises. In attempting to act out characteristics opposite to their usual modes of self-presentation with others (the opposites being assigned to them by their spouses and other members of the group), members were concentrating on the (for them) distinct realm of external, interpersonal, focal awareness, yet supposedly doing so within a conceptual-emotional-sensory structure at variance with their usual structural sense of themselves. To do so with any sense of authenticity would require them to to be in touch with a conscious sense of identity or, to use a term from the model in chapter 1, a sense of ultrastability. Otherwise, the different structure would merely seem alien and inauthentic.

By contrast to enacting this new role with authenticity or conscious genuineness, members might also make contact with consciousness as observer of structural-behavioral conflict. For one can imagine that in attempting to agree when one usually negates or to frown when one usually smiles—that is, to take on one's opposite—one's words, gestures, tones of voice, and facial expressions could sound and feel odd to oneself. One would experience conflict at the structural and behavioral levels between accustomed ways of organizing and carrying out behavior and kinds of behavior which do not fit into the accustomed sense of what is appropriate. And that conflict, if recognized and borne, would be registered, not by one's accustomed structure, which would be out of equilibrium precisely because it could not encompass the task at hand, but by consciousness.

Still another reaction to a momentary impression of disharmony would be the return one's ordinary structural attitude, evaluating the disharmonious effort as somehow valueless, and thus not appropriating consciousness.

As could be expected, the exercise itself was filled with tension, noise, explosive hilarity, and awkward silences. Members' senses of timing, appropriateness, interpretation of events, and inner-strategizing——aspects of their ordinary structural definition of their roles in situations—were thrown out of kilter. Afterward they reported experiences such as the following (not in direct sequence):

Member 1: I had trouble seeing anything out there or translating it through this role into behavior.

Member 5: I felt like I was concentrating too hard on behaving the way I was supposed to be behaving and not really feeling anything. I kept looking for places where I could be assertive.

Member 1: There was more of a pressure to say something than there usually is.

Member 7: I just felt agitated and out of touch completely.

Member 6: Usually I play things over in my mind and know what I want to do, but with those two [roles] it was as if I were up against a stone wall. I, in a way, felt as if someone were holding me back, or that I was at the end of the earth and about to fall off. . . . I couldn't even imagine what I would do, and it was just a big blank.

The various qualities of awareness that we have just denoted as "conscious genuineness," "consciousness of structural-behavioral conflict," and "lack of appropriation of consciousness through evaluation" were all reported or observed after the exercise. Two members reported a sense of genuineness about their role-behaviors:

Member 3: Yeah, I'm really glad that the role was given to me because I really meant everything I said. It was really a mind-blowing experience. It allowed me to really let out.

Author: I kept scaring myself by throwing these flip comments around and finding out that they were arrows not frisbees. I was finding myself really twisting things in. You know, seeing a side of myself, well, part of my role was to not be accepting, and yeah, it was sure there in me.

Two other members noted during the discussion *after* the exercise that some members were at that point more genuinely enacting their role-opposites than they had been able to during the exercise itself, even though everyone had presumably ceased acting:

Member 11: I don't mean to—I *do* mean to interrupt—[here it might be appropriate to interpolate that Member 11's role-opposite had been to be dominating] I'm really struck by Jane. I've rarely seen you act like this—not taking back statements or qualifying them. Maybe it's an aftertaste of her role [which had been to act self-assured].

Member 9: I can't get over the carryover though. Even though it was hard to get into, I and others still seem to be operating through [the roles].

These observations suggest the speculation that members initially decided to take part in the exercise from within their ordinary cognitive-emotional-sensory structures which, in turn, resisted temporary displacement during the exercise. Then after the exercise the ordinary structures relaxed this extra resistance against the usually suppressed qualities, which, stimulated by exercise, now expressed themselves.

The second quality of awareness—consciousness of structural-behavioral conflict—was clearly expressed by one member:

Member 8: I guess I had a different reaction. I'm feeling a lot of pain now. And I found it impossible to be just agreeing, and it's very painful for me to realize that. I am spontaneous in some ways, but I am also very supercontrolled and it wouldn't come out. I just wanted to follow what was happening, but I kept analyzing it.

As long as this member operates within the structural configuration that ordinarily controls her perceptions, interpretations, and behaviors, she can feel herself to be spontaneous. In other words, the transformations between her structure and behavior are congruent and unnoticed. Attempting to perceive and behave in ways contrary to what is "natural" for her, however, she encounters the "supercontrolled" quality of her structure, which denies her the freedom she assumed she had.

The third quality of awareness experienced during the exercise —that of returning to one's ordinary structural mode to evaluate an initial impression of disharmony and blocked effort as not worth pursuing—is revealed, in the following comments, to have occurred in Members 7, 6, and 11:

Member 7: I found it very difficult. I didn't have a role I could jump into. First, I was listening. The role I wanted to try was to be very critical and harsh. At first I tried to get at it by saying "This is a great big put-on." But then that didn't make any sense, because why should I be harsh to somebody for not being themselves?

Member 8: I have the perfect role for you: not being so logical.

Member 5 (who is Member 7's spouse): That's what I told you [before the exercise]!

Member 6: I think I made the mistake of picking four roles and then splitting myself among them.

Member 13: Why did you try four rather than one?

Member 6: I guess because I knew I couldn't do one. So I just did the two that were easiest and sloughed off on the two I couldn't do. I don't think that was conscious.

Member 11: I had trouble with my role completely. I mean, I couldn't do it at all. Bill told me to be dominating, and frankly I usually experience myself as dominating and any other mode seemed ridiculous.

The automatic, nonconscious, absorbing quality of the evaluations ("that didn't make any sense," "I just . . . sloughed off," "any other mode seemed ridiculous") contrasts sharply with the wide vistas of awareness evident in the quotations from the earlier exercise, and highlights the difficulty of achieving and maintaining consciousness in action.

In sum, the exercises of the second and third experimental-group meetings and the members' responses to these exercises indicate the scale and subtlety of the effort of contacting the level of consciousness and congruently transforming its perspectives and initiatives through thought, feeling, and inner sensation into behavior. Central existential dilemmas in this learning process seem to be:

(1) how to reconcile inner, sensual, personal, meditative, trans-focal subsidiary awareness with external, cognitive, interpersonal, calculative focal awareness; how to interpret conscious tastes and intents congruently at the structural level and realize them authentically at the behavioral level; more specifically:

(2) how to interpret, understand, and act upon the negative emotions aroused by the conflict between conscious awareness and mystery-mastery self-images; and

(3) how to identify transcognitive awareness in oneself without thereby dispersing it and becoming reabsorbed in cognitive evaluations of impressions; how to experience thought as but one aspect of one's total presence without thereby blocking, dismissing, or devaluing its function.

These dilemmas face the group members both as persons desiring to be in fuller contact with the lives they are living and as scientists concerned to see phenomena and their interrelations more clearly.

IMPLICATIONS

After reading preliminary drafts of this chapter, a number of people have asked some fundamental and related questions about its practical, theoretical, religious, and political significance and implications.

(1) The appropriation of full consciousness, even though it seems immediately to involve a subtle sort of relaxation, seems in the long range to involve a formidable spiritual effort. Is it genetically possible, psychologically advisable, and socially desirable for everyone? Isn't there a practical need to filter out some of the complexity of reality if we are to act at all in day-

to-day matters? Doesn't this need to filter reality constitute both man's potential for commitment and man's tragedy?

2) Why is a broad distinction made in these meetings between focal and transfocal awareness rather than the tripartite division of focal, subsidiary, and intentional elements of attention introduced in part I?. In particular, why is the quality of intentional attention so little discussed?

3) If the personal discipline necessary to purify one's temple to receive the holy fire is initially diminished by the author's and group's support of persons only peripherally committed to such an effort, will this process not make it more difficult later for the persons involved to discipline themselves and not fall into despair?

4) The author's authority during these meetings appears more paternal than fraternal, his language more academic than personal, his appeal directed more to a leisurely elite than to the common man. Under these circumstances, how can he possibly be exploring revolutionary consciousness?

These questions seem highly legitimate. They verify the extent to which people related the resistances, conflicts, and emotions aroused by this investigation to the core of human destiny. And they indicate that the conditions appropriate to "training investigators" are not describable by a scientific methodology that aims to isolate variables from the broad context of man's political and religious experience. If, indeed, the author tended to take social conditions for granted in introducing group members to the terms and processes of inward vision suggested in this section, then these questions quickly oblige aspiring investigators of subsidiary and intentional processes to focus on social realities. And the questions demand responses that will be visible in terms of the future scientific, political, and religious styles of the investigators—mainly, of course, of the author, since his responsibility is greatest. Such responses are primarily generated by living, not arguing, so my responses here will not exceed the following short comments on the questions. These comments are not intended as final answers, but rather as my way of framing the questions in an effort to keep them maximally alive.

1) The need to focus on day-to-day experience and to choose *what* to focus on *within* daily experience is not denied by this model of attention; but the genetic, psychological, and social questions raised will not be solved by an awareness limited to focal objects. Moreover, no matter how far the effort to appropriate full consciousness will lead those who initially attempt it, they will be that much closer to understanding and accepting their actual role in the world, that much less likely to project inner dissonance on the world, unless they permit themselves to be led down some path which only espouses the rhetoric of consciousness toward other ends. Since the choice of path is partly a focal issue, man's potential for commitment and for tragedy is excited rather than abridged by an effort to appropriate full consciousness.

2) The lack of independent evidence regarding the intentional element of attention fits with the lack of overt focusing in the meetings upon religious or political issues, which represent man's ultimate investments regarding the meaning of the world and his relative role—his intention, purpose, life form —in it. Conversely, the intentional element of attention is most readily discriminable in the context of religious or political questioning, if, indeed, one is able to remain self-questioning when one is aware that religious or political foundations of meaning are at stake. At such moments, the intentional element of attention can be the active element. At other moments, it may take the less obvious denying or reconciling forms. Further study by the experimental group could have led its members to recognize the distinction between subsidiary and intentional attention, even if the intentional element continued to manifest itself primarily in denying and reconciling forms.

3) The danger of tempting another away from personal discipline is always real, but an isolated spiritual quest is not the only solution. Another is that new social forms be evolved to provide continuing support for such a quest.

4) For six years I have been attempting to explore the interaction and integration of the various levels of experience that I

try to codify in this work and I am uncertain what kind of authority this experience creates for me in relation to others. I am certain that I am not yet fully and permanently conscious and that my behavior thus betrays patterns and assumptions of which I am not aware. I am also certain that each man arrives at the continous revolution of consciousness by his own path and that no single pattern of behavior reveals the necessarily haphazard exploration toward one's center, periphery, and translation process between center and periphery. On the other hand, the entire model of "levels of experience" and "experiential consciousness" is initially foreign to culturally ingrained patterns of thought and therefore intrinsically difficult to understand. To what extent this factor contributes to what some readers experience as an academic and paternal style is difficult for me to estimate. Also, not my behavior but my structuring of the three meetings may be what strikes some as paternal. Since this book does not address the question of patterns *among* units of behavior, the criteria for determining whether my structuring of the meetings was coercive or liberating are not obvious.

Chapter Six

CATEGORIES FOR OBSERVING VERBAL
BEHAVIOR

A framework for categories of verbal behavior to distinguish between behaviors conducive and not conducive to experiential learning was introduced in chapter 4 (p. 97). Three levels of analysis categorize the interactions between consciousness and cognitive-emotional-sensory structure, between that structure and behavior, and between behavior and the world outside. The three levels of analysis are named, respectively, conscious appropriation of behavior, structural modes of behavior, and focal functions of behavior. These categories deserve to be defined and exemplified with some care because they become the basis of reliability and validity studies in chapters 7 through 9.

Of the three systems of inference, conscious appropriation of behavior is most fully developed in operational terms in chapters 7 through 9, for it most directly measures the degree of consciousness of the speaker. Since, according to the model offered in chapter 1, experiential learning occurs when a person is conscious, this system of inference should, in theory, most directly measure the degree of experiential learning occuring for the speaker.

Nevertheless, discussion and exemplification of the other two systems of inference can serve several purposes for readers and scorers. First, such discussion indicates what attributes of behavior are not scored by the categories of conscious appropriation of behavior. Second, it helps to relate this theory of verbal behavior to other previous work in the behavioral sciences. Third, it may be of interest to the reader in reflecting about the permutations, themes, and emphases in his own behavior.

THE FOCAL FUNCTIONS OF BEHAVIOR

Six focal functions seem to me to represent the problematic issues in day-to-day life for any three-level human system, whether it be completely formed and in permanent contact with consciousness, not yet completely formed, or not regularly in contact with consciousness. They include: (1) setting and achieving goals in one's environment, or *work;* (2) determining boundaries that reflect one's differentiation from and integration with the environment, or *identity;* (3) defining what sorts of information it is appropriate to exchange with other systems, or *intimacy;* (4) discovering what thoughts, feelings, and behaviors are authentic, effective transformations of conscious intentions, or *education;* (5) fixing responsibility for the sequence in which events occur among systems, that is, for group leadership and for the source of meaning-structures, or *authority;* and (6) transforming structural-level configurations by behavior outside the comprehension of existing structures but nevertheless demanding response, or *action.*

Let us approach these six functions, one at a time, more comprehensively:

WORK. Setting, checking, adjusting, and achieving goals and paths to goals in the environment. Work is the most general function of behavior in relation to the environment. However, the transformation of the world outside is not the sole function of behavior. In contrast to this productive function of behavior, the five other focal issues perform expressive functions. That is, behavior is also concerned with the reconciliation of disparities among the "inner" levels of experience of different people. Such disparities can be expressed as mutually hostile emotions, ideologies, perceptions, and actions that disrupt work in the absence of a common struggle toward consciousness. Or these disparities can fire a common struggle towards consciousness, complementing and dignifying work.

From this high rhetoric, let us turn to a few examples of the kind of comments people might make in everyday conversation that would be categorized as work according to our definition:

Executive at a business meeting: There are ways. (This statement deals, on the surface, with paths to goals. There are no clues, besides its surface meaning, what its behavioral function is, so it is categorized as work.)

School official to consultant: Well, what do you have in mind for this conference? (This statement invites the setting of goals, or the expression of goals.)

At a cocktail party: There's an amusing example which actually ampifies your point. (Here an activity is justified by relating it to a goal—amplifying a point.)

Student at group meeting to determine a course project: The thing I was trying to say was that I'm not sure it's going to be easy to get people to talk about what their real anxieties are. (The determination of focal function is made here on the basis of the main clause—"the thing I was trying to say was"—rather than on the basis of the content of the thought. The speaker is using a second path to achieve the goal of expressing an idea.)

Social researcher in the early stages of a collaborative study: What I'm thinking now is that the whole thing is being too objective-oriented. The way I'm seeing this group is subjective and not worrying about accurate data samples. (The speaker is disputing the path chosen to accomplish a goal.)

Teacher to student: I'm not sure what you're saying. I'm not sure if it's that you're having a hard time integrating formal requirements with the possibility of a relationship—or if you're asking me to respond to you. (Here the speaker is checking to determine what the other person's goal is.)

The examples indicate that verbal behavior fitting the category of work consists predominantly of setting, checking, and adjusting goals and paths to goals, rather than actually achieving goals. The actual achievement of goals often has to do with the organization of the inanimate world rather than talking to others. Authoritative orders to do work, which in a pyramidal organization tend to be a first step in goal achievement after the goals have been set by a higher level of management, are not regarded as work by this scoring procedure, but rather as fitting the category of *authority,* to be described next.

Stories, historical descriptions (i.e., past tense), and logical analyses, when offered directly in principal clauses, are all considered work in this scoring procedure, unless a context shows that a story fulfills one of the expressive functions.

AUTHORITY. Discovering, setting, asserting, fixing, or acknowledging responsibility for the naming and sequencing of events, for the source of meaning, and for the source of leadership. If the varying levels of human experience were not distorted in their mutual interaction by the tendency to concentrate all attention into focal awareness, the issue of authority would not occur overtly at the level of behavior. It would merely be implicit in the kind, pace, and sequence of work done. However, because current science, technology, education, and cultural myths regard the world as restricted to what is focally observable and tangible, effort is made to control focal experience by manipulation. Consequently, it also becomes a task to rediscover the organizing function that different levels of experience exert in relation to one another.

Both the effort to organize by manipulation and the effort to recognize interlevel organization can be expressed verbally in ordinary conversation. The following examples are drawn from situations in which the speakers tend to be somewhat more self-reflexive than would usually be the case. This tendency helps us in our initial exemplification of authority:

During a discussion of a theory in a class: My only problem with this sort of scheme is that the words are contaminated for us with other meanings. (This statement is explicitly concerned with establishing a source of meaning for words.)

Son to father in a family conversation: No, no, that's not what I was saying at all. (Again the issue is the meaning of words.)

Teacher to student about a course project: Well, it sounds like in all of that is something like "commitment." And the thing that tastes bitter to you around final product is "final." Like, are we building something or not? (This statement is concerned with naming.)

In a group: People never challenge me when I suggest we do something next, but the group never does it. (This statement exposes the relation between sequencing and leadership.)

In a voluntary political action group: It's a question of who will take the first step. (Again, the issues of sequencing and leadership arise.)

In an encounter group: Don't resign yourself to passivity; don't accept it as a personality and internal problem. The group must be doing something that you are defining as "not being interested in you." It might help us if you could tell us what cues we're giving that make you think that we're disinterested in your ideas. (Commands always involve asserting responsibility for the sequencing of events. In this case, the content of the command concerns the meaning of an event—the group's disinterest in one person.)

Member of meditation group to author during first half of first session: The evening seems to be sort of a vacuum which you've created for us. Maybe it isn't up to you to establish a structure . . . even though it's arbitrary. (This speaker is concerned with naming events—"vacuum," "arbitrary"—and with fixing responsibility for leadership—"Which you've created for us," "maybe it isn't up to you.")

In a T-group: I have trouble figuring out when to raise feelings when I'm not interested by what is going on. (This statement explores the speaker's responsibility in sequencing events.)

In some ways, the concept of authority offered here is more restricted than in ordinary usage. Discussion of rules, for example, does not fall under the heading of authority here, but rather is an aspect of *identity,* because rules concern the structure of a group or situation or institution. The same thing is true of group norms. Although, speaking outside the framework of this classification system, one may say that rules and norms are distinctive precisely because they are authoritative—and although this manner of speaking gives us a clue about the connection between structure and process—nevertheless, in this scoring procedure, structural features of discussion are considered identity issues.

IDENTITY. Determination or exploration of boundaries, structures, or processes that characterize, distinguish, and specify a given individual by contrast to its environment. The individual in question may be a person, a group, a situation, an organization, or a society. Identity becomes a focal issue overtly because entities do not remain stable at the level of focal experience, yet the process of change is invisible since it is an interlevel phenomenon, so persons living only with focal awareness repeatedly face the question whether a given individual "is himself."

A second orientation to identity occurs when a person begins exploring beyond focal awareness. Identity remains a focal issue as he attempts to check what *he* in particular is discovering beyond focal awareness as compared to others' experience.

The following comments all express the issue of identity:

At a party: I forget things from hour to hour. (An example of personal process.)

In a T-group: I feel I am not a member because I do not accept to learn in this way. (Here the speaker distinguishes himself from a group by specifying a process characteristic of the group—"to learn in this way"—which falls outside his boundaries as he sees them.)

At a school staff meeting: Who belongs to this faction? (The speaker is exploring one aspect of the boundaries of a sub-group.)

Leader at outset of a T-group: The rules are that we stay in the here and now, and we try to find out what is going on within and between us. (The speaker is characterizing the structure of this situation.)

In a T-group: Your delivery is soft-spoken, like people who know they will have an impact and don't need to pound it in. (Here another individual is characterized by linking a particular element of his process—delivery—with an inferred structure—a sense of self based in knowledge that one's presence is experienced by others.)

Member of meditation group during first half of first session: I have a different image. I have a sense of being withdrawn, for myself anyway I feel distant . . . maybe partly because I'm being more reactive than active. (This speaker characterizes an element of momentary personal emotional structure—being withdrawn, distant—relating it to a more general sense of personal structure—being reactive.)

Engineer at meeting on company sales policy: I guess I felt that I didn't have the credentials to discuss that topic. (Here the speaker reveals how he structures his behavior—in terms of assessing his credentials to participate in discussion.)

The reader will recall that when the event described is past history, even if it is internal to the person, it falls under the category of work, rather than identity. Thus, for example, the following statement is categorized as work.

Member of meditation group: I did a very heavy and rich kind of trip. I started off being conscious of the people in this room, hearing the noises and shoveling outside, then the heater and a sense of this house as a life-support system.

The reader may also wish to contrast the final example of the identity category with the examples of *intimacy* offered next. The engineer gives a sense of what kind of information gets exchanged in this group (part of the definition of intimacy), but entirely from the point of view of his personal structuring of the situation.

INTIMACY. Defining or exploring what sorts of information it is appropriate to exchange with other individuals, or what is regarded as informative; or describing the present conditions, qualities, and effects of exchange. Two basic orientations result in discussion focused on the issue of intimacy. One orientation is that personal habit or social custom automatically determines appropriate forms of information for exchange, and that within these forms the moment-to-moment relational process is inevitable or arbitrary, but certainly always *inappropriate* to exchange. This orientation results from confining awareness to the focal level of experience, which in the case of conversation tends to be the content of what is said. From this orientation, intimacy is focused on primarily in negative terms: when one individual expresses himself in a way which another finds inappropriate, the other is somehow nonresponsive or punishing.

The other orientation occurs in exploring the interaction of the various levels of experience. This exploration indicates that what information it is appropriate to exchange depends upon the participants' conscious aims in the given situation and can therefore not be taken for granted. Second, the exploration indicates that in fact there is often wide variance in personal structurings of what is said in particular situations, so that describing the present conditions, qualities, and effects of exchange can be necessary to ensure actually effecting the exchange.

The following comments belong to the category of intimacy:

In a T-group: You push for clarification in your terms rather than letting him explain it in his terms. (The speaker is describing the present quality of exchange, indicating a disparity in personal structurings of what is said.)

In a T-group: I'm disappointed that we've given up already. Every time someone tries to start something or say anything it gets put down. (The speaker reveals the effect of the exchange upon him, as well as the conditions—everything gets put down—that have led to the present quality—everyone giving up.)

Son to father: Lecturing isn't going to help now. (This statement identifies an inappropriate form of exchange.)

One participant to another in meeting at a drug drop-in center: I wonder whether you wanted to say anything. (An invitation to another to explore what can be exchanged between the speaker and the other.)

In a T-group: Saying "Thank-you" genuinely is owning up to your dependence on him—I think that's what we find embarrassing about it. (Here the quality of an exchange is assessed and its effect upon a third party, the speaker, is described.)

In any context: Yeah. (Even without context or verbal tone this statement is responsive, indicating that, at a minimum, the speaker has heard the information previously given.)

A white to some blacks at a public meeting: Your glances at one another and knowing smiles make me feel that what I just said sounded ridiculous rather than relevant, and I wonder if that is how you feel. (The speaker is exploring what kind of exchange seems informative and appropriate, as well as reporting the effects of others' behavior on him.)

Discussion of roles falls into the category of intimacy, since roles are social agreements intended to define appropriate patterns of interaction among role-incumbents. For example:

Dissatisfied student in a meeting with the professor: I'm talking about my professor as a person with him, not even as a kind of role of professor serving in the classroom, but the way that person is serving as human being. I feel like I wanna be open, but you are the professor and I am the student, and that's a hassle.

The reader will note that, although the category of intimacy concerns the quality of exchange, it is discriminated on the basis of discrete comments, just like the other categories. Simply because one comment in a conversation is responsive to another in terms of a further development of the same content does not mean that it falls into the category of intimacy. For example, the professor referred to in the previous quotation responded to the student as follows:

We got a lot of educating of each other to do. I find it difficult to remember how it feels to come up against "the professor" for the first time. . . . It's obviously damn real and damn powerful and I'm denying, so you better remind me that you're having a hard time with me.

Although this statement is responsive to the student, it concerns authority, not intimacy. This conclusion derives from the commanding quality of the first sentence and of "you better remind me," as well as from its concern with the source of meaning in what the student said—"I find it difficult to remember how it feels"; "it's obviously damn real."

EDUCATION. Discovering what behaviors are authentic transformation of conscious aims and intentions; or, in other words, what behaviors are congruently translated from consciousness through one's cognitive-emotional-sensory structure into behavior.

The process here alluded to is an inverse of the process referred to by the authority category. In that case, the movement is from behavior toward a conscious sense of sequencing or meaning. In the case of education, the movement is from consciousness toward behavior. ("Movement" is not a fully appropriate term, since the different levels interact simultaneously. Rather, one might say that in the case of authority one's behavior actively asserts leadership or explores meaning, while one's structural framework passively conducts this action to the conscious level, where it is reconciled by one's sense of aim and integrity. By contrast, in the case of education one's conscious aim is active and is translated or reconciled with the passive behavioral result by one's structure.)

There are two circumstances in which discussion reflects education. The first is when a person who has been out of touch with consciousness begins to try to discriminate between the active impulses of his structural level and active conscious impulses which are being translated by the structural level. By expressing his exploration he will reveal to a person who is more aware of the quality of tranformations among levels whether he is in fact learning from experience or merely acting from his structural level.

The second and empirically more common expression of education occurs when a person attends to an external social structure as though it were his consciousness, attempting to translate its dictates passively into his behavior, and attempting to develop an internal structure which reconciles his behaviors as his own. This second process is the one labeled internalization in chapter 1 and differs from genuine experiential learning.

Examples of education include:

In a T-group: You're saying "I want to change," and *you're* saying "I understand." We accept, understand, identify—everything but help. (The speaker implies that the aim is to help, yet members' verbal behavior is not authentically realizing this aim.)

A corporate executive at a workshop: Yes, I see now—I really pushed. (The speaker recognizes an aspect of his structuring of behavior—pushing—which evidently distorted his intention without his being aware of it at the time.)

In a T-group: We're talking analytically again and I don't know how to get to it. I try to find another way of talking, but I look inside and just see a blank and after a while that's frustrating. So

I'm frustrated inside and outside. Where does it get us to say that? (This statement both expresses a search for a reconciling structure—"I look inside"—and recognizes itself as part of that search, with the uncertainty about whether it is itself an authentic transformation of conscious aim—"Where does it get us to say that?")

Client in therapy: Of course, you know, that, that makes me—now wait a minute—that probably explains why I'm primarily concerned with feelings here. That's probably it. (This example fits two categories, authority and education. Other examples of combinations will be offered below. In this case, the authority element is indicated by the "wait a minute," which reveals a concern with sequencing. Then the speaker's behavior passively reflects the shift from one structuring to another, i.e., from the thought with which he began the sentence to the thought he finally expresses. Having discovered a more authoritative source of meaning in mid-expression, the speaker permits it to act through his thought to his expression.)

The small number of examples offered for *education* reflects the rarity of the occurrence of this category in ordinary conversation. The category occurs rarely because most individuals in our culture neither experience nor imagine reality to consist of simultaneously interacting levels of organization and because internalization is rarely expressed except after the fact as contributions to *work*.

As the final example above indicates, statements can reflect combinations of any two of the foregoing five categories. Several more examples can illustrate such occasions:

I see you with a lot of props. I don't know, sort of a bag of tricks or something, and partly, you know, metaphorically. And almost at the beginning, you said almost too quickly, I was glad you said what you did, but there was a part of me that couldn't quite believe you. (The statement begins and ends by focusing on another's and then his own identity, using a focus on the questionable appropriateness of an exchange—intimacy—as the transition.)

Did you feel that I kind of cut you off by saying I didn't want your support? Because I didn't mean to. (The initial focus is on intimacy—questioning the effect of an exchange. Then the focus turns to authority—what the speaker really meant.)

I think one of the reasons why there's so much silence is that
we're not dealing with the real issues. Like, one of the issues is
that I might be laying my own trip on this group; one of the issues is, what do we really want to do. (There is a concern with
authority, evidenced by the search for source of meaning in the
phrases using "real" and "really," as well as in the concern with
leadership in "I might be laying my trip on this group." And a
focus on identity in the characterization of group and self
processes—group silence, "my own trip.")

ACTION. This category is a complement to work and a mix of the
other four categories—authority, identity, intimacy, and education. Whereas work involves transformation of the world outside,
action involves transformation of the structural level.

Examples of verbal action are even harder to find and describe
than examples of education. We must turn to the unusual for
help. Let us examine a Zen master in *action:*

A monk came to Gensha and wished to know how he was discoursing
on the principle of Zen. Said Gensha: "I have very few listeners."
Monk: "I wish to have your direct instruction." "You are not deaf?"
came straightway from the master (Suzuki, 1955, p. 83).

We can imagine the thoughts and feelings structuring the
monk's focal awareness as he approaches the master, Gensha,
hoping to gain admission to the hearing of the true word. We
can imagine his feeling of elation when he finds that Gensha in
fact has few listeners. Perhaps the monk also permits himself a
slight sense of pity or superiority about the poor master currently
bereft of students. But these thoughts and feelings are not the
issue at all: Gensha has few listeners because few can hear the
voice of consciousness. And you, monk? At this moment how do
you stand? We are already in the midst of instruction, yet you
imagine it as a dream of the future, clouding your present awareness. If the monk really hears the master, the entire structure of
his thoughts and feelings, his implicit sense of when things start
and finish, what is appropriate, and how learning occurs all are
overturned. If he is indeed deaf, the master's reply will seem to
be nonsense. But this conclusion too will overturn the monk's
cognitive-emotional-sensory structure because he has already for-

saken worldly possessions in the belief that through his own efforts and a master's responses he may attain enlightenment.

We can see how action implicitly involves the other behavioral functions, by analyzing the master's second reply. It questions what is the effect of the master's words on the monk (intimacy); it defines the identity of the master's listeners—those few who can hear the voice of consciousness; it also can serve to reconstruct the meaning of the master's first response for the monk (authority); and it challenges the monk to respond in a manner that similarly reflects simultaneous contact with the three levels of experience (education).

There is a second circumstance when action is expressed behaviorally. This is in the case of socially sanctioned activities—such as acting, wars, sports, or drinking at cocktail parties—in which one is permitted or expected to step outside one's ordinary structural framework by "playing another role," "forgetting oneself for the cause," "playing over one's head," or "going out of one's mind."

In both circumstances it is necessary to know the context in order to be able to identify a piece of behavior as action. (For example, any of the examples of the other focal issues would be action if spoken by an actor in a play. And in the case of Gensha and the monk, the comment "You are not deaf?" would be scored as identity if encountered in isolation.)

RELATIONSHIPS AMONG THE FOCAL FUNCTIONS

These six issues are highly interrelated, as the foregoing discussions have suggested. The reader may recall (chapter 1, p. 15 ff.) that the setting of behavioral goals, if they are to be truly his own goals, can only occur when a person is in contact with his conscious purpose; thus, *work* and *education* are interrelated. Obviously, whether or not the person is in contact with his consciousness will also deeply affect the quality of his boundaries; thus, *education* and *identity* are interrelated. Furthermore, the person's sense of his structure describes in part both his boundaries and his determination of what is information and what information it is appropriate to exchange with another; thus *identity* and *intimacy* are interrelated. The kinds of structural limits a person places on information that he considers appropriate to exchange with others will, in turn, influence strongly whether his behaviors (e.g., what he says and how he says it) are authentic transformations of conscious purposes (in the case of mystery-mastery structures, what the structure of the system deems appropriate will tend *not* to be an authentic transformation of consciousness); thus, *intimacy* and *authority* are interrelated. It has been implicit throughout this book that conscious purposes, interpenetrating systems that are distinct at the behavioral level, can, if appropriated, serve as the source of meaning and sequence relative to the structural and behavioral levels; thus, *authority* and *education* are related.

The concept of authority operating *through* all members of a group appears relatively strange when, in the socially common mystery-mastery mode, authority tends to be viewed as externalized in leadership roles, rules, and laws within an organizational or social structure and as acting *on* persons. However, Mills (1965) supports the possibility that authority works through rather than on persons when he speaks of the potential for all group members to assume the "executive role" concurrently. In order to change from mystery-mastery personal and social structures of authority to conscious sources of authority requires persons to face practical, focal dilemmas that they wish to resolve but cannot resolve from the mystery-mastery perspective; thus, *authority* and *action* are interrelated.

We can theorize that whether a person is aware of their interconnection or not, the issues of work, identity, learning, intimacy, authority, and action cannot be resolved independently. Nor can they be resolved in human systems in a nonconscious state. At most they can be covered over.

Earlier theories of experiential learning have tended to focus on one or two of the six issues as central to experiential learning. For example, Bion (1961) sees the primary aim in experiential learning to be developing a work group, that is, a group capable of setting and achieving goals overtly rather than colluding or conflicting covertly. Slater (1966) and W. Schutz (1967) see an enlargement of one's sense of who one is—of one's boundaries—as the primary result of experiential learning. Mann (1966) and Mills (1964) focus on the issue of authority in a self-analytic group. Culbert (1968) and Jourard (1968) have focused on the issue of self-disclosure, or intimacy. And Argyris (1967) has focused on self-education through experimenting with new behaviors. The emphasis on one or two issues and the lack of a systems model led these authors to theoretical propositions not only partial by comparison to the theory offered here, but actually in conflict with it.

For example, Bion equates work with education in his therapy groups. Such an equation is considerably different from relating the two issues, since the patients will develop little sense of the connection of education to practical work in their therapy groups if education is their work. On the other hand, Argyris (1967) has used a model of setting and achieving goals for oneself (i.e., work) to conceptualize how a person can increase his self-acceptance and self-awareness (i.e., learn from experience). Such an equation makes experiential learning a subsidiary process or by-product of work; but according to my model and theory, experiential learning may be a process subsidiary to the other focal functions as well (measured by the system of inference I call conscious appropriation of behavior), or itself be expressed as a focal function in education. Although my model and theory indicate the interrelation of work and education, they do not equate them in the way Argyris and Bion seem to. Their equation results in a little-noticed but severe theoretical stumbling block: a critical distinction between work-goals and education is overlooked. Work-goals involve transformations at the behavioral level of things in the world outside. Learning, however, is not a goal in this sense at all, for it involves realizing a conscious intention in one's behavior. In work one's behavior is active in transforming the environment, whereas in education one's behavior is receptive to, or the result of, the action of the conscious level. If we overlook this distinction, we will tend to regard increasing self-awareness as a function of specific kinds of behavior, irrespective of whether they represent authentic transformations of conscious intentions (leading to the substitution of a limited coping process for learning, such as the feedback-and-change mechanism discussed in chapter 1). (See also the differentiation between goal-setting-and-achievement and self-recognition, chapter 2, pp. 46–49.)

Another study which links two of the six behavioral level issues (Mann, 1966) views a self-analytic group's initial inability and later ability to work cooperatively as correlated with its changing relations to its leader (authority). Other studies have viewed two or more of the six behavioral issues as related by the temporal sequence in which they are encountered during the group's life. S. Culbert (unpublished paper) has applied a theory of learning whereby the issues of intimacy and identity counter each other in successive phases. Bennis (1964) has suggested that the authority issue must be dealt with first in T-groups. Only after the members and leader have resolved their relationship are they persons to one another rather than roles, and thus ready to focus on intimacy. On the other hand, W. Schutz (1967) has written that identity (is a person included in or excluded from the group?) precedes the issues of authority and intimacy (or, as he names them, control and affiliation).

On the basis of the systems model of man, I do not recognize any single sequence of focal issues as proper and most effective. According to this model, the six issues are indissolubly interrelated and one cannot be fully solved, in the sense of being made fully conscious, without solving the others concomitantly. Moreover, none is absolutely primary. This is not to argue, however, that there will be no sequence whatsoever in the way a group or person attends to the six issues. For focal attention is perspectival —things are perceived from one side at a time (Husserl, 1962; Schachtel, 1959a)—and will therefore tend to focus on the interrelated issues one at a time, changing focus with difficulty, until members' structures congruently transform their conscious intuitions. Increased contact with consciousness will bring comprehension of the actual complementarity of the issues.

If the six interrelated behavioral issues are treated sequentially by a group devoted to experiential learning, the sequence results from two factors. One factor is a certain openness to such learning on the part of the members, an openness which can by no means be assumed to exist. Bion (1961) has offered some highly insightful analyses of therapeutic situations in which patients are *not* open to experiential learning. In such cases the same issues arise, but covertly rather than overtly. Thus, the authority issue arises in terms of unacknowledged dependency by the members on the leader for direction. The identity issue arises in members' fight-or-flight reaction when unresolved group boundaries are approached. The intimacy issue is reflected in members' tendency to pair up in any discussion.* The phenomena according to which Bion determines what is the salient issue at a given time are not verbal. The leader, the group boundaries, or sexual pairing is not necessarily being discussed when evidences of dependency, fight-flight, or pairing present themselves. In fact, these modes of resolving the issues of authority, identity, and intimacy function precisely so as to avoid overt recognition by the group that they were ever unresolved issues. They all fall within the mystery-mastery mode of operation, prevent contact with consciousness, and consequently do not actually resolve the issues in question. As a result, they will be used recurrently rather than in some definite sequence. Early in an experiential learning process we can expect that at least some of the group members will tend not to be open to this kind of learning and will obstruct a sequential focusing on the different issues by the group.

The second factor which determines whether the six behavioral issues are treated sequentially is members' tendency to treat all learning as occurring in terms of their focal attention. So long as they treat learning in this manner, the only way they will be able to deal with interconnections they see between the various issues is to talk first about one and then about another; or, later in the group's life, as the issues gain some common definition, it may be possible to talk about the interaction of two issues. Under these conditions, the focal functions will tend to be treated sequentially, although the change of focus from one issue

---

* The difference between Bion's and my analysis is that I would look for covert ways a group handles the work, learning, and action issues, as well as the authority, identity, and intimacy issues. And, on the other hand, I would expect all six issues to be handled differently in what he narrowly calls a work group. This difference may be less substantive than a result of the more systematic explicitness of the present theory.

to another will result from chance, or from factors outside the group's awareness, or from the mastery of some person or faction, rather than from a common, conscious intention.

As subsidiary processes and conscious intentions gain recognition as critical, but not focal, aspects of personal and group functioning, members' verbal and nonverbal behavior will become increasingly subtle, ironic, and symbolic in attempts to manifest authentically the moment-to-moment mix of focal, subsidiary, and intentional elements they experience. At this point, as in the case of the covert treatment of issues, what a member is talking about will not define the full function of his behavior. In this case, his treatment of a focal issue will be overt, but his behavior will also communicate at the subsidiary and intentional levels in ways that increase the meaning of what he says. The Zen master's statements illustrate this. The shift from one focal issue to another may be swift, dictated by a logic beyond the verbal level of experience. Thus, to someone aware of only the focal level of experience it may appear that the focal issues are being treated in a mixed and inconclusive fashion.

What distinguish the covert, the overt but merely focal, and the multilevel treatments of the six focal issues are the structural modes and degrees of conscious appropriation involved in different behaviors. We can turn now to a discussion of structural modes of behavior.

THE STRUCTURAL MODES OF BEHAVIOR

The *mystery-mastery* structural mode, to which we have referred numerous times, approximates what is often called "putting up a front," or "playing games." At the opposite extreme from mystery-mastery behavior is behavior organized by structures in contact with consciousness. I distinguish among three such structural modes, naming them *supportiveness, self-disclosure,* and *confrontation.* Unlike the mystery-mastery mode, these three modes are open to consciousness and are concerned with the congruence of transformations among levels of experience. Unlike the imprisoning mystery-mastery structure, they represent alternative structures available to the conscious person, who is able to let go of a given structure and try another.

Between these two extremes lies the range of ambivalent behavior that occurs when a person strives to explore but is restricted from full exploration by mystery-mastery assumptions he makes and fears to question. We can call such behavior *exploration of structure*.

In principle, these different structural modes define the differences between covert, overt but merely focal, and multi-level treatment of the six focal functions of behavior. Since the mystery-mastery mode tends to supress existential exploration altogether, it characterizes the covert treatment of the focal functions. By contrast, exploration of structure characterizes the *overt but merely focal* treatment of focal functions, since it attempts to recognize and explore such existential dilemmas, but does not achieve conscious access to the multiple levels of immediate experience. Finally, the structural modes of supportiveness, self-disclosure, and confrontation, having access to the multiple levels of experience, treat the focal issues as *multi-level* phenomena.

THE MYSTERY-MASTERY MODE. Mystery-mastery behavior treats what goes on within persons, including oneself, as mysterious, inaccessible, irrelevant, or inappropriate for conversation (or other outer behavior). At the same time, it relates to the outside world (including other people, who are treated as external objects) by trying to control or master it. In short, this kind of behavior aims at *mystery* about oneself and *mastery* of others.

This mode is revealed partly by what is missing from behavior, that is, by a lack of attention to or a denial of personal feelings, perceptions, and purposes. It also reveals itself partly through attempts to pressure another person to conform to one's own expectations. It includes statements that treat external appearances as facts to be taken for granted.

The first two examples have already been discussed in terms of their focal functions.

There are ways. (Work. Stated as a fact to be taken for granted.)

The rules are that we stay in the here and now, and we try to find out what is going on within and between us. (Identity. "The rules" are presented as though they were external facts rather than social agreements.)

The next two examples occurred during the first half of the first meeting of the meditation group.

Well, she's charged me and then retreating behind a wall to assess. (Intimacy. The words "charged," "retreating," and "wall" are all perceptions and interpretations of the speaker, and the word "assess" involves an inference, yet they are all presented as unequivocally descriptive of external events.)

No, I really don't have feelings towards you personally. Do you see what I mean? (Intimacy. Denial of feelings.)

We can take a short excerpt from an encounter-group meeting as a further example of the mystery-mastery mode. This excerpt illustrates how, even in a situation where the avowed intent is to reduce alienation and enhance freedom, the actual behavior may encourage withdrawal and conformity:

Bill: What do we want from Linda right now?

Andy: The truth.

Educator: We want to know *her*.

Andy: I want to know the truth and why she puts up these fronts.

Carla: I want to see some real feelings come out of her.

Andy: Me, too.

Tim: Yeah.

Carla: That's all I want to see.

Dennis (to Linda): Everything you do, it just seems phony as heck.

Carla: Linda, have you ever tried giving to somebody?

Art: She just wants to take.

Carla: Have you ever tried to give to somebody, Linda?

Linda: Uh-huh.

Andy: What happened, Linda?

Linda: He walked away.

(Argyris, 1967, p. 175)

Ironically, other members prevent Linda from opening herself to them by pressuring her to be open. Her "mystery" is heightened rather than dissolved by their effort at "mastery." Moreover, the other members preserve their mystery too, revealing almost nothing about themselves. This mode of behavior is particularly evident and ironic in settings supposedly devoted to learning from experience because there is no "external organizational structure" to justify mystery-mastery behavior as "necessary for survival in a competitive world." It contrasts starkly with the avowed intent of the group to create open, noncoercive climates.

EXPLORATION OF STRUCTURE. A second structural mode of behavior can be named *exploration of structure,* the behavior of a person accustomed to putting up a mystery-mastery front but who now tries to be more exploratory. Exploration of relationships between one's thoughts and feelings, one's own behavior, and others' thoughts and feelings is directly contradictory to the fundamental orientation of the mystery-mastery mode. Consequently a whole new structure of thought and feeling—a whole new set of assumptions about human relationships—is necessary for true exploration. A person who habitually operates in the mystery-mastery mode inevitably finds himself groping for an appropriate structure each time he undertakes any exploration. Since the exploration of structure, the challenge to his basic assumptions, tends to be more than he bargained for in an emotional sense, and since his mystery-mastery assumptions tend to inhibit exploration in any event, he will tend to swing back and forth between exploratory and mystery-mastery behavior.

His behavior will tend to be ambivalent; he becomes more vulnerable by his questioning, but simultaneously avoids vulnerability by becoming aggressive, defensive, or self-qualifying. The ambivalence arises because the person is uncertain (thus the exploration), but uncertainty is experienced as weakness by a person accustomed to the mystery-mastery mode. The person is therefore on the lookout (at least subconsciously) for any suggestion that his "weakness" will be used against him.

Exploration of structure characterizes statements that show uncertainty how to define information, what information is relevant, how to act at the moment, or what question to ask, when these are accompanied by hesitations, false starts, and introductory or concluding qualifiers. In another aspect, exploration of structure is indicated by openness to exploration by another person without any indication that the speaker is himself open to

levels of experience besides that of the world out there. Or, in
still another aspect, attacking others through an analysis that simultaneously reveals real dilemmas for the group exhibits the
characteristic ambivalence. In all three cases the speaker gives evidence of tending to speak within the mystery-mastery mode,
which is not open to exploration, but at the same time evinces
recognition that exploration is appropriate or unavoidable.

The following three examples of exploration of structure have
already been described from the point of view of their focal functions:

Well, what do you have in mind for this conference? (Work. The
speaker invites exploration by the other without indicating his
openness for exchange across varying levels of experience.)

I'm disappointed that we've given up already. Every time someone tries to start something or say something it gets put down.
(Intimacy. The speaker attacks the group, presenting interpretations as facts, yet the dilemma may be real, and the speaker indicates clearly that he feels it.)

It's a question of who will take the first step. (Authority. The
speaker indicates an openness to others' taking a first step, but
not his own experiencing in relation to that possibility.)

The following longer excerpt portrays the ambivalence characteristic of exploration of structure. The exchange between Joan,
a person who tends to be quiet and withdrawing, and Jane, who
is relatively aggressive and assertive, occurs as part of a staff meeting at a school (of which the author was director). The meeting
includes a discussion of the results of some research the staff has
done on itself in an effort to improve its functioning as a team.
One aspect of the research asked each staff member to estimate
the level of conflict between himself and each other member of
the staff. The results show that Jane consistently estimated *lower*
levels of conflict between herself and others than they did with
her. We join the conversation as Joan, who is usually quiet, tries
to explore why she feels conflict with Jane:

Joan (hesitatingly): With me I think it *is* a conflict. I don't know
whether to bring this up. You seem to be always so dramatic that
I don't know when you're being Jane.

Jane (assertively): Well, that's Jane.

Joan: Well. . . .

Jane (interrupting, slowly and forcefully): I am a dramatic personality.

Joan: But it's still hard for me to decide whether you're being real or not.

Jane (sincere, demanding): How do you feel this? In what way do you assess me as being dramatic?

Joan (pause): Well, in every way.

Jane (immediately, loudly): My speech. . . . (Pause, then softly, reflectively.) People have brought this up before—terribly offends and bothers many people. I can't hear my speech and I don't know if I could change my speech to please people. I don't know if this is something one should ask me to do.

Joan begins in the mode of exploration of structure (the hesitant "I don't know whether to bring this up.") But Jane initially responds in the mystery-mastery mode, pressuring for conformity to her view that "that's Jane." When her two comments fail to quiet Joan completely, Jane questions Joan, overtly indicating openness to a response from Joan. However, in this case her overt openness falls within the mystery-mastery mode because her demanding, dramatic tone of voice is precisely what Joan mistrusts; so Joan is caught in a bind: on the one hand, it is difficult for her to take the risk of owning up to her feelings when the very way she is asked increases her distrust of the other person's genuineness; moreover, if she discloses her feelings straightforwardly, Jane will have gotten away with presenting the very style that creates the problem; on the other hand, Jane appears open to Joan's feedback that might help to correct the problem. The struggle among these emotional strands (not necessarily explicit to Joan) yields her limp, "Well, in every way." Jane rushes on, but seems to stumble by accident into an exploration of structure when she recalls previous feedback she has received from people about the quality of her voice. The tone of her voice changes, and a sense of hesitation, uncertainty how to behave ("I don't know if this is something one should ask me to do"), and ambivalence creeps in.

SUPPORTIVENESS. All three conscious structural modes—supportiveness, self-disclosure, and confrontation—are characterized by an underlying acceptance of oneself and the other person as being more than meets the eye and as experiencing dilemmas and incongruities among values, rhetoric, and behavior that can call forth work on oneself. Such acceptance goes beyond *what* is said to *how* and *why* it is said—to the rhythm and tone of voice, posture and gestures of the speaker, and to his social and temporal context.

Supportiveness does not involve agreeing with *what* the other person says, as much as dwelling in the other's experiencing as far as possible (the whys and hows as well as the whats), and thereby encouraging further exploration through the listener's willingness to experience it with the speaker.

This mode of behavior has been extensively researched in the field of psychotherapy, and is especially associated with Carl Rogers (Rogers, 1961b; Truax and Carkhuff, 1967). A major aspect of supportiveness has been named "accurate empathy" and another aspect "nonpossessive warmth" or "unconditional positive regard." It has been suggested that these qualities help another person explore his inner structure because (1) he does not have to defend an inadequate structure from attack by another; (2) his sense of relatedness to and support from the other person reduces his fear of "losing control" if he questions his structure; (3) he experiences the other's attentiveness as a positive reinforcement of his exploratory behavior; (4) the other's attentiveness acts as a catalytic factor in reconciling the person's new-found sense of himself as one who can question structures with his previous sense of total identification with a single structure (Haigh, 1968; Truax and Carkhuff, 1967). The following excerpt from one of Rogers' (1961b, p. 89) therapeutic interviews both demonstrates the therapist's supportiveness and portrays a point at which his client begins to accept a wider sense of herself than what her previous structure defined as appropriate. After a pause of several minutes the client (C) speaks:

C: You know that is kind of goofy, but I've never told anyone this (nervous laugh) and it'll probably do me good. For years, oh, probably from my early youth, from seventeen probably on, I, I have had what

I call to myself, told myself were "flashes of sanity," I've never told anyone this, (another embarrassed laugh) wherein, in, really I feel sane. And, and pretty much aware of life. And always with a terrific kind of concern and sadness of how far away, how far astray that we have actually gone. It's just a feeling once in a while of finding myself a whole kind of person in a terribly chaotic kind of world.

T: It's been fleeting and it's been infrequent, but there have been times when it seems the whole of you is functioning and feeling in the world, a very chaotic world to be sure—

C: That's right. And I mean, and knowing actually how far astray we, we've gone from, from being whole healthy people. And of course, one doesn't talk in those terms.

T: A feeling that it wouldn't be *safe* to talk about the singing you— [referring to something the client said earlier].

C: Where does that person live?

T: Almost as if there was no place for such a person to exist.

C: Of course, you know, that, that makes me—now wait a minute— that probably explains why I'm primarily concerned with feelings here. That's probably it.

T: Because the whole you does exist with all your feelings. Is that it, you're more aware of feelings?

C: That's right. It's not, it doesn't reject feelings and—that's *it*.

T: That whole you somehow lives feelings rather than pushing them to one side.

C: That's right. (Pause.) I suppose from the practical point of view it could be said that what I ought to be doing is solving some problems, day-to-day problems. And yet, I, I—what I'm trying to do is solve, solve something else that's a great, that is a great deal more important than little day-to-day problems. Maybe that sums up the whole thing.

The therapist has focused entirely on the client, but has not pressured her to move in any direction, instead communicating his investment in, and encouragement of, her capacity for self-initiated exploration of structure by his efforts to reflect her experience accurately.

SELF-DISCLOSURE. By contrast, in the mode of self-disclosure, to which we can now turn, a person expresses and questions his *own* experiencing, thus modeling effective exploratory patterns of behavior. If a judgment or evaluation is made, it is expressed as part of one's experience, and as relating to the current situation rather than treated as the basis of all experience. Often a statement in this mode will relate two levels of experience, such as the speaker's thought or feeling in relation to his perception or behavior.

Several researchers have focused upon self-disclosure as a method of encouraging experiential learning (Culbert, 1968; Jourard, 1968). In a similar vein, others have emphasized the importance of "genuineness" or "authenticity" in presenting oneself effectively (Argyris, 1962; Truax and Carkhuff, 1967).

Two examples of self-disclosure may furnish a more concrete sense of this structural mode. The first piece of dialogue is a continuation of the exchange between Joan and Jane (p. 158). Jason enters the conversation in a self-disclosing mode that seems to help Jane proceed a bit further with her exploration of structure:

Jane (end of previous excerpt): . . . I don't know if this is something one should ask me to do.

Joan: No, I don't think so.

Jane (haltingly): My tone—and John brought this up last spring —my tone of voice—I don't know how one would describe it. . . .

Jason: Your tone of voice to me is different now than it was a few minutes ago.

Jane (neutrally, warily): I have a great range.

Jason (with positive concern): It seems to have softened and deepened.

Jane: It's still Jane though.

Jason (to Jane): Do you feel it's *more* Jane? I have a more sympathetic reaction to this tone of voice than to the other, although. . . .

Jane: This is certainly a more relaxed voice because I'm trying to talk to Joan. When I'm trying to insert something in a more anxious way it may not be the same voice.

Jason's three comments here are self-disclosing. They express his perceptions of and reactions to what is happening without demanding conformity from Jane. It is interesting to note that his last comment, if it were just the question "Do you feel it's *more* Jane?" would have exerted some pressure on Jane. However, the succeeding self-disclosure shows why Jason would like to think her softer tone was more Jane and thereby releases the pressure on Jane to give the answer implicitly called for, "yes." Jane can acknowledge experiencing different states (anxiety, relaxation) at the end of this excerpt, in contrast to her monolithic "I am a dramatic personality" at the outset of the first excerpt. But the ambivalence involved in the mode of exploration of structure shows in her lack of initiative in exploring the implications of the feedback she is receiving from Jason, and, in fact, her wariness about dealing with the information at all.

A second example of self-disclosure is taken from a meeting of a recruiter with job candidates for positions at the same school. The school's staff has already made preliminary evaluations of the candidates on the basis of applications and interviews. The organization is concerned to hire those candidates most capable of experiential learning, since they must learn on the job, because this school brings together blacks and whites, rich and poor, in a mix that is initially culturally alien to everyone. Consequently, both as a way of demonstrating to the candidates how the organization attempts to combine processes of inquiry and action in its structure and as a way of identifying for the organization those candidates most able to combine the two processes in their behavior, the organization is asking the candidates to collaborate with the recruiter in selecting themselves. They are to combine inquiry and action in deciding whom to select, using the information already gathered and the preliminary evaluations by the staff as examples of possible selection criteria.

The particular candidates in the following excerpt have received the most negative initial evaluations. The recruiter (R), returning to each applicant the information gathered from him, reminds the group that it can now share in the decision-making. Then:

Ben: What do you want us to talk about? What do you want us to say? I mean, I don't understand.

R: I'm not sure. I think I've told you what I hoped we'd do, but I didn't bring you here to *make* you do anything.

Ben: Oh, I know that.

R (continuing): I'm uncertain. I can only see going where you want to go. I feel I've done my part. We've made a preliminary evaluation. I'm willing to go anywhere you want.

Greg: Okay, how do we get out of our preliminary evaluations?

R: I guess, for me, I'd have to be convinced you understood the evaluation. Then, either I'd have to see behavior that made me revise my judgment—of course you're free to come back next week anyway, these are just my criteria—or you'd have to make a strong commitment to work on yourself. It depends, too, on the issue with the specific person—is the problem goals, or skills, or interpersonal style?

Sam: One of the weaknesses is that we are not with you when you consider the applications and I think that could be very valuable if you really want to make it a two-way experience. Personally, I feel left out. Nothing is written on me. I would have been interested to have been there.

R: We didn't consider them much together. In your case, it was mostly me. I'm primarily responsible for your evaluation; it's true you don't know what I thought because it's not written, but I feel perfectly ready to let you know.

Sam: Well . . . I don't think that's worth doing now, but can we do it after we're finished?

R: That's a problem for me: I hoped to be able to respond here because of limited time and resources; I would prefer to do it here if possible. If there's a problem about doing it as a group, maybe we could do it individually.

(*Pause.*)

Ben: With me individually, I recognize what they say is wrong with me, but I don't see any way I could change it. It says "naive, vague." That's a real weakness. I'd like to know how to overcome it. I'm at a loss.

The recruiter focuses on giving all the information relevant to his behavior that he can. The information he discloses concerns both his personal and organizational structure, as well as personal feelings and organizational events. However, he makes no effort to sell his point of view or lead the group in particular directions. Nor does he present himself as having all the answers. He presents his uncertainty straightforwardly, rather than reflecting it through ambivalence. These characteristics distinguish self-disclosure from the mystery-mastery mode and from exploration of structure.

CONFRONTATION. We can turn now to the mode of *confrontation*. In this mode the speaker differentiates himself from the person to whom he is speaking, either explicitly by noting their different patterns of behavior, or implicitly by being able to note contradictions between the other's expressed values and actual behavior (between *what* he says and *how* he says it). In either case, the speaker poses the opposition as a dilemma for the person to whom he is speaking as well as himself, one that must be explored if the interpersonal or intrapersonal contradiction is to be resolved.

The mode of confrontation brings the speaker's intellectual framework into play overtly, since he is describing patterns of perception and behavior. Moreover, it may be associated with a feeling of commitment on the part of the speaker to his own framework (in the case of comparison between his and the other's behavior patterns). If the other person appears unwilling to work on resolving the difference, the speaker's confrontations may involve increasing anger or attempts to structure the situation so that the other's mystery-mastery avoidance of the issue is stymied, leading him to experiment with another structural mode (such an attempt would correspond to the focal function of *action*).

Superficially, such confrontation may appear to contradict rather than complement the supportive mode of behavior, but this is not true theoretically (and practically, assuming the educator is indeed conscious) because the educator's aim is still to help the other person break through behavior patterns and self-images in the mystery-mastery mode and to attain congruent transformations among his aims (whys), behaviors (hows), and statements (whats). The anger and action of the speaker are aimed not at the sinner but at the sin, to use religious phraseology. He is not accepting of the other's self-presentation only because that self-presentation is not accepting of that person's full, three-level experience.

Of the three structural modes of behavior that facilitate learning from experience, confrontation has been the least discussed in scholarly writing on experiential learning. T-group or therapeutic forms of interaction, which comprise the most researched forms of verbal behavior, have tended to occur at times set aside from the usual behavioral-level concerns, time limits, and commitments. Consequently, it is not surprising that the value of confrontation in experiential learning has been noted primarily by educators who have intervened in on-going organizations (Davis, 1967; Whyte and Hamilton, 1964, in reference to Argyris' [1962] style).

Another reason that the mode of confrontation has been largely overlooked is that its distinction from mystery-mastery directiveness is subtle. Industrial studies of leadership have differentiated two factors of leadership called "consideration" and "initiation of structure" (Fleishman, Harris, and Burtt, 1963; Kahn and Katz, 1963). Aggressive behavior on the part of the leader consequently tends to be associated by behavioral scientists with "initiation of structure," i.e., directiveness (and this tends to be true empirically, given the prevalence of the mystery-mastery mode). However, this connection between aggressive initiative and directiveness is not imperative. For example, a therapist may command his client to act out a neurotic symptom (e.g., a tic or a tone of voice). If the client does so, it may appear to an observer of this sequence that the therapist has merely succeeded in creating conformity to his dictate (mastery). However, if the patient has already exhibited total dependence upon the therapist for solving his problem, but at the same time has claimed he is unable to control (i.e., to voluntarily act out) his neurotic symptom, the therapist's command will have placed him in a double bind. Whatever the client's response, he must experience himself in a new way, outside his previous self-image. If he refuses to adhere to the command, he will exhibit independence from the therapist; if he adheres to the command, he has controlled his symptom (Watzlawick, Beavin, and Jackson, 1967).

The therapist, in this case, has seen the client's "blind spot" in regard to the interaction between his own structure and behavior and has so manipulated the social situation as to force the client to experience the blind spot emotionally, that is, to see directly what his usual sense of self prevents him from seeing. The therapist has brought the client into confrontation with himself. But the therapist does *not* control what the client actually does—he does not manipulate the client. He simply makes it impossible for the patient to do what he habitually does. The result is an enlargement of the client's sense of what is possible for him rather than a specification of what is good for him. Thus, what appears to be directiveness can be a form of confrontation, and distinguishing between the two is crucial if we are to understand how to encourage experiential learning rather than conformity in settings where initiation, choice, and aggressive action are necessarily operative.

Yet another reason why confrontation has received relatively little attention is that most research and theory in the area of experiential learning has focused on the interplay between behavior, on one side, and thought and feelings, on the other (i.e., on the interplay between behavioral and structural levels). The interplay between the structural level and intuitive consciousness has been largely overlooked. For example, the concept of congruence has been applied to the undistorted transformation of feelings into verbal behavior (Dyer, 1969), but not to the transformation of consciousness into structural-level thought, feeling, and inner sensation.

As a result of this oversight, the scale of the problem of changing from a mystery-mastery mode of functioning and awareness to a more facilitative, effective, and aware mode is misconceived. For example, the supportive mode of facilitation is advocated without recognition that many of a person's own initiatives result from, or are interpreted by himself in terms of, the mystery-mastery mode. If this is true, then the supportive mode must be used judiciously by the conscious person, chosen at times when the other's initiative is toward contact with consciousness. And when the other's initiatives are not toward consciousness, a friend may wish to turn towards imaginative forms of confrontation instead. This sort of confrontation is particularly visible among Eastern masters who have attempted to link the living of daily life with the awakening of intuitive consciousness. The example of action by a Zen master in relation to a monk, described on p. 148, could also be presented as an example of confrontation.

A reading of lives of other masters such as Sri Yukteswar (Yogananda, 1968) and Gurdjieff (de Hartmann, 1964; Ouspensky, 1949) also reveals an emphasis on confrontation as a mode of behavior. These educators most explicitly behave so as to shock their students out of habitual structural patterns of thought, feeling, and inner sensation. This form of confrontation is deemed necessary because so long as a student's efforts toward consciousness remain framed by a mystery-mastery structure they will be self-contradictory.

A specific example of the mode of confrontation can be taken from the same meeting of a recruiter with job candidates described earlier (p. 164). The reader may have noted that the different candidates who spoke had already begun to differentiate themselves from one another in their behavior. Ben and Greg seemed to be oriented towards exploration of structure (personal and situational), while Sam began in a condemning, mystery-mastery mode. This difference continued, and there came a time when the recruiter felt that Sam and another candidate with a similar behavior pattern were preventing the rest of the group from obtaining the kinds of feedback and exploration they seemed to want. So the recruiter confronted Sam and the other as follows:

I see you as expressing a lot of aggression towards the judgments we've made and which you claim we haven't shared with you. And yet as I see this session it could be for sharing information and I don't see myself as hindering that process right now. I see *you* as hindering it. (Coldly.) I don't feel terribly moved by what you're saying.

In other words, the recruiter is claiming that Sam's pattern of behavior is contradictory to what Sam himself says he would value. The effect of this comment is to quiet Sam and the other for a time, giving the rest of the group a chance to proceed with setting up an information-sharing structure. Thus, the intervention is clearly facilitative for the group as a whole. Although Sam and the other later rejoin the conversation in a participative rather than condemning mode, it is unclear whether the confrontation has lasting value and meaning for them.

Another example of confrontation derives from a workshop of top executives of a corporation (Argyris, 1962, pp. 190–91). (Group members are numbered 1 to 10; the educators are lettered A and B. The excerpt is only part of a dialogue.)

No. 5: I feel badly inside when I disagree with my boss but don't say anything. In fact, I act as if I agree. Then I leave the meeting and act as if I never agreed. I ought to say to my boss, "I disagree."

No. 7: Let's assume we made a decision, and you didn't like it, and you defended it to others. This isn't dishonest. You're part of a team. You shouldn't feel you're a hypocrite. Your conscience shouldn't bother you.

B: I hear you're telling people around the table that they shouldn't have some of the feelings that they have.

No. 10: The point is not whether I should or should not feel badly. It is: Do you help me explore my feelings?

No. 2: Why should anyone want to hold onto and explore his feelings? What good does it do?

B: Let's ask No. 10.

No. 10: I'm not sure I understand your question.

No. 2: What good does it do to have these feelings?

A: Is it a matter of good? He has them.

No. 2: Okay, but if you say to me that you have strong feelings and it hurts me, I'd say, "Okay, change them." You ought to rationalize yourself to the point of not having them. The feelings are purposeless.

No. 10: You're using me as an example, let me answer. That comment would really hurt me. Worse than telling me to jump overboard.

No. 4: Wait a minute. You brought your point up so that we can discuss it.

No. 10: Yes.

A: But what encouragement do we give him if we tell him he is wrong for feeling this way?

No. 2: Wait a minute—that's unfair, darn it.

B: If we are going to make it unfair, let me add another aspect. I felt, No. 2, that you were saying to No. 10 that if he were as intellectually bright as you, he could intellectually rationalize his feelings just as you can.

No. 2: Maybe that's it. Let me say what I *really* thought. I've had the same problem—it hurt me too, and I kick myself for it, then I have to say, "What good does all this do to me?" I was trying to convey this to No. 10.

No. 10: This is a great difference.

No. 2: Yes, I see—I really pushed.

B: And one of the values about this learning is that you became help-ful to No. 10 when you told him the problems that you had in this area and how you strived to solve them.

No. 2: That's an interesting observation.

B's first intervention is not empathic, nor is it self-disclosing. In-stead B deliberately reorganizes what No. 7 said to show its con-tradiction to a value No. 7 is presumed to hold, something like "people's feelings are their own business." Likewise, B's second intervention begins to turn a somewhat rhetorical, intellectual-ized question ("Why should anyone . . .") into a personal one that can receive an answer. A's first intervention confronts No. 2 with the problem of specifying what he means, giving No. 10 something to respond to. A's second intervention reorganizes what No. 4 said to show how he and others discourage the very discussion they say they want to have. B then exposes an implied invidious comparison between No. 2 and No. 10 in No. 2's ear-lier comment. At this point, No. 2 again reformulates his earlier question, this time organizing it in the self-disclosing mode rather than as a mystery-mastery attack. B is then able to use No. 2's self-disclosure as an example for an intellectual model of how one encourages learning. Thus, at every intervention the educa-tors bring a different perspective to what has just been said, reor-ganizing it according to an intellectual framework which presents the situation as an existential dilemma for a particular person or the group as a whole. Like Zen masters, the educators here are not moving towards conformity to their view of the world, but rather are concerned to open the members to the question of the moment, a question to which no one can have the answer beforehand.

STRUCTURAL MODES CONDUCIVE TO EXPERIENTIAL LEARNING

I have suggested that the three modes which facilitate learning from experience are mutually complementary, but I have given only hints by way of the examples as to the different situational factors, timing, and purposes that determine which of these three modes will be the most effective at a given moment.

The idea that a fully effective person will be able to behave authentically in all three modes gives a sense of the scale of the project of becoming fully effective. At present, most educators in the fields of therapy, T-groups, and consulting to organizations tend in practice and often in theory to value one of these modes more highly than the other two.

It has been suggested that trainers using different facilitative modes may be equally effective when each mode derives from a cognitive map congruent with the particular educator's personality (Bolman, 1968). Moreover, Schoeninger (1965) has shown how ineffective one of the modes can be if it is incongruent with the educator's personality or previous training. He found that high levels of educator self-disclosure were viewed favorably by clients in only one of three cases; after further investigation, he concluded that this mode was incongruent with the previous training of the other two educators. These findings indicate that at a given time in their lives two persons may indeed be equally effective although they use different modes, because only one mode is authentically transformed through the personality structure of each.

Other findings, however, indicate that both educators would be more effective if they could authentically transform their intentions through all three modes of behavior. For example, Culbert (1968) found that high levels of educator self-disclosure early in the life of a group were associated with increased member growth during that period compared to a group in which the trainers manifested relatively low levels of self-disclosure. But continued high levels of self-disclosure in the first group eventually became less effective at promoting member growth than did the continued low levels of self-disclosure in the other group. This finding suggests that self-disclosure on the part of an educator is particularly effective early in the life of a group, or, more generally, that a particular style is especially effective at certain times.

How are we to reconcile these apparently contradictory findings? In simplified terms, one group of studies indicates that a particular mode is more or less suited to a given person at any time. Another study shows a particular mode to be more or less suited to a given time for any person. These findings can be reconciled by recognizing that a difficult learning process is necessary for a person to become authentic in any of the three facilitative modes: because one's ordinary social behavior tends to have a mystery-mastery character, it is necessary to go through a period of exploration of structure in order to achieve authentic supportiveness, self-disclosure, or confrontation. Hence, without undergoing such a learning process, or before he has completed it, a given person will be ineffective using a particular mode.

On the other hand, if the person does not create opportunities for himself to integrate all three modes into his behavior, his style will be relevant only to certain situations, although he will apply it in all situations. In such cases, the person will tend to feel that his style is the way he must present himself in all situations in order to be effective. He will therefore tend to be less interested and more threatened by feedback indicating how effective he actually is. And, in the long run, under these circumstances he will tend not to increase his effectiveness. He will cease learning.

CONSCIOUS APPROPRIATION OF BEHAVIOR

I have characterized supportiveness, self-disclosure, and confrontation as structural modes that theoretically reflect contact with consciousness. Earlier, I described the different manifestations of each focal function as theoretically depending upon whether it is organized by the mystery-mastery mode or by consciousness. Throughout these discussions, however, the specific qualities that characterize conscious appropriation of behavior have remained implicit. Let us now describe this quality of behavior explicitly.

In general, we are moving from many-sided appearance (the six focal functions) toward a singular essence (conscious appropriation). This movement is reflected in the different kinds of measurement at each level of analysis. The focal functions of behavior are a series of distinct, mutually unordered, nominal categories. The structural modes of behavior are also distinct categories, but they are related to one another along a continuum. That is, the mystery-mastery mode occurs at one extreme, the mode of exploration of structure lies in the middle, and the three conscious modes lie at the other extreme. Thus they represent ordinal measurement. Finally, the categories of conscious appropriation result in interval measurement.

All three categories of conscious appropriation to be described (*intentionality, relationality,* and *momentary validity*) are applied to each unit of behavior. The analytical question for an observer is not to which category the behavior belongs, but rather whether the behavior is positive, neutral, or negative in relation to each category. All three categories describe aspects of a single quality, the conscious appropriation of behavior. The results for the three categories are additive, counting postitive as $+1$, neutral as 0, and negative as -1. Consequently, scores of conscious appropriation for a given unit can vary between $+3$ and -3, with 0 indicating lack of evidence or conflicting evidence.

INTENTIONALITY. One index of conscious appropriation is the extent to which a person regards his activity as *intentional* on his part, rather than as externally caused. There may indeed be strong environmental pressures or influences, but the person who exhibits conscious appropriation of behavior regards himself as deciding whether to take them into account and then as personally causing his own behavior. The reader will recall that for a conscious system this state of affairs does exist: effective structure and behavior and the very definition of feedback from the environment are all dependent for their organization upon the conscious purpose of the system (chapter 1; see also de Charms, 1968 Husserl, 1962; Merleau-Ponty, 1963).

A conscious system would tend to express verbally rather than deny the self-determined, intentional quality of its behavior. Examples of denial of responsibility for behavior, where one's behavior is viewed as externally caused and beyond one's control, would be:

I can't help it if I get angry after a long day.

The orders came down from the top, so of course I had to obey them.

Examples of high levels of realized intentionality would be:

I'm angry at you because I become defensive at demands uttered impersonally; I want to be appreciated and loved.

I decided to obey the orders, afraid of what would happen if I didn't.

These examples have been chosen to emphasize the point that conscious appropriation of one's intentionality does not mean that one is uninfluenced by one's environment, but rather that one recognizes oneself as author or origin of one's behavior even when environmental influences play a part.

To put this concept another way, in the egocentric mystery-mastery mode either the ego or the environment is viewed as controlling a given transaction. Environmental influences are perceived as pressures on the ego. By contrast, when the single-structured ego dissolves through continued contact with consciousness and with the alternative structures that that permits, one recognizes that the view of consciousness as within the body and environment as outside the body holds only at the behavioral level. At higher levels, whether one controls oneself is not determined by distinguishing between personal and environmental influences and seeing which predominate, for the two are not fully distinguishable.

This perspective is not easily illustrated, but the following account describes one way in which I occasionally experience the interpenetration of self and others:

In conversations of four or five people, when we are exploring near the edges of what is comfortable for us, I find myself growing cautious about my choice of words and tones so as not to break through the delicate web of solidarity and risks, stretched tight by our fears and resistances. I sense a transition in myself from reacting to others' points of view, tones, and gestures as though they were external pressures necessitating caution on my part, to actually feeling the various fears and resistances inside myself and approppriating them as my own. The whole web of emotion enters into me, and my perception of the others changes to seeing them as projections or manifestations of feelings I own. I come to experience my words and gestures as part of a rhythmic dance, influenced by the inner rhythm just as are the others' words and gestures.

The sense of intentionality is personal or transpersonal, transmuting itself through one, not impersonal, not manipulative. A sense of intentionality can be expressed behaviorally as a statement of one's intention as one acts, a recognition that there are different ways in which one can organize given external events, or as an effort to dwell in, understand, or reproduce the way another person is organizing his moment-to-moment experience.

Denial of intentionality is the reverse: a sense that external forces operate upon one and cause behavior that one does not feel ownership of or responsibility for. Also, a sense that external facts are objective, or, put another way, that only the organizing scheme one is currently using is legitimate.

RELATIONALITY. The illustration of "interpenetration of self and others" suggests how closely related intentionality is to a second aspect of conscious appropriation of behavior, named abstractness or complexity by theorists concerned with cognitive structures (Harvey, Hunt, and Schroder, 1961), and here named *relationality*. By abstractness, theorists refer to an ability to recognize the "relational linkages between alternative views" of a situation by the persons present (Schroder, Driver, and Streufert, 1967); hence, the term relationality. Whereas intentionality can be thought of as concerning "vertical" interrelations among levels of experience, such as thought and behavior, relationality can be thought of as concerning "horizontal" interrelations among aspects of a given level, such as two persons' behavior.

In terms of the model of experiential learning presented in chapter one, consciousness interpenetrates the various structures through which members view events in a group, so that he who is conscious realizes that his behavior influences and is influenced by others' view of a situation even in cases where two members' expressed views are directly contradictory on a given issue. Consequently, another person is never viewed or treated as totally alien by the conscious person. The conscious person may directly contradict another at the behavioral level by confronting him, but will recognize the continued interdependence of the two systems at the structural and conscious levels. Hence, his behavioral contradiction of the other will not extend to a total devaluation of him, but rather involves a testing of his own position in front of the other person.

At the extreme, total devaluation of the other person (or devaluation unless the other changes to conform to the speaker's expectations) is implied in what are commonly called personal attacks. In contrast, at high levels of conscious appropriation the person places differences within a relational context. For example, the conscious person may say:

I know, in a way that seems distant to me now, that you and I are both concerned to help these children, but I am more vividly aware at the moment of a feeling of real anger and antagonism at you for cutting me off, which makes me think you are unconcerned with anybody but yourself. I guess *you* must feel *I'm* not really concerned to help the children since you cut me off, and I wonder what I am doing to make you feel that way.

This statement shows an appreciation that both members are behaving and structuring their perceptions of each other's behavior in ways that create their mutual conflict. It may indeed be that one member will, after further exploration, decide that both his behavior and his way of structuring his perceptions of the other's behavior can be more effective if changed, while the other member may find both his earlier behavior and perceptions confirmed. Nevertheless, at the time of the initial interaction it is still true that both members behave in ways that create their mutual conflict.

Relationality can also be exhibited in terms of different aspects of oneself or in comparing the present situation and some past situation.

Denial of relationality is the reverse sense: that one's perceptions and behaviors are absolute, uninfluenced, and unchanged either within oneself, over time, in different contexts, or by others; that the issues at hand in no way depend on or have implications for personal relations; that right decisions are determinable in terms of abstract principles unrelated to personal influences; and that conflict is a sign of illegitimacy and breakdown.

MOMENTARY VALIDITY. A third aspect of conscious appropriation of one's behavior is the recognition that its validity extends to and is restricted to the moment of time of its performance or to specified other times. In the simplest case, momentary validity occurs whenever a person expresses a current thought or feeling as an experience that he is having. Another simple case occurs when a person relates a current thought or feeling to current behavior. An example will help us discuss more complex aspects of momentary validity. In the example, a T-group has focused on several different issues in rapid succession, a few members dominating the conversation. The silent members, as it turns out, are uncertain whether the issues are interesting to them, whether their own comments would add to the value of the discussion, or whether the issues are being dealt with in sufficient depth to produce any learning. As these reservations emerge and develop into a conversation about the implicit norms of the group as to who speaks when and how, one of the previously silent members begins to say, "I think we're politely leading up to the point—" only to be interrupted by one of the members who earlier dominated the conversation, saying, "—that *I* talk too much ! Yeah, I know I do, I'll admit it."

At first glance, we may respond to this statement as perceptive and open on the part of the member who owns up to talking too much. Next, however, we note that the statement is self-condemning (and thus in the mystery-mastery mode) and not very helpful analytically (i.e., at this level of analysis it could equally be said of others that they talk "too little"). Further, we might interpret the statement as a preemptive defense rather than the open owning it claims to be. By condemning himself the member preempts others from expressing their feelings towards him or prevents such feelings from having an impact on him (he can respond, "I already know that").

If we ask ourselves what it is about the statement that leads us to interpret it as defensive, we find that it neither extends itself nor restricts itself to the moment of his present behavior. In short, the member has talked too much in the very act of stating that he talks too much. That is, he does not appropriate the effect of his behavior in cutting off the other. (Moreover, the other person might not have raised this issue at all.) Certainly the interruption will tend to discourage the other from further participation, reinforcing the dynamics that lead him to talk "too little."

The insight implicit in the statement "I talk too much" and the act of stating it are mutually contradictory at this moment and consequently cannot represent the authentic transformation of a conscious intention. In this sense the validity of the behavior does not extend to its own performance. Conversely, the generalization inherent in the statement attempts to extend its validity to all moments, thus obscuring the fact that the speaker chooses to speak at certain moments, not at all moments. In this sense the validity of the behavior is not restricted to its own performance.

Rogers (1961a) contrasts a rigid, undifferentiated view of one's experience (e.g., "I talk too much") to "process experiencing," in which "experiencing has lost almost completely its structure-bound aspects. . . . The situation is experienced and interpreted in its newness. . . . The self is much less frequently a perceived object, and much more frequently something confidently felt in process" (pp. 152–53). This distinction of Rogers suggests how the concept of the momentary validity of behavior connects to the systems model I have proposed. Earlier, in chapter 1, I distinguished between rigid, structure-bound self-images that are out of contact with consciousness (e.g., "I say what I believe" and "I see myself on a pedestal") and conscious ultrastability that permits one to change structures as one's intentions and situations change. To the differences between these two system-states and their experiencing we can now add a different sense of time.

In the structure-bound state, what is true now will be true later, since the structure determining truth will remain unchanged. Moreover, the problem of whether what is true now conceptually is also true behaviorally (i.e., whether there is a congruent transformation between the structural and behavioral levels) is not considered at all in the structure-bound state, for the system is not in contact with the conscious vision that can interpenetrate thought and action. By contrast, the conscious system is concerned with the problem of whether its intentions are authentically transformed into behavior from moment to mement, and, because it can operate through many structures, it recognizes that the validity of any one mode of presentation is restricted to the momentary situation.

The one example I have offered is protypical in that it overtly concerns the issues of talking and timing. It should be noted, however, that numerous other statements are or are not extended and restricted to the moment of their performance. For example, the following statement lacks momentary validity:

I really think you ought to grow up and make your own decisions. Don't pay any attention to people who try to tell you what to do.

The speaker both generalizes to all occasions and fails to extend his opinion to the present, since he is clearly attempting to tell his listener what to do.

GENERAL COMMENTS

The three qualities of conscious appropriation are highly interrelated, as the examples show. If the reader reexamines the examples of high and low intentionality (p. 174), he will note that the examples of high intentionality also involve a high recognition of system-environment relationality. Similarly, the example of high recognition of system-environment relationality also reveals an effort to extend and restrict the validity of the statement to the moment of performance. And, completing the circle, there is no evidence of appropriation of intentionality in the examples of statements which do not appropriate their momentary validity.

In general, the sense of intentionality, relationality and momentary validity must come from the speaker's present verbal posture in the conversation, not merely from the content of what he says. Thus, all statements that are expressed entirely in the past tense, or as hypotheticals, present no evidence of conscious appropriation of behavior.

Interferences with establishing intentionality, relationality, or momentary validity, such as proforma qualifiers, are scored as negative (for example, "I may be wrong, but . . . ," "I don't mean this personally, but . . . ," "I don't like to say this, but . . .").

Responses such as "Yeah" or "Oh," if in isolation, are neutral in regard to all three categories. "No" is scored as negative relationality unless it is somehow qualified.

Some examples of appropriation and denial of intentionality, relationality, and momentary validity follow. They have already been analyzed in terms of their focal functions and structural modes.

I'd like to talk about the group norms here now. (Work, self-disclosure. The "I'd like" indicates appropriation of intentionality and the "now" indicates restriction of validity to the present. Thus, +2.)

The evening seems to be sort of a vacuum. Which you've created for us. Maybe it isn't up to you to establish a structure . . . even though it's arbitrary. (Authority, mystery-mastery. The "which you've created for us" indicates denial of intentionality; the validity of the comment is not restricted to the present, nor does it include the present even though it is in the present tense, since the speaker is evidently creating this comment. She shares in creating the evening in the act of claiming someone else had created it for her. Thus, −2.)

It's a question of who will take the first step. (Authority, exploration of structure. Although there is a reference to a relation outside the speaker—"first step"—there is no evidence about the speaker's relation to that event. Nor is there evidence regarding the intentionality or momentary validity of the statement. Thus, 0.)

The rules are that we stay in the here and now, and we try to find out what is going on within and between us. (Identity, mystery-mastery. "The rules" are treated as an external force, impersonal, denying the speaker's intentionality. They are taken as absolute rather than related to the present time and situation, denying relationality. And, by the same token, they are generalized but not applied to the speaker's own behavior. Thus, −3.)

You push for clarification in your terms rather than letting him explain it in his terms. (Intimacy, mystery-mastery. The speaker shows no awareness that he is using *his* terms in this statement to clarify something for the other, so validity is not extended to his own behavior in speaking; again, although he describes a relationship outside himself, there is no evidence of his own relation to the person he is addressing. Thus, −1.)

I'm disappointed that we've given up already. Every time someone tries to start something or say something it gets put down. (Intimacy, exploration of structure. The speaker relates his inner state to an external situation, yet the validity of his statement does not extend to itself, since by offering an analysis he is starting something rather than giving up. Thus, $+1 -1 = 0$.)

Lecturing isn't going to help now. (Intimacy, mystery-mastery. The speaker restricts the validity of his statement to the present, but does not extend it to the present, since he himself can be viewed as lecturing. Hence the evidence regarding momentary validity is contradictory. There is no evidence regarding the intentionality and relationality of the statement. Thus, 0.)

Yes, I see now—I really pushed. (Education, self-disclosure. The "now" indicates momentary validity; the "yes" indicates appropriation of his present relationality; the "I see" followed by what he sees indicates his intentional reorganization of his experience. Thus, +3.)

Table 3 presents an overview of all the theoretical categories introduced in this chapter.

Table 3. Theoretical categories based on the model of learning

Levels of analysis of each behavior unit	Categories
focal functions of behavior	authority intimacy identity work education action
structural modes of behavior	mystery-mastery exploration of structure supportiveness self-disclosure confrontation
conscious appropriation of behavior	degrees of denial or appropriation of: intentionality relationality momentary validity

BEHAVIOR CONDUCIVE TO EXPERIENTIAL LEARNING

According the the model in chapter 1, experiential learning occurs only when there is contact with consciousness. In terms of verbal behavior scored by the foregoing categories, contact with consciousness is operationalized as *conscious appropriation of behavior*. Consequently, the degree of experiential learning achieved by a person as he speaks is directly reflected in the degree of conscious appropriation scored. Negative scores can be taken to reflect the fact that a person can actually mislearn in a situation, that is, get farther away from the real structure of experience in his own fantasy or in a fantasy he shares with many other people.

We would also expect, by the theory , that the mystery-mastery mode would be correlated with negative experiential learning, the exploration of structure mode with somewhat more (i.e., less negative) learning, and the modes of support self-disclosure, and confrontation with positive experiential learning. This expectation is confirmed, in an illustrative sense, by the eight examples of conscious appropriation and denial presented on the preceding pages. The statements in the mystery-mastery mode average $-1\frac{1}{2}$ learning; those in the exploration of structure mode average 0 learning; those in the other modes average $+2\frac{1}{2}$ learning.

The elaboration and illustration of the three levels of verbal analysis in this chapter raise several questions. Are the clinical analyses of behavior discussed in this chapter merely subjective interpretations by the author? Or are the criteria of interpretation sufficiently specified to permit several scorers to agree on how to apply the categories? Further, if it is possible to score behavior reliably using these categories, do the resulting scores really reflect experiential learning? That is, do they indicate in practice, as they do in theory, contact or lack of contact with consciousness? How do scores of learning determined by this procedure compare to other estimates of learning? In short, how valid are these categories?

These questions will be addressed by chapters 7 through 9.

III

MEASUREMENT OF EXPERIENTIAL LEARNING

Measurement generally presupposes agreement about a unit of measure. However, in a study of how units of experience become defined and gain subjective, intersubjective, and objective value, it is obviously impossible to presuppose agreement about a unit of measure. Instead, a primary task becomes development of an agreeable unit of measure, as well as an agreeable structure for measurement and agreeable instruments of measurement. Moreover, these three tasks necessarily intermingle, even if they can later be separated analytically into distinct parts and chapters in a book.

The following part describes efforts to develop an agreeable (i.e., reliable and valid) empirical unit of measure for experiential learning. It reports the scoring of two series of group meetings, described earlier, in which members attempted, in different ways, to learn from their experience. The first half of the first and third meetings of each group were transcribed from tape recordings and scored, after the author and two other scorers obtained high reliability using the scoring procedure.

Chapter 7 describes the process and results of developing reliable application of the scoring procedure by three scorers.

Chapter 8 investigates the validity of the scoring procedure in terms of its quantitative determination of the relative degree of learning of the two different groups and of different members within each group.

Chapter 9 characterizes the validity of the scoring procedure

by analyzing individual cases in which the scoring procedure's
determination of who learned much or little differed sharply
from participants' evaluations of each other's learning.

Of course, the influence of the scorers' work and of the group
meetings extends beyond providing data on a unit of measure.
The scorers' work helped to mold the theoretical structure of the
scoring procedure, reported in chapter 6. And the instruments of
measure themselves were developed in the very process of using
them, in that the scorers became the final instruments of empirical measurement and the members of the meditation group became the final instruments in the phenomenological studies reported in chapter 5.

Chapter Seven

ACHIEVING AGREEMENT IN SCORING
OF LEARNING

This chapter reports the process and results of three persons' efforts to reach agreement in their use of the theoretical categories of behavior, described in the previous chapter, to score transcripts of group meetings. It may, therefore, be of greater interest to behavioral scientists than to other readers.

Some readers may prefer to skip the chapter after this one-sentence summary of its outcome: the three scorers achieved a respectable level of agreement among themselves on the exact scoring of units of behavior and a very high level of agreement on the scoring of units relative to one another (the latter kind of agreement being particularly important for comparisons of aggregate learning averages among individuals and groups).

The process of reaching these levels of agreement sheds light on the model and theory of learning in much the same way as did the process of the meditation meetings described in chapter 5. Some readers may find this process of interest, even if they prefer not to negotiate the few statistical tests at the end.

INITIAL EFFORTS TO OPERATIONALIZE THE
THEORETICAL CATEGORIES

In a first effort to operationalize the theoretical categories of behavior presented in chapter 6, I observed several T-groups in action. My overriding impression was that much of the dialogue at these meetings reflected low levels of learning, even though the groups were intended to create climates conducive to experiential learning. The following are my initial impressions, jotted down after several weeks of observation:

When I first entered several on-going T-groups as an observer, attempting to learn how to distinguish the theoretical categories in actual conversations, I sensed myself to be floating rather uncomfortably in the backwash of the conversations, rather than applying my scoring procedure vigorously to each succeeding comment. At first I explained my behavior to myself as resulting from the speed of the dialogue combined with my unfamiliarity in applying these categories to behavior. I would simply take down pieces of occasional sentences for later analysis.

Gradually, however, I became aware of a number of different feelings within me that were making me much less than the efficient, impartial observer I may have appeared outwardly to be. First of all, the excitement of the interaction in which I could play no part made me feel very lonely, especially since my work on my dissertation had for several months been a predominantly solitary occupation. Second, I found myself looking at persons' behavior as though I were the group's trainer, attempting to gauge appropriate moments and forms of intervention, and feeling increasingly frustrated at being unable to help the group at such moments. These negative feelings intensified rather than dissipated, leading me, on the one hand, to self-pitying imaginings about how I was being stunted emotionally by my work on the disseratation and, on the other hand, to self-congratulatory fantasies about how helpful and potent the group atmosphere would be if I were the educator. These musings distracted me from the group's interaction even more than the earlier sensation of floating in the backwash. Attempts to banish my imaginings and regain impartiality only made me feel sealed off from the group by a thick layer of skin, through which sights and sounds scarcely penetrated, so engrossed was I in my own inner dialogue.

I realized I was building up resistance against a caring involvement in the groups I was observing, but that this resistance was making me less rather than more perceptive about what was happening around me.

I made an effort to focus again on members' comments, remembering that my role as researcher was a valuable one— simply going about the business of discriminating which of my scoring categories applied to each comment. Still, the behavior I was observing did not seem to fit my scoring categories. Again I gave up the intensive effort, but this time let my mind float right with the conversation unanalytically. Now the conversation took on for me the semblance of a dense wood through which I wandered, happening upon occasional clearings. These "clearings" were comments or sequences of comments that seemed to me to have idiosyncratic potency. That is, they really seemed to "get something said," to shake the conversation out of neutral gear and into forward motion. I tended to copy these comments down, and later, when I attempted to analyze them, I found that they were relatively easy to categorize, unlike the earlier comments I had jotted down more or less at random.

One of the main difficulties in categorizing many comments, I found, was that *the speaker commonly showed no awareness that what he said was itself a piece of behavior* and served some behavioral function for him and the group. Consequently, since the group was supposed to be focusing upon its own functioning, the comments tended to be analyses of *past* behavior. As such, they were confusing for me to categorize since they would be comments about behavioral functions that they themselves did not represent. For example, a person could say, "Learning is not something I do easily," or "I don't think we were doing the sort of learning we said we wanted to do." Initially, hearing the word "learning," I would think of the behavioral function *education.* However, neither of these statements obviously involves testing nonhabitual behavior to see whether it will authentically transform a conscious intention (i.e., experimenting, taking a risk). Rather, the first portrays boundaries (*identity*) and the second is a historical description concerning goal-attainment (*work*).

These difficulties obviously arose from three sources: my lack of training in applying the theoretical categories; the interpretive nature of my scoring procedure; and the generally low level of conscious appropriation exhibited by group members. Early comments by other behavioral scientists also reflected these difficulties. They felt that the scoring procedure was so demanding of both scorers and behavior scored that they doubted whether it would be possible either to achieve agreement among scorers or to find behavior that would receive high scores on my measure of conscious appropriation. So rare, they felt, was the kind of behavior regarded as learning by my theory that they questioned whether my theory was scientifically useful. What could its use be if it did not in fact distinguish among different units of behavior—if it scored behavior as uniformly low in terms of conscious appropriation?

NECESSARY DILEMMAS

A possible response to these early impressions would have been to give up the effort altogether. But this would have been an irrational choice, because my models of learning and science explained both difficulties as necessary dilemmas. Low conscious appropriation of behavior was to be expected as a statistical norm, given the prevalence of the mystery-mastery mode of behavior. This fact in no way lessened the significance of establishing a reliable and valid procedure for measuring which behavior does lead to learning (given agreement that learning is or could be a significant human process). As to the high demands made on scorers by the scoring procedure, these too were to be expected if one took seriously the need to reach agreement on *ways of structuring phenomena into observable categories* rather than merely *taking existing cultural and linguistic conventions for granted in observing phenomena.*

The difficulty in finding behavior that reflected high conscious appropriation became the original impetus for inviting a group of friends to the experimental meditation meetings, in the hope of generating high conscious appropriation of behavior among them. (The fact that the approach and content of these meetings were originally no part of the plan of this study, yet later assumed a still more central role (chapter 5) than I foresaw when I held the meetings, illustrates the vagaries of scientific investigation, despite orderly and apparently premeditated outcomes.) As the following chapter will show, even in these meetings the group average for conscious appropriation of behavior never reached $+1$ (on the $-3/+3$ scale). Nevertheless, the meetings did provide enough variance in conscious appropriation and enough examples of high scores to determine what kinds of distinctions the scoring procedure made.

We can also study in greater detail the difficulties facing the scorers. Two aspects of the scoring procedure challenged the scorers as they attempted to obtain reliability using the categories. The first problem is that, even as finally presented in chapter 6, the various categories do not receive a high degree of operationalization in passing from theory to scoring procedure. They remain highly interpretive, demanding creative rather than unambiguously programmed judgments by the scorers. Hence, it is not surprising that I should have found it so difficult to anchor the categories to particular phrases or words such as "learning." The second difficulty is that, because of its highly interpretive nature, the scoring procedure requires continuous effort in application, and thus a degree of motivation on the part of the scorer that exceeds what is necessary to hurry through a routine job as quickly as possible. The scorer's continuing motivation must be deep enough to surmount the feelings of resistance I felt during my early efforts to apply the categories.

Two fellow graduate students joined me in attempting to learn how to score behavior reliably with my categories. Many of the guidelines presented in the previous chapter for defining and discriminating among categories were developed or modified during our sessions together. Before our first meeting the other two scorers read early drafts of chapters 1 and 6 and expressed both personal and professional commitment to mastering the scoring procedure. I warned them that the commitment was likely to be demanding of both time and energy, and they accepted the task with this understanding.

The three of us met five times for three-hour sessions, doing some practice scoring, comparison of scores, revision and rehearsal of categories, and theorizing in each session. At our fifth meeting we obtained a percentage of agreement among our scores that was high enough, in our judgment, to warrant scoring the transcripts of the group meetings, with which I planned to test the validity of the scoring procedure.

Short sections and random units from these group meetings were among the materials used in practice scoring. The scorers practiced both on isolated units and on units in context and reviewed their results after every ten units or so, determining together what scores seemed to be accurate for each unit. Consequently, after the full transcripts were scored, two kinds of final reliability checks were possible: a comparison to scores earlier determined to be accurate and a comparison to short sections of the transcripts that had been scored by another scorer.

BASIC DECISIONS DEFINING THE SCORING PROCEDURE

The scoring procedure deals with units of verbal behavior. Presumably a scoring procedure based upon the same principles could also be devised for nonverbal behavior. Presumably, too, a scoring procedure based upon the same principles could be extended to take into account varying settings. The reader should be aware that the restriction to verbal behavior means that the scoring procedure does not encode the full range of behavior conducive to learning.

Moreover, the limitation of any empirical scoring procedure to externally observable phenomena such as behavior means that it can measure awareness of the structural and conscious levels only when they are congruently transformed into behavior. All forms of conscious irony, in which relations among levels are revealed through apparent contradictions at a given level of experience, are inaccessible to this scoring procedure. This limitation is reflected in the discussion of the focal function *action* in the previous chapter, which points to the necessity of knowing the context before being able to identify a piece of behavior as action.

As the reader has by now probably inferred, the scoring procedure treats each occasion of a person's talking as a single unit of behavior, no matter how short or long it is. Each unit of behavior receives three distinct scores, corresponding to the three levels of analysis—focal function, structural mode, and degree of conscious appropriation. It might be possible to construct a theoretical justification for choosing occasions of speaking as the units for this scoring procedure. The argument could take the form that the occasion as a whole reveals the gestalt of the person's intuitions or habits relating to verbal behavior at that moment. And since the scoring procedure is an attempt to elucidate the experiential meaning of behaviors for the engaged persons (which is not to say that these persons are always intellectually aware of this meaning), it is just this general gestalt that we are concerned with illuminating. Such an argument is not offered with confidence, however, since there is no reason to believe a priori that whole occasions of behaving *do* form single gestalts for persons. Rather, the decision to treat each occasion of a person's talking as a single unit of behavior was reached, first, because it was an obvious discrimination for scorers, virtually eliminating the problem of obtaining reliability in identifying units of behavior and, second, because preliminary practice with the procedure indicated that scorers encountered little difficulty in treating whole occasions of behavior as single units.

The scoring system can probably be used not only to compute individual and group scores on experiential learning in verbal interactions (its dominant use in this book), but also to trace trends, dominant issues, rhythms, and turning points of interactions.

So far, the most useful way to score dialogues has been to go through them three times, scoring comments at one level of analysis each time, and not referring to levels already scored when assessing subsequent levels. This process not only helps to ensure that the decisions on scores are not distorted by theoretically expectable connections among the levels (such as between mystery-mastery and denial of responsibility for behavior), but also seems to be less confusing for the scorer, increasing speed and reliability.

THE PROCESS OF LEARNING THE SCORING PROCEDURE

The learning process of the three scorers was slow and arduous. The reader may recall that I attempted unsuccessfully to introduce the scoring procedure as a conceptual-interpersonal aid during the meditation meetings described in chapter 5. The reverse phenomenon occurred among the three of us in learning to use the scoring procedure. We attempted for three meetings to approach the job of obtaining reliability as a conceptual-interper-

Table 4. Agreement among scorers in early stages of their work

Meeting	Units scored	Total scores	% Initial agreement among all 3 scorers	% Initial agreement between any 2 of the 3 scorers
first	8 random	24	.25	.79
second	10 random	30	.27	.90
third	9 random	45	.29	.84
	13 in context	65	.31	.82
fourth	20 random	80	.21	.91
fifth	13 in context	52	.52	.87

sonal task requiring clarification of the categories and consensus among the scorers regarding operational boundaries between categories. Then, unable in three meetings to raise our level of average agreement (see table 4), we attempted some meditation exercises similar to those described in chapter 5, in hopes that intuitive-experiential familiarity with the qualities of intentional and subsidiary awareness might aid us in discriminating their presence in verbal behavior. Instead, the other two scorers found the meditations confusing because they seemed to encourage a free-floating rather than a concentrated awareness. Although they found the exercises intriguing and challenging in themselves, the percentage of agreements among all three scorers in the practice scoring that followed the meditation fell below those attained in the second meeting (see table 4). Thus the felt conflict between focal, calculative, interpersonal awareness and transfocal, meditative, intrapersonal awareness seemed to suggest itself once again.

% Agreement of each to accurate scores	Average agreement to accurate scores	Average agreement at each level	Range of categories used in sample scored
author .79	.60	conscious .54	13 of 18
scorer 1 .50		structural .77	
scorer 2 .50		focal .63	
author .80	.69	conscious .67	15 of 18
scorer 1 .54		structural .77	
scorer 2 .73		focal .70	
accurate scores not determined			16 of 22
author .90	.64	conscious .63	18 of 22
scorer 1 .50		structural .60	
scorer 2 .52		focal .64	
author .88	.65	conscious .63	11 of 15
scorer 1 .49		structural .69	
scorer 2 .56			
author .75	.82	conscious .83	8 of 11
scorer 1 .85		structural .79	
scorer 2 .87			

Another confusing factor was my introduction of the first draft of a scoring manual (now interpolated into chapter 6) between the second and third meetings. The other two scorers studied the manual, and subsequent scoring was based upon it; but the connections between the theory and operationalization of intentionality, relationality, and momentary validity were little discussed until the fifth meeting. The other two scorers still tended to focus upon the *content* rather than the *impact* of what was said for evidence of intentionality and relationality. Emphasis on the lack of evidence of either dimension in any past-tense utterances, no matter what their content, helped to counter this tendency. At this time I was also able to offer a useful way to distinguish the two dimensions, by defining intentionality as concerned with "vertical" interactions among levels of experience and relationality as concerned with "horizontal" interactions at a given level of experience.

I presented the other two scorers with an explanation of each of the 80 scores of the fourth session for review at the outset of the fifth meeting, and this technique seemed to stabilize their criteria (as indicated by the rise both in initial agreement among all three scorers and in our average agreement to scores we later determined to be accurate after comparing our individual scores).

Another difficulty during the first four sessions was that I would vary the quality of practice transcripts as widely as possible. For example, the thirteen units in context that were scored during the third session were drawn from the meditation that is in large part transcribed in chapter 5. It was the first time the other two scorers had ever encountered dialogue of that quality and they felt themselves to be both overfascinated by it and underprepared for it. In the fifth meeting, for the first time I presented units of dialogue that could be considered to be within the frame of reference already developed by the scorers.

Prior to the fifth session the scorers would find at times that, after discussions of differences among them, they would merely trade their conflicting criteria, each adopting the other's previous criterion, rather than adopting common criteria.

Discussion during these five meetings was not limited to units scored. The scorers brought to the meetings for diagnosis some of their own critical encounters with others in daily life, using the categories of the scoring procedure both to test the validity of the categories and to gain insight. This process arose spontaneously and seems to me to reflect the structural-level change demanded by this scoring procedure in order to obtain the behavioral-level operational consensus. As one of the scorers put it, reliability in using this scoring system requires congruence among scorers' values as much as congruence among their perceptions of observable events. For example, a person may say to another who has just spoken,

You push for clarification in your terms rather than letting him [a third person present] explain it in his terms.

The scorer's first reaction may be that this comment shows high awareness of relationality on the speaker's part. However, the comment gives no evidence whether the speaker is aware that he is related to the person to whom he is speaking. It also shows no evidence of the speaker's intention. Still, the statement seems so insightful that it must receive a positive learning score. So the scorer might be tempted to score the comment positively for momentary validity, since one might infer that the speaker is referring to a specific behavior of another person and not generalizing to all of the other's behavior. However, the speaker shows no compunction about using his terms to clarify something for the other person, even while criticizing the same practice by the other. Thus, the statement should receive a negative score for momentary validity, since its "preaching" is incongruent with its "practice." Although at first glance, especially to anyone familiar with the T-group emphasis on "descriptive feedback," the comment appears to be a positive contribution to the conversation, it receives a -1 learning score by this procedure, indicating denial of responsibility for one's behavior.

The scorer must not merely look for evidences of relationality or momentary validity as he ordinarily thinks of these terms, but must reconceptualize these words to apply to the form rather than the content or context of the comment, in order to score accurately. His habitual value judgments regarding the positive or negative quality of statements may be quite the reverse of judgments of learning by this scoring procedure.

In the language of this model of learning, such reconceptualizing by a scorer involves structural-level change. Structural-level change requires conscious motivation, and such motivation, it seems to me, could arise from the need for new conceptualizations to account for and guide one's own experience. The scorers may have found the motivation to work on reliability through their discovery in analyzing their own critical encounters that the concepts of the scoring procedure helped explain and guide their own lives.

One further comment will conclude this discussion of the scorers' initial work. The scorers found they had to prepare themselves before each occasion of scoring. The task, quite simply, felt difficult. It felt as though it would require more energy and concentration than were present or could be mustered at any given time. This problem was somewhat alleviated by the elimination of the behavioral level from consideration after the third session and the collapsing of the structural categories into nonconscious modes (mystery-mastery and exploration of structure) and conscious modes. Thus, the final emphasis was upon accurate scoring of degrees of conscious appropriation. But the psychic demand made by the scoring procedure continued to be felt after the number of operative categories was cut from 22 to 11.

Even when the scorers moved to the lengthy transcripts, the scoring never became an easy, automatic process. Each unit of dialogue seemed to require active thought before it would yield to interpretation. And the scorers found themselves guarding against, rather than looking for, obvious indicators as consistent operationalizations for categories, returning instead time after time to the theoretical meaning of the categories to seek clues for the scoring of a particular comment. These experiences may occur because successful discrimination of conscious appropriation of behavior requires the scorer himself to be conscious and thinking actively rather than merely thinking along the lines of his habitual structural configuration.

THE FINAL RELIABILITY TESTS

With the achievement of over 80% agreement to "accurate" scores during the fifth session, we decided we could move to the task of scoring the four transcripts. I scored the first meetings of each group and short sections of the later meetings, and each of the other two people scored one of the later meetings. These scores were the basis both for the final reliability tests and for validity tests to be described in the chapters eight and nine.

The reliability tests first showed that one other scorer and I had obtained high agreement to scores determined to be accurate in earlier practice sessions. The third scorer, however, only obtained about 50% agreement with earlier scores and with a short section that I had scored in the same transcript he was working on. The third scorer and I discussed the discrepancies between our scores for the short section I had scored (but not the discrepancies between his and the earlier accurate scores). He then rescored his total transcript. His agreement with two other short sections I had scored rose to 80%, and his agreement with the earlier accurate scores rose to 60%. His overall level of agreement was 73%. I obtained 81% agreement with the earlier scores. The second scorer obtained 72% agreement with the earlier scores and the sections I had scored.

On the basis of the transcript scores, I performed two other tests of reliability that were more directly relevant to the validity tests based on the scoring procedure than to absolute agreement among categories. These tests related to the aggregate -3 to $+3$ scores of degree of conscious appropriation for each scored unit. They indicated whether any two scorers agreed on the amount of conscious appropriation of any two units or aggregates of behavior, relative to one another.

The scores for each spoken unit were to be summed in two different ways in the validity tests. First, averages of scores for each member of the group were to be compared to one another. Second, averages of scores for contiguous sections of meetings and for whole meetings were to be compared to one another. One would hope to show thus that contiguous scores could be reliably discriminated from one another, leading to accurate differentiations among either individual or group learning averages for different meetings or parts of meetings.

Kendall's tau correlation performed the first function, and the Pierson product-moment correlation performed the second function. In the case of the tau, the ratings by two scorers for individual spoken units are compared to see whether both people agree about the relative ratings for all units within a given sample. The correlation is raised whenever the two scorers agree in scoring unit x higher or lower than unit y, and it is lowered in all instances where one person rates unit x higher than unit y, but the other person rates unit y higher than unit x. If the tau correlation were high, one could be confident that differences in mean learning scores for members of a group reflected reliable differences in unit-by-unit scores and not simply random variation.

In the product-moment correlation, average scores by two scorers for different sections of contiguous units or several units from the same meeting are compared to see whether scorers agree about the relative magnitudes of, and intervals among, the different averages. The correlation is raised as the two scorers tend to agree about the relative rank of a given average in relation to the other averages and about the relative interval between the given average and the other averages. If the product-moment correlation were high, one could be confident that average learning differences for different meetings or parts of meetings resulted from reliable scores and not from random variation.

The three scorers achieved tau's of .55, .47, and .47 on the basis of comparisons between 10, 13, and 20 units, respectively. These correlations are comparable in magnitude to those obtained by Dollard and Auld (1959) for a scoring procedure of similar complexity that was intended to infer the motives of patients in therapy settings. The comparative scores for all 43 units included in the reliability tests are shown in table 5.

Table 5. Reliability of unit-by-unit scores

		Earlier accurate score or later score by author						
		−3	−2	−1	0	1	2	3
Score by scorer of total transcript	−3							
	−2				1			
	−1							
	0			1	13	5		
	1				9	3	3	**1**
	2					3	1	
	3						2	1

The table indicates that in only two out of forty-three comparisons (those in bold face) did scorers disagree by as much as two points in a range of seven. This straightforward result is the basis for confidence in the reliability indicated by the tau statistics. The table also suggests that there is no strong systematic tendency for scorers of the transcripts to err on the high or low side in relation to the comparative scores for the given unit.

This latter suggestion is strongly supported by the product-moment correlation performed on nine average scores of learning from distinct samples, totalling 85 units and including the 43 units measured by the tau's. Each sample represents scores from a similar context, either directly contiguous to one another or from

Table 6. Reliability of aggregate scores by context

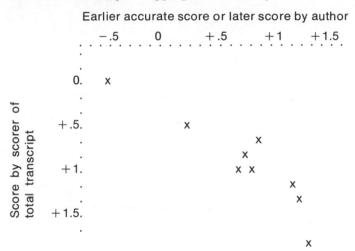

Earlier accurate score or later score by author

the same meeting. The correlation is very high, .95, and significant beyond the .001 level by the t-test. Table 6 illustrates the relationship of the scores to one another. Again, we find no extreme deviations between average learning scores of two scorers
for the same sample. The largest deviation between averages for
the *same* sample is .31, whereas the range of deviation *among*
samples is 1.74.

It seems safe to conclude on the basis of the tau and product-
moment correlations that a high enough level of reliability
among scorers has been achieved to warrant testing the validity
of the scoring procedure. Just what, in practice, does the scoring
procedure discriminate, and how does its measure of learning
compare to other perspectives on learning? We turn to these
questions in the following chapters.

Chapter Eight

CORRELATIONS BETWEEN LEARNING SCORES
AND OTHER CRITERIA OF LEARNING

Having seen that reliability was obtained in the use of the scoring procedure, we can turn to questions about what the scoring procedure actually measures. In some respects, chapter 6 answered the questions. It offered theoretical justifications for each scoring category (yielding construct validity) and also extensively exemplified each category (yielding content validity). However, the question of external validity remains. How does what the scoring procedure measures as learning compare to other criteria of learning?

To answer these questions we turn to the transcribed tape recordings of the meetings of the two groups that were invited to participate in experiential learning, and to the questionnaires the members filled out after each meeting on their perceptions of their own and others' learning.

The first group, called the "meditation" or "M" group in the following pages, was the group that participated in the meditations and related exercises described in chapter 5. For more details about the composition of the group, the reader can refer to the description at the beginning of that chapter.

The second group, here called the "friendship" or "F" group, was composed of Yale undergraduates, mostly freshmen, who joined an informal experiential-learning seminar that I had designed around the topic of friendship. This group was also invited to participate in various exercises, but of a more interpersonal than meditational nature. For example, during the second

half of the first meeting, when the M group was first introduced
to meditation, the F group engaged in a role-playing episode.
And during the second half of the third meeting, when the M
group attempted the role-reversal exercise described toward the
end of chapter 5, the F group engaged in eyes-closed, nonverbal
milling around in which the members had to decide how to meet
and interact with one another physically.

Thus, the two groups were comparable in some respects but
not in others. They were comparable in that they were both led
by the author; the members of both groups participated from
some basis of personal interest; both groups developed over similar time periods; both were engaged in experiential exercises of
some sort; both filled out and received feedback on the same
questionnaires at the same time-intervals; and the scored transcripts are derived from the first half of the first and third meetings of each group. The two groups were not comparable in that
the members of the M group were older, closer friends of the author to begin with, and more familiar with the idea of experiential learning through T-groups, communes, and meditation than
were members of the F group; also, the exercises in which the M
group participated were directly related to the theoretical propositions of this book, whereas the exercises in which the F group
participated were drawn from the existing repertoire of techniques for facilitating group learning.

THE AMBIGUITIES OF TESTING HYPOTHESES

The process of testing the external validity of the scoring procedure cannot be a straightforward one of proposing hypotheses
concerning expected configurations of learning scores for individuals and groups. Every conceivable hypothesis contains assumptions about the content or the way of measuring experiential
learning that are challenged by the model and theory upon
which this scoring procedure is based.

For example, an obvious hypothesis is that persons with previous experiences in meditation, T-groups, or communal living
would be more attuned to experiential learning initially and con-

sequently would score higher in terms of average learning than other members at the first meeting. However, since no single model has heretofore guided experiential learning, different prior methods may result in wide variance in these scores. This variance may be greater than the variance between members with and without previous contact with experiential learning. Thus, my hypothesis could be negated although my theory was capable of explaining the negation.

Another criterion for the validity of the scoring procedure might be group members' perceptions of who learned most and least. Adopting this criterion, I would hypothesize that members who were perceived as learning most would score highest in terms of individual average learning scores. Yet my model of learning points to the rarity of and resistance to experiential learning and the widespread tendency to view internalization as learning. Consequently, I have reason to predict that members' perceptions of who learned most will not correlate highly with the determinations made by the scoring procedure.

In short, the combined novelties of the model, the theory, and the operational measure introduced here make it impossible to find external criteria which can be taken for granted as valid and against which this measure's validity may be tested.

Short of retreating to the model and theory introduced in earlier chapters and standing behind them as though behind fortress walls, in empty, solipsistic triumph, I must choose a number of lines of inquiry to follow and discover how learning as scored here actually does relate to other ways of discriminating learning. Each discrimination and comparison will be interpreted as thoroughly as the quantitative and clinical evidence permit. This process should reveal the flavor and consistency, the potency and limits, of the scoring procedure.

EFFECT OF PREVIOUS EXPERIENTIAL LEARNING

The first line of inquiry concerns the question whether members with previous contact with experiential learning are measured by this scoring procedure as learning more than members without previous contact with experiential learning. The question can be investigated quantitatively in two ways. We can see whether the M group, with a higher percentage of members who have participated in settings supposedly conducive to experiential learning (58% as opposed to 27% in the F group), had a higher average learning score at the first meeting than the F group. And, second, we can see whether the specific members of each group with previous exposure to experiential learning settings had a higher average learning score than those without.

The answer to both of these questions is positive. For the first half of the first meeting, before any exercises were introduced to either group, the mean learning score for the M group is +.95 whereas the mean learning score for the F group is only +.31. This difference in means is significant beyond the .01 level by a t-test. At the same time, in the M group the members with previous experience averaged +1.05 learning, whereas the members without previous experience averaged +.70 learning. In the F group, the members with previous experience averaged +.81 learning, while the members without previous experience averaged only +.27 learning for the first half of the first session. The difference in means within the M group is significant only beyond the .10 level, while the difference in means within the F group is significant beyond the .025 level. And, when one compares all members with previous experience in both groups to all members without, the difference in means is significant beyond the .01 level.

Although these findings appear to support the ability of the scoring procedure to discriminate behavior conducive to the kinds of learning broadly intended by meditation, T-groups, and communal living, alternative explanations have not yet been ruled out altogether. Two other initial differences between the M and F group members were average age and degree of previous friendship with the author. Either of these differences could conceivably be the basis for the difference in average learning between the two groups. However, equally convincing theoretical explanations could be constructed to show that increased age and friendship would have the effect of *lowering* average learning in a group. Moreover, when I compare the older to the younger members or close friends to acquaintances within the M group I find no significant differences in average learning (younger members rank 3, 4, 7, 9 and acquaintances rank 3, 4, 6, 9, 11, 13 in terms of relative individual learning averages). Also, differences in age and degree of acquaintance with me do not explain the difference in means based on relative previous contact with experiential learning by individual members.

EFFECT OF THE MEETINGS

The second question we can ask is whether both groups increased their aggregate learning, as measured by the scoring procedure, from the first to the third meeting. We could expect such an increase in a commonsense way on three grounds: (1) both groups were becoming increasingly acquainted with processes reputed to be conducive to experiential learning; (2) I supposedly have some skill at facilitating such learning; and (3) I viewed the meetings as generally successful.

One can imagine a considerable number of alternate ways in which learning could "increase" in the group. Figure 1a repre-

Figure 1. Cumulative learning

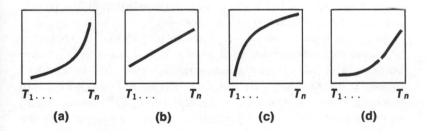

$T_1 \ldots$ T_n	$T_1 \ldots$ T_n	$T_1 \ldots$ T_n	$T_1 \ldots$ T_n
(a)	(b)	(c)	(d)

sents a situation in which each session contributes more to cumulative learning than the previous one, in terms of higher mean learning scores. Figure 1b, a situation in which each session contributes equally to cumulative learning (i.e., each succeeding session yields similar mean learning scores). In figure 1c, each session contributes a diminishing, but still positive, amount to cumulative learning. And, last, in figure 1d early sessions contribute increasingly to cumulative learning but, after a certain level is reached, any further sessions contribute equally (i.e., an upper limit exists beyond which a group's average learning per meeting will not rise). Since the scoring procedure establishes an absolute upper limit of $+3$, figure 1d is necessarily a more realistic expectation for a group's learning in the long run than is figure 1a.

All the foregoing kinds of increases in learning by a group over time are based on changes in mean learning of the group in succeeding sessions. One can also imagine that variation in the way learning occurs during each session, despite similar learning averages across different sessions, might indicate increases in learning from session to session. Perhaps a pattern of increasing average learning among contiguous units within a session is indicative of more learning than a pattern of decreasing average learning among contiguous units, even though the two sessions in question show similar learning averages overall. Perhaps occasional peaks of learning represent insights that are not attained at all in a session where learning scores remain at a given plateau; or vice-versa.

With two sessions of two groups as our range of data, we cannot hope to explore the full scope of possible learning patterns outlined above. But their exposition alerts us to the complexity of determining whether a group has increased its aggregate learning from an earlier session to a later one.

In a first exploration of the data, table 7 shows the comparative learning averages for each group at each session (T_1 represents the first half of the first meeting; T_2 represents the first half of the third meeting). In the case of the F group, the mean learning score rises from T_1 to T_2, the difference in means being significant beyond the .01 level by a t-test. This represents the most obvious possible confirmation that an increase in learning, as measured by the scoring procedure, has occurred from one session to the next. By contrast, the mean learning score for the M group drops slightly, but the difference between the means is not significant. Thus, in terms of overall average, the M group has increased evenly in terms of cumulative learning, but does not appear to have done more learning during the third meeting than during the first.

Table 7. Mean learning scores
for each group each time

	T_1	T_2
M Group	+.95	+.87
F Group	+.31	+.93

There are two reasons why a straight comparison of aggregate averages may hide increased learning by the M group. The first is that the increase in learning may be shown by a different distribution of scores within each meeting. If so, another way of analyzing the scores may reflect increased learning. This possibility will be pursued below. The second reason is that the increase in learning is hidden by the greater opportunity for regression toward the mean in average learning scores of members of the M group, since their scores were nearer an extreme in the first session than were those of members of the F group. In other words, random error in scoring and change in learning due to incidental variables not taken into account is more likely to lower the average learning score of the M group than of the F group. Consequently, merely maintaining their average learning at the same level suggests that an *increase* in learning has occurred in the M group to counterbalance the tendency to regress toward the mean.

Inspection of mean learning for individuals in the two groups at each session tends to support this interpretation. Half the members of the M group increased their average learning scores nearly as much as the two-thirds of the members of the F group who increased their average learning scores. Starting from an average base of .54, these members of the M group increased to 1.06 on the average, while the members of the F group who increased in learning average went from an average base of .32 to .97. Further analysis shows that the three members of the M group whose average learning scores decreased most had higher scores at the first meeting than any F group member did at either session, and two of these three were members with no previous contact with experiential learning. These findings support the possibility of regression toward the mean operating in the slight drop in mean learning on the part of the M group at its third meeting.

Turning to the possibility that an increase in learning is indicated by a different distribution of scores, we find that the variance among units at the third meeting of the M group is significantly greater than the variance among units at the other three meetings (beyond the .01 level by Hartley's F_{max} test for homogenity of variance [Winer, 1962, p. 97]). By contrast, the variances for the other three meetings are homogeneous with one another. This finding suggests that there may have been portions of the third M-group meeting that yielded particularly high average learning scores, whereas other portions yielded low average scores. A further possible inference is that more learning may have occurred at this meeting than at the first meeting as the result of certain particularly intense interactions carried through to the end, by comparison to uniformly lukewarm or interrupted interactions in the first meeting.

Choosing the hundred contiguous units representing the highest scores in each meeting and grouping them by tens (fig. 2), we find our inference confirmed impressionistically. In this comparison the mean score for the third meeting is higher than for the first meeting. Also, at the third meeting there are longer exchanges, with average scores for groups of ten that are above 1.0, uninterrupted by behavior less conducive to learning.

To determine whether our interpretive inference is correct that such concentrations of high learning scores actually result in more learning than shorter peaks, we can turn to a comparison of the two transcripts. The long sequence of high learning scores at the third meeting concerned and included the meditational exercise, excerpts of which are quoted in chapter 5. Thus the sequence does represent a unitary interaction carried through to the end. By contrast, the following ten comments represent the learning peak (average: 2.1) in the first meeting:

Author: I've been having the feeling, if I'd been sitting in Member 10's place, I think my reaction to what you've been saying would

Figure 2. **Comparison of one hundred contiguous units from each M group meeting**

	Average learning for groups of ten units										Average for total
T_1	1.0	1.4	0.4	0.6	2.1	1.1	0.1	0.7	1.8	1.1	**1.03**
T_2	0.5	1.5	1.3	1.8	0.3	1.2	1.3	1.5	1.4	0.5	**1.13**

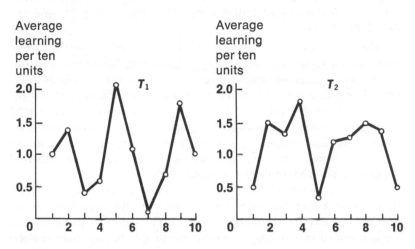

be "Why should I put more into it? If you don't hear it in my words, well, too bad."

Member 10: Those words didn't exist in my head, but they really resonate.

Member 7: I like you.

Member 10: Can I ask why?

Member 7: I don't know. You're constantly surprising me. Somebody said before that ever since they came in they've been noticing you and I have too. Maybe it's. . . .

Member 13: Yes, I've been aware of you since I came in too.

Member 1: I've thought of you as active because when you said about being demonic I had sort of that feeling too, but from a passive point of view, like "I wonder what's going to happen next," feeling that something else was, you know, required.

(*Silence.*)

Author: I have a sense that—the image that keeps coming into my head is whirlpools—that we're all whirlpools. That so far the closest we've come to not being individual whirlpools is that we've almost gotten sucked into Member 10's whirlpool, and we came pretty close to being sucked into Member 8's whirlpool at the very beginning. But it's this very continuing sense—I had it about five minutes ago and it's still with me—that each one is somehow very separate.

(*Silence.*)

Member 9: I have a different image. I have a sense of being withdrawn, for myself anyway I feel distant . . . maybe partly because I'm more reactive than I am active. I don't have too much of a personal whirlpool.

Member 7: Yeah, I don't know what you mean by whirlpool. I'm very much here. I don't feel very close to everybody here as a group, but I don't find my attention wandering to things outside of here. Is that what you had in mind?

Here we find that the topic changes within this short exchange from a focus on an interaction between two members, to a characterization of persons' reactions to one of the participants in the interaction (Member 10), to a description of the group atmosphere, using the image of whirlpools. The discussion of whirlpools extends only one unit beyond the excerpt. The interruptions are not behavioral in nature—they do not involve cutting somebody else off; rather they seem to reflect an inability by the group to integrate ideas and feelings beyond a certain point.

The increased integrating energy in the third meeting seems to derive from the author's intention to attempt the meditational exercise. This interpretation suggests that the qualities of intentionality, relationality, and momentary validity may be measurable not only in terms of individual units of conversation, but also in terms of the setting, structuring, and flow of the conversation as a whole. For example, the third meeting of the M group was characterized by two related themes rather than many unrelated ones. The first was a discussion of members' learning at the first two meetings and of what learning meant to them, which was introduced and kept alive by a number of members. (It can be noted parenthetically that much of this discussion was in the past tense, accounting for relatively low learning scores, because it showed no evidence of conscious appropriation rather than actual lack of conscious appropriation.) The second was the effort to learn through the meditation, introduced by the author and kept alive by the learning-filled comments of the other members. The increased intentionality and relationality suggested by the unity and flow of the two dominant themes of the meeting are not simply a matter of the author having "taken control of matters" after an "unstructured" first meeting, since the first part of the third meeting was organized by members other than the author.

In any event, the distinction among (1) conversations organized by high degrees of intentionality and relationality, (2) conversations organized by directive control, and (3) disorganized conversations, may be pursuable by operationalizing a measure of conscious appropriation to be applied at the level of whole conversations rather than individual units within conversations. Or further research may show that such distinctions are regularly determinable on the basis of the configuration of unit-learning scores of a meeting, just as in this case the test for homogeneity of variance highlighted the distinctiveness of the third meeting of the M group.

For the present, we can simply confirm that the scoring procedure indicates the quality and extent of learning in a group in other ways besides mean scores for the aggregate. The degree of variance among scores and the concentration of high unit-learning scores seem to be additional indicators of the degree of learning at a meeting.

The reader may wonder, however, about the validity of the underlying assumption that more learning did occur for the M group at the third meeting. I began with some commonsense reasons for thinking that it might have (p. 207), and the foregoing comparison of some first meeting dialogue to the meditation sequence seems to me to provide further evidence. It may also be noted, as further confirmation that in some sense "more" learning occurred at the third M group meeting than at the first, that its members perceived more learning to be occurring, based on relative responses to the question and scale in table 8, after each average rating for the third meeting was 5.5. This difference is significant beyond the .001 level by a t-test. However, given my mistrust of *perceptions* of learning, I can hardly introduce this evidence as any more conclusive of greater learning than the other fragments.

Table 8. The question and scale used to measure participant perception of group learning

On the average, how much would you say group members learned at this group meeting?

Little and insigni-ficant learning		average for a compar-able period of time			extraordinary amount of learning	
1	2	3	4	5	6	7

THE RELATION OF LEARNING SCORES
TO PERCEPTIONS OF LEARNING

Another series of investigations involves the relationship between members' perceptions of one another's relative learning within groups and the determinations of relative learning by the scoring procedure. We have already noted that we would *not* expect rank orders of learning perceived by group members to correlate highly with the rank order determined by the scoring procedure. Conversely, we must remember that members of the M group tended to be more familiar with experiential learning than members of the F group and that they were also introduced to exercises that were related in theory to the behavior scoring procedure. Consequently, we might anticipate that the correlations between their perceptions of their own and other members' relative learning and the determinations of the scoring procedure would be higher than for the F group.

The rank orders based on the scoring procedure and those based on members' perceptions are determined as follows. In the case of the scoring procedure, individuals are ranked according to their average learning scores. The only exception to this procedure is that an individual's average is slightly reduced if he has a very low level of participation, on the assumption that one or two high learning scores could unreliably inflate his average in such a case.* In no case during the four meetings does such a reduction result in a drop of more than one place in the rank order for the individual in question.

In the case of members' perceptions, two potentially different rank orders derive from the questionnaire administered. The questionnaire asks members to list the three members they see as being highest and lowest on a number of dimensions (new behaviors, contributing to a group atmosphere conducive to learning, experiencing strong feelings, and coming to new insights) and also to rank all members on learning, each member defining learning as he wishes. One rank order is based on the sum of the number of times a member is mentioned as highest on the dimensions, minus the number of times the member is mentioned as least along the dimensions. These particular dimensions have been chosen because various theories and methods of experiential learning emphasize them as critical to learning.

The second rank order is based on the rank of learning made by each member, using his own criteria of learning. Two aggregate rank orders are derived and then are averaged together into a composite from these individual rank orderings. One aggregate is based on the average rank assigned each member by the other members. The second aggregate is based on the relative rank each member assigns himself. These two aggregate rank orders can be named "other-perceived learning" and "self-perceived learning." They are averaged together on the assumption that there is no *a priori* reason to trust others' perceptions more than

* The formula for reducing averages is based on the reasoning stated. The actual numerical transformations are chosen rather arbitrarily. A member's average is divided by 1.19 (the fourth root of 2) if he participates less than one-half the quotient of the total number of units for the session divided by the number of members present.

self-perceptions, yet self and others may have different and complementary data, yielding a more accurate rank order when combined than either would alone.

Table 9 shows the correlations between perceptions and scor-

Table 9. Correlations between rank orders of learning based on scoring procedure and rank orders based on members' perceptions

Rank orders correlated	M group	
	$T_1 (n = 14)$	$T_2 (n = 12)$
summation of dimensions : scoring procedure	+.50**	+.46*
other/self perceptions : scoring procedure	+.30*	+.38
	F group	
	$T_1 (n = 11)$	$T_2 (n = 8)$
summation of dimensions : scoring procedure	+.19	−.41
other/self perceptions : scoring procedure	+.12	+.05

* Significant beyond .10 by t-test.
** Significant beyond .05 by t-test.

ing procedure for each group at each session that was analyzed. The table shows that seven of eight correlations between perceptions and scoring procedure are positive, but that for the F group the correlations are uniformly low and insignificant. All the correlations between perceptions and scoring procedure are higher, as anticipated, for the M group (significant beyond the .02 level by a Mann-Whitney U test). For the M group one of four correlations is sufficiently positive to be significant beyond the .05 level by a t-test, and in two cases the correlations are significant beyond the .10 level.

These data tend to confirm the expectation that persons more familiar with processes called experiential learning will rank learning more in line with the scoring procedure than will persons previously unfamiliar with them. Since the correlations for the M group are not uniformly significant beyond the .05 level and since the data base is relatively small, this confirmation cannot be considered conclusive.

A second line of inquiry can also test the relationship between learning scores and perceptions of learning. We may ask whether members who learn most at a given meeting, according to the scoring procedure, will themselves rank learning within the group most nearly in conformity with the scoring procedure's rank order. The theoretical explanation of such a result would be that high learning as measured by the scoring procedure reflects the person's contact with consciousness, and contact with consciousness, in turn, prevents perceptions of others from being distorted by the person's habitual structuring of experience or by defensiveness at structural-level changes in others. Contact with consciousness theoretically gives one the ultrastability necessary to bear rather than defend against the experience of changing structures in oneself or others.

On the other hand, if most persons are unfamiliar with conscious perspectives and if conditions conducive to experiential learning initially lead only to brief moments of contact with consciousness, then the initial attempts to estimate others' learning might be confused as much as enlightened by the divergent criteria offered by one's habitual sense of learning and the occasional conscious intuitions. Such confusion seems a likely initial response when we recall the comments of members in the M group, reported in chapter 5, concerning the conflict they experienced between intrapersonal and interpersonal awareness. Inner efforts to transcend their habitual structuring of experience when they were in interaction led to feelings of confusion rather than heightened perception.

We can pursue this line of inquiry by determining, in each group, Spearman rank-order correlations comparing each member's rank order of learning with that derived from the scoring procedure. These correlations are then themselves ranked, starting with the most positive, and a Spearman correlation is determined comparing this rank order of "relative accuracy of perceptions of learning" to the scoring procedure's rank order of learning. Such operations, performed for both groups at both meetings, show virtually no correlations or, if anything, slightly negative ones. The correlations are:

$$M_{T_1} = -.03 \qquad F_{T_1} = -.04 \qquad M_{T_2} = -.05 \qquad F_{T_2} = -.25.$$

A longer period of effort at this kind of learning than occurred during the three meetings would be necessary to determine whether the lack of correlation between accurate perception and learning results from members' unfamiliarity with this kind of learning and consequent inability to maintain continuing contact with consciousness, or from a theoretical misformulation that reduces the validity of the scoring procedure. We do, however, have a number of hints that the former interpretation is correct. The disconnection between learning and accurate perception exposed here is paralleled by the discussion in chapter 7 of the scorers' inability to score reliably after engaging in this kind of experiential learning. And we have already noted the further parallel to members' comments that they experienced conflict between analytic, interpersonal awareness and meditative awareness.

In review, we can see that the scoring procedure generally scores persons, groups, and processes reputedly conducive to experiential learning as associated with increased learning. Also, the group more familiar with experiential learning tends to identify learning in a way more like the scoring procedure than does the other group. At the same time, individual members who score relatively high in terms of learning do not tend to perceive relative learning more like the scoring procedure than do other members. None of these findings has the strength of testing and confirming a hypothesis.

Some limitations of the scoring procedure have been encountered. Regression toward the mean may distort comparisons among aggregate scores. The lack of procedures for scoring the structural and nonverbal elements of interactions may create a gap between scores of learning and *actual* learning.

Further investigation will be necessary to increase our confidence in the scoring procedure. The next chapter will move from the quantitative emphasis of this chapter to a clinical analysis.

Chapter Nine

DEVIATIONS BETWEEN LEARNING SCORES AND OTHER CRITERIA OF LEARNING

Since we are not testing hypotheses, deviations between the scoring procedure and other criteria of learning are as likely to be helpful in characterizing the scoring procedure as are correlations. Moreover, if we can examine cases of extreme deviation between members' perceptions and scores of who learned most or least, we may find reasons to favor one or the other estimate of learning.

In each of the four meetings analyzed there was a member who learned a great deal relative to others, according to the scoring procedure, but little relative to others according to members' perceptions. In each meeting there was also a member who learned a great deal according to others' perceptions but not according to the scoring procedure. Four illustrative cases are described below.

CASES OF LOW PARTICIPATION

In two cases, the members who ranked relatively high according to the scoring procedure (ranking 6 and 1) but low according to perceptions (14, 8 with $N = 14$, 8, respectively) participated very little in that meeting (3 of 213 and 7 of 229 units, respectively).

The first member's three comments are rated $+1$, -1, and $+3$, yielding a 1.00 average, reduced to .84 because of her low level of participation. The first two comments refer to controlling the family dog (this was the author's wife, and the meetings were all held at the author's home: the home and the dog are two other factors common to both groups!). The third comment is quoted below, along with the comment preceding it:

Member 9: I feel a lot less anxious now that everybody else has said that they feel anxious. (Scored +2.)

Member 6: I feel really good by what Member 9 said, but at the same time am sort of struggling inside to keep my mind here rather than thinking of next year and those of us who are leaving, and my thought in particular will be sad. I find that my head is sort of going away and something in my chest is sort of bringing it back to me. I kind of feel as though I have a head and a chest and nothing else. (Scored +3.)

The content of this comment concerns the member's difficulty in concentrating on the present, yet in form the comment is wholly concentrated in the present, and the member is reporting an active inner dilemma and struggle in a way that leaves open a continuing question for her about her commitment, role, and posture in the conversation.

In retrospect the comments relating to the dog are not insignificant either, for the member reported uncertainty after the session about how to behave, given her role as hostess to the group. (The +1 comment was "I'm getting anxious," in relation to the dog barking outside.) The member thus managed to express an existential dilemma in a manner sufficiently clear conceptually and sufficiently open emotionally that it remained alive for her even after the meeting.

The reasons why members would perceive her as learning little, relative to others, also seem clear. She participated little, and six members later reported using amount of participation as a criterion for determining amount of learning. She may also have appeared to risk little and to work through little. Members may also have heard the content of her third comment more loudly than its form and concluded she was simply not "with it."

The second case is similar to the first in that the member in question participated little and spoke about having difficulty fully entering into the interactions:

No, I was just feeling like tonight I didn't feel like expending energy or anything. I just felt like lying back and doing nothing. But I came, and you know I'm not quite sure how I will feel by the end. Joe at least seems to feel a little bit confident that he'll feel good about it. (Scored +2.)

This statement has a quality similar to the openness to an existential dilemma that we noted in the first member's quoted comment. This member is not sure how he will feel by the end of the meeting. In fact, at the end of the meeting he reported being disappointed by his inability to be more participative, and still later phoned to ask whether he might bring a girl friend with him to future meetings. Thus, lack of participation, dissonance, bad feelings, and lack of working through to a solution seem in this person's case to have had the effect of increasing his commitment to questioning rather than decreasing it. Yet others seemed to regard him as learning little on the basis of having expressed his condition as an issue.

In reflecting over the first two meetings, a member of the M group expressed the different concepts of learning implicit in the divergence between the scoring procedure and members' perceptions. At first, she maintained that she had both enjoyed and learned more at the second meeting than at the first because the author had presented some clear concepts at the second meeting which she could grasp, whereas the first meeting had left many matters unresolved. After this statement she caught herself up and remarked that she and her husband had discussed the first meeting at much greater length than the second meeting and that she could still remember incidents and issues of the first meeting, whereas the events and concepts of the second meeting had faded.

The quality of learning that the scoring procedure seems to have identified in the two cases reported above is an opening to dilemmas in such a way that they remain alive for the person at later moments and directly influence him, rather than a kind of learning where solutions are ingested and the dilemma precipitating the solutions either forgotten or never recognized in the first place. There is reason to believe that in these two cases the

members' lack of participation reflected the nature of their dilemmas rather than a reluctance to deal with dilemmas.

We may turn now to the other two illustrative cases. In these,
the persons were ranked high in terms of members' perceptions
of learning (1.5, 3) but low by the scoring procedure (13, 11, with
$N = 14$, 11, respectively). Both persons participated considerably
(19 of 226 units and 84 of 393 units). The first member received
negative scores for comments such as the following:

I think one problem at least that I'm having is that this is basically a very artificial situation being with this group. You can be
most yourself in a relationship with one other person, talking to
one other person, but this is very awkward to just be confronted
with a group of people and to be told to be yourself and to present yourself. It's not real. (Scored negative intentionality, negative relationality, positive momentary validity: − 1.)

Yeah. . . . I still think that's different when you feel you are
working with an audience, if that's the right way of expressing
what this situation is like. Maybe we shouldn't think of ourselves
as on a stage, or should we? Is that a good image of what's happening? (Scored same as previous comment: − 1.)

The evening seems to be sort of a vacuum. Which you've created
for us. Maybe it isn't up to you to establish a structure . . . even
though it's arbitrary. (Scored negative intentionality, negative relationality, neutral momentary validity: − 2.)

From their comments it appears that other members perceived
this person as actively dealing with the unfamiliarity of the struc-
tureless "T-group" setting. The fact that the setting was unfamiliar to her may have indicated to them that she had "more to
learn" than the others who could be more relaxed, and her active
grappling with it may have suggested to them that she was learning more.

The scoring procedure, however, focuses on this person's tendency to present her organization of the world as though it was

not her organization of it at all—indeed, as though there were no question of her organizing and responding to events cognitively and emotionally—but rather as if it was objective fact ("this is basically a very artificial situation"; "it's not real"; "if that's the right way of expressing what this situation is like"; "it's arbitrary"). She denies the extent to which she creates what she sees through her structuring of it ("The evening seems to be sort of a vacuum. Which you've created for us."). The form and language of her comments, rather than opening to the existential dilemmas that the comments actually imply, instead camouflage the ongoing reality of interaction between inner person and outer world by their assumption that reality is predefined but temporarily hidden, like a stage-set still in the wings.

From the perspective of the model of learning presented in this book, any conclusions based on such assumptions about reality (for example, "this is . . . artificial") must be mislearning rather than learning. And the effect of such mislearning must be to alienate the person increasingly from the direct experience, meaning, and inherent creativity of encounter, leading him instead to treat all matters as predefined, unchanging, or resolved. The result is well illustrated by the individual in question. Toward the end of the meeting I said that I felt something like resentment or anger towards her:

It had something to do with "my game is so different from yours that we can't even pretend it's the same game." Whereas the other people were close enough so I could—so that I didn't have to feel resentment maybe—this is all just coming out right now, and I'm not sure. I'm not sure "resentment" is the right word, more "anger."

She made no response to this comment at the time. When I visited her and her husband during the following week to give them feedback results from the questionnaires, she did not refer to the incident during a pleasant conversation about the philosophical implications of different forms of meditation. Her husband returned home at this point and asked whether we had discussed "it." He then related that after the meeting my comment quoted above had evoked the strongest emotional response he had ever seen in his wife. She had felt utterly condemned and hated by the author, utterly worthless, and utterly incompetent.

In the conversation that followed this revelation, I felt able to establish a fuller and firmer relationship with the husband and wife. Although they initially did not intend to return to further meetings, they changed their minds after our conversation. But the matter of prime interest here is the manner in which the wife dealt with the comment. She initially misread my explorations of a feeling towards her and of its basis, viewing the intended exploration as an attacking evaluation of her. Second, she could not respond either at the time or later in the week in private to check whether her perception of me correlated with my intention towards her. Third, she was able to recognize and deal with her emotionality only in the context of "giving up" on herself and me rather than permitting it to enliven the relationship. My exploration of a feeling became transmuted into an unchanging, objective fact by virtue of her reaction, and only a lucky visit prevented my relationship to the couple from being totally disrupted. Where I had sought to open myself to an existential dilemma, the other individual had seen no opportunity for learning, but rather a need for closure. It is just this quality of closing oneself off from recognizing, experiencing, and owning existential dilemmas that the scoring procedure identifies as negative learning.

The second member's negative learning scores were related to quick exchanges, such as the following (the member in question being "M"):

Member M: People were moving across the floor, each one with different reasons. Some were playing games, and that's why I went quickly. I think it was the games that I didn't like.

Member I: I really felt that way when *you* were doing the thing with your hands.

Member M: Games? Oh, I don't know.

Member I: In one sense it really seemed superficial.

Member C: Yeah, I felt that way too.

Member M: There were people playing the "let's crawl over as many people as possible as slowly as possible game."

Member C: What did you think about that finger thing?

Member M: The what?

Member C: That finger thing that *you* were doing.

Member M: Well, I was just writing a word.

(M's comments scored +1, −2, −1, 0, −1)

Member C: Where are you, M?

Member M: Where am I?

Member C: Yeah.

Member M: Sitting up here against the wall, watching. I'm watching the group.

Member E: Where are you at?

Member M: Where am I at? I'm feeling pretty good, if that's what you mean, E.

Member C: What?

Member M: I'm feeling okay.

Member C: I get sort of pissed off by the way you set yourself up here.

Member M: Absolutely not. I'm not mad at anybody at all. I'm just watching.

(M's comments are scored 0, −2, +1, +1, −3)

Author: Do you feel responded to, M?

Member M: No, not really. But I don't really care.

Member I: You don't care?

Member M: Well, yes I do. But I'll find out.

(M's comments scored −1, −1)

One feels that this person's behavior is largely oriented toward getting or keeping him off the hook, uncommitted ("Games? Oh, I don't know."). His reflex questions ("The what?" "Where am I?") delay and defuse encounter. His deflection of conversation from himself saves him from exposure. Not only the form, but even the content of what he says expresses noninvolvement ("I'm just watching"; "I don't really care").

Yet he is in fact heavily involved in the group, speaking more than one-fifth of the units. This contradiction bespeaks denial of responsibility for his own behavior. His average learning according to the scoring procedure reflects this denial of responsibility in being the only negative score in all four meetings analyzed (−.28).

On what basis was this person perceived as learning a lot? A majority of members of the F group listed degree of participation as one of their criteria of learning, and he participated frequently. Also, he viewed himself and was viewed by others as quick, intelligent, and perceptive, and this quickness may have set the pace for the meeting as a whole, since it registered almost twice as many units of speech as any of the other three meetings for a comparable time period.

There is an interesting parallel between this case of negative learning and the previous one. This member, too, decided not to return to further meetings. His reasoning was different, however. According to a friend, he decided that he was "too far ahead" of the group for it to be of value to him and that the author was "an uninteresting psychologist." In this case I did not visit the member after the meeting, and the member did not, in fact, attend further meetings. Given the controlling amount and quality of his participation, his absence may have made it considerably easier for the F group to raise its learning average at the third meeting.

BIASES IN MEMBERS' JUDGMENTS OF LEARNING

The analysis of these four cases indicates that there are certain biases in members' perceptions of learning that are corrected by the scoring procedure. The members tend to weigh amount of participation heavily in judging level of learning. This tendency is confirmed beyond these cases by 24 out of 45 reports of participants (across the four meetings) that indicated that they used participation as a cue to learning in determining their rank order. No other single cue was mentioned even half as many times. By contrast, the behavior-scoring procedure does not place so much reliance or such undiscriminating reliance on participation as a cue to learning. It can recognize little participation as sometimes more learning-filled than much participation.

Underlying the bias toward perceiving high participation as indicative of high learning, there seems to be a bias among members to regard focusing on topics defined by the group as conducive to learning, whereas dilemmas that impede one from participation are regarded as preventing one from learning. This view of learning can be called a bias because it implies that one must conform to predefined topics if one is to be regarded as learning. By contrast, the scoring procedure seems to regard a dilemma outside the current focus of the group as conducive to learning if the member experiencing it can express it and the tension between it and participation in the group.

DISCREPANCIES BETWEEN SELF- AND OTHER-PERCEPTIONS OF LEARNING

In addition to the cases of discrepancy between members' perceptions of learning and the determinations by the scoring procedure, there were two instances in the M group of sharp discrepancy between self-perceived and other-perceived learning during the first two meetings. The basis of these discrepancies was discussed during the third meeting. It will give us a further indication of the quality of the scoring procedure to ask how the procedure treats these cases.

In one case, others ranked the person as learning much in each of the first two meetings, whereas the person ranked herself as learning little. In the first meeting she experienced strong feelings at not having enough situations like the present one "where I can get a lot for myself." So strong were her feelings that she could hardly speak for a time and found herself weeping. Later she was involved in the most intense confrontation with another person that occurred at that meeting. During this confrontation she insisted that she did not experience to be genuine a feeling that another member was expressing. She also received feedback at that time, indicating that she had a way of showing herself to be vulnerable but then refusing support from others. Her response was:

Well, I didn't really want to cut off traffic, you know—that's very helpful, what you're saying to me. When you said that, it reminded me of something I've learned so many times and forget so many times—when you said I didn't want support. I think I have a reservoir of strength and I'm strong, but I don't want you to get that message—I don't want you to leave me alone.

This theme of learning, forgetting, and relearning reemerged in her discussion of her tendency to rank herself low on learning in the first two meetings:

I wasn't learning new things was what I was thinking. I was relearning things that I've learned a lot of times before. Like, I've been very peaceful with myself many times [a reference to the second meeting], but it is a state that doesn't last, and that I consider like relearning, but it isn't new learning.

These comments connect to the statement about learning used earlier: the member managed to express an existential dilemma in a manner sufficiently clear conceptually and sufficiently open emotionally that it remained alive for her after the meeting (p. 220). In this case, somebody else expressed a dilemma in encountering the member in one instance (regarding her refusal of support), and in that and other instances the member was reminded of emotional truths about herself (or, perhaps better, intuitive possibilities for herself) that she had known before but tended to forget.

The criterion for this kind of learning seems that to be known it must be alive, i.e., both emotionally and intellectually present in the moment. But to maintain a sense of feeling and thought as distinct yet related, one must stand outside both while experiencing them—one must be conscious. Since, according to this book, we are rarely conscious, this sort of learning constantly escapes us and must be relearned. As a friend of mine once remarked, "It is the most important things, not the least important things, that we constantly forget."

The scoring procedure seems to identify such "relearning" as learning. Overall, the scoring procedure ranked this person fourth of fourteen in learning at the first meeting, with a high average learning score of $+1.24$. A discussion of Plato's view of all learning as remembering might serve to justify this identification of relearning with learning. But we can also see from the preceding discussion that such an identification is consonant with the theory of this book, since such relearning implies current contact with consciousness.

The second case of a discrepancy between self- and other-perceived learning involved a person who participated relatively little during the first two meetings (6 of 226 units at the first) and was ranked low on learning by others, yet ranked himself high. In one of his comments, already quoted in the previous chapter in the ten-unit example of the dialogue of the first meeting, he suggests that a certain passivity is characteristic of him:

I've thought of you as active because when you said about being demonic I had sort of that feeling too, but from a passive point of view, like "I wonder what's going to happen next," feeling that something else was, you know, required.

The sense of passivity reemerges during the third meeting when the member explains why he ranks himself as learning much relative to others, though he does not appear to others to be doing so:

Well, I think I view myself as being and am quite passive in a group, so people don't get very much information about me. And so there's not too much that people can say about me. And that would tend to make me rank low in terms of these categories. Also, you know, the same kind of passivity could overlap into my seeing what's going on. Maybe it's true, but I don't think that's true. I have a pretty good idea of what's happening within me.

Author: How do you formulate the kind of learning you felt you were doing?

Well, uhm, I guess I see sort of two *modus operandi* which sort of split and I'm on one side. One is to get the situation stirred up and see what happens because of your stirring. And the other way is to sort of sit beside it and do what it does. And I sort of think of myself as doing the second kind of thing. It's that kind of learning, I think: seeing what the shape of things and people are.

In this case, the scoring procedure does not rank the member high on learning relative to the other members of the group (11th of 14), although his average learning score is not low: $+.84$ adjusted to $+.71$ because of his low participation. (The learning averages of the three members below him dip sharply, averaging only $+.26$.) More directly, his perception of himself as accurately "seeing what's going on" is justified in terms of the scoring procedure, in that his ranking of members' learning correlates most highly of anyone at the first meeting with the rank order of learning determined by the scoring procedure.

In his case the scoring procedure justifies both the self- and other-perceptions of learning, in different ways. Furthermore, the analysis of this case suggests that the scoring procedure directly measures active, behavioral learning in contrast to passive, perceptual learning, which is more directly tapped by the level of congruence between an individual's rank ordering of his learning and that of the scoring procedure. This distinction between "active" and "passive" learning is, however, offered with reservations. Earlier analysis has shown that the so-called active behavior scored as learning by this procedure can be an openness to dilemmas rather than a solving of problems, thus sounding relatively passive. And, on the other hand, the theory of attention introduced in chapter one stresses that so-called passive perception is in fact an active selection of what to look at. But however unified the active and passive, perceptual and behavioral learning may ultimately be, this case demonstrates a felt divergence that is discriminated by the scoring procedure.

We can conclude this discussion of cases of discrepancy in judgments about whether learning occurred for a certain person at a certain meeting with a sense that the validity of the scoring procedure is supported in highly convincing ways. In sum, we have found ample evidence in the discussion of the validity of the scoring procedure in this and the previous chapter that the procedure is capable of making a variety of discriminations among differently composed groups, different sessions of the same group, different flows of conversation, and different members. Moreover, when such discriminations do not accord with participants' perceptions of learning, the determinations of the scoring procedure seem more convincing. When participants' perceptions are themselves in discord, the scoring procedure reflects and explains this discord. Furthermore, in attempting to explain the basis for discriminations made by the scoring procedure, we find ourselves returning easily to the theoretical language in which the procedure is rooted, showing that the procedure congruently operationalizes the theory.

CONCLUSION

To observe and recognize one's full intent, constructive and destructive; to feel and acknowledge one's actual relatedness to others, the familiar and the alien; to relax and strive towards momentary validity in one's behavior, whether the result be dramatic or mundane—these disciplines I find demanding, unavoidable, and worthy.

The scale of the task of achieving continuing consciousness often appears awe-ful, as well it might, for through it we are brought into the presence of our life as a whole. We are not accustomed to lifetime tasks. We—and I must create an adequate word here—enhabit finite jobs, ideologies that make us right to begin with, and relationships that match our expectations. In this book I have tried to introduce a way of doing science and a way of thinking about personal experience that can open towards truths on the scale of a lifetime. Its success depends more than that of most formal work on the response of its readers.

I would like to close on a personal note, an excerpt from a letter I have written that strives to translate the structure of thought in this book into my daily life with a friend.

In your letter to me you say: "I am becoming more and more in need of some kind of truth. . . . I need more and more to know the reason for every thing I do. . . . No one knows."

In other words, you will refuse to be satisfied by all that ordinarily passes for truth. It will not sustain you. Your truth must ring tangibly in your body-mind-feeling/life—must make a difference. Stated this way it's so obvious that this must be the criterion for anyone's truth, yet you see no one around you actively in search for such truth with convincing intensity and humility. So, despite its obviousness to you and to me, we must conclude that there is something evasive about it, that those around us are not likely to help us toward it, and that some special effort is required by each alone. Without this special effort, the body constituted by our life-experience will become more and more heavily weighted with untruth each passing day, and the pain of our separation from truth will naturally become greater and greater.

This is how I understand your cry.

What the quality of your effort can best be, I'm sure neither of us knows. That *some* special effort is necessary for you to begin to feel more at home in this life seems to me terribly clear.

For a time our meditation together seemed to hold some meaning for you; the group meditation less; for Mary, I tried to describe a form of work that derived from relating to Jennifer as spirit to matter, noting failures of in-formation; for you an effort connected to working with your hands might help; I think I am finding that movements of body and voice, unattended except in passing, are especially potent for me.

We are not searching for a knowledge that superimposes some pattern over our experience, but rather for a direct illumination of experience; to feel with acceptance the patterned interplay of spirit and matter through us, the interplay of force and interruption, of energy and form, light and shadow.

So deeply woman, the universe resounds in you involuntarily in its full cacophony; your task: somehow to translate it through your life into tune (as I see you so magnificently beginning to do with pots and with me) *and* to feel your translation acceptingly. For me, the disciplines of illumination and translation emerge as favored and the more frightening task that of risking the shadows and permitting the primitive interruptions.

All spiritual experiences are sensations in the body. . . . What is a true spiritual discipline? It is a known rhythm of the harmonized body. All is there. Nothing could be more material than to use the body for acquiring a right sensation of God. . . . A well-conducted discipline makes it possible to identify and recognize at its base a unique sensation which is a sensation of the universe. What is known as meditation is the interiorization of this "pure sensation" outside of time. It is a taste of eternity (Reymond, 1971).

BIBLIOGRAPHY

Allport, G. 1967. The open system in personality theory. *Current Perspectives in Social Psychology*, ed. B. Hollander and R. Hunt. 2d ed. New York: Oxford U. P.

Argyris, C. 1962. *Interpersonal Competence and Organizational Effectiveness*. Homewood, Ill.: Dorsey.

Argyris, C. 1965a. *Integrating the Individual and the Organization*. New York: Wiley.

Argyris, C. 1965b. *Organizations and Innovation*. Homewood, Ill.: Irwin.

Argyris, C. 1967. On the future of laboratory education. *Journal of Applied Behavioral Science* 3: 153–83.

Argyris, C. 1968a. The nature of competence acquisition activities and their relation to therapy. In *Interpersonal Dynamics*, ed. W. Bennis, E. Schein, D. Berlew, and F. Steele. 2d ed. Homewood, Ill.: Dorsey.

Argyris, C. 1968b. Some unintended consequences of rigorous research. *Psychological Bulletin* 70: 185–97.

Argyris, C. 1969. The incompleteness of social-psychological theory: Examples from small group, cognitive consistency, and attribution research. *American Psychologist* 24: 893–908.

Bakan, D. 1967. *On Method*. San Francisco: Jossey-Bass.

Bakan, P., ed. 1966. *Attention*. Princeton, N.J.: Van Nostrand.

Bales, R. 1951. *Interaction Process Analysis*. Cambridge, Mass.: Addison-Wesley.

Bartos, O. 1967. *Simple Models of Group Behavior*. New York: Columbia.

Bennis, W. 1964. Patterns and vicissitudes in training groups. In *T-Group Theory and Laboratory Methods*, ed. L. Bradford, K. Benne, and J. Gibb. New York: Wiley.

Bergin, A., and Solomon, S. 1967. Study summarized in C. Truax and R. Carkhuff, 1967.

Bion, W. 1961. *Experiences in Groups*. New York: Basic Books.

Blalock, H., and Blalock, A., eds. 1968. *Methodology in Social Research*. New York: McGraw-Hill.

Blumer, H. 1969. *Symbolic Interactionism*. Englewood Cliffs, N.J.: Prentice-Hall.

Bolman, L. 1968. The effects of variations in educator behavior on the learning process in laboratory human relations education. Ph. D. dissertation, Yale University.

Boulding, K. 1968. General systems theory. In *Modern Systems Research for the Behavioral Scientist*, ed. W. Buckley. Chicago: Aldine.

Bradford, L., Benne, K., and Gibb, J., eds., 1964. *T-Group Theory and Laboratory Methods*. New York: Wiley.

Brenner, C. 1957. *An Elementary Textbook of Psychoanalysis*. Garden City, N.Y.: Doubleday, Anchor.

Brown, N. 1966. *Love's Body*. New York: Vintage.

Brown, R. 1965. *Social Psychology*. New York: Free Press.

Bruner, J. 1966. Theorems for a theory of instruction. In *Learning about Learning*, ed. J. Bruner. Washington, D.C.: Government Printing Office.

Buber, M. 1965. *Between Man and Man*. New York: Macmillan.

Buckley, W. 1967. *Sociology and Modern Systems Theory*. Englewood Cliffs, N.J.: Prentice-Hall.

Cadwallader, M. 1968. The cybernetic analysis of change in complex social systems. In *Modern Systems Research for the Behavioral Scientist*, ed. W. Buckley. Chicago: Aldine.

Campbell, D., and Stanley, J. 1963. Experimental and quasi-experimental designs for research on teaching. In *Handbook of Research on Teaching*, ed. R. Gage. Chicago: Rand McNally.

Camus, A. 1955. *The Myth of Sisyphus*. New York: Knopf.

Carson, R. 1969. *Interaction Concepts of Personality*. Chicago: Aldine.

Cohn, R. 1968. Training intuition. In *Ways of Growth*, ed. H. Otto, and J. Mann. New York: Grossman.

Culbert, S. 1968. Trainer self-disclosure and member growth in two T-groups. *Journal of Applied Behavioral Science* 4: 47–73.

Davis, S. 1967. An organizational problem-solving methodology of organizational change. *Journal of Applied Behavioral Science* 3: 3–21.

de Charms, R. 1968. *Personal Causation*. New York: Academic.

de Hartmann, T. 1964. *Our Life with Mr. Gurdjieff.* New York: Cooper.

Deutsch, J., and Deutsch, D. 1969. Attention: Some theoretical considerations. In *Attention,* ed. P. Bakan. Princeton, N.J.: Van Nostrand.

Deutsch, K. 1966. *The Nerves of Government.* New York: Free Press.

Dewey, J. 1922. *Human Nature and Conduct.* New York: Holt.

Dollard, J., and Auld, F., Jr. 1959. *Scoring Human Motives: A Manual.* New Haven, Conn.: Yale.

Dunphy, D. 1968. Phases, roles and myths in self-analytic groups. *Journal of Applied Behavioral Science* 4: 195–225.

Dyer, W. 1969. Congruence and control. *Journal of Applied Behavioral Science* 5: 161–74.

Erikson, E. 1958. *Young Man Luther.* New York: Norton.

Erikson, E. 1959. Identity and the life cycle. *Psychological Issues,* monograph 1.

Evans-Wentz, W. 1960. *The Tibetan Book of the Dead.* New York: Oxford. U.P.

Fahey, G. 1942a. The questioning activity of children. *Journal of Genetic Psychology* 60: 334–55.

Fahey, G. 1942b. The extent of classroom questioning activity of high school pupils. *Journal of Educational Psychology* 33: 128–37.

Festinger, L. 1950. Informal social communication. *Psychological Review* 57: 271–82.

Festinger, L., and Carlsmith, J. 1959. Cognitive consequences of forced compliance. *Journal of Abnormal Social Psychology* 58: 203–10.

Fink, E. 1962. Response to speech by Alfred Schutz, as quoted in A. Schutz, 1962.

Flanders, N. 1959. Teacher-pupil contacts and mental hygiene. *Journal of Social Issues* 15: 30–39.

Fleishman, E., Harris, E., and Burtt, H. 1963. Leadership and supervision in industry. In *People and Productivity,* ed. R. Sutermeister. New York: McGraw-Hill.

Franck, A. 1967. *The Kabbalah.* New Hyde Park, N.Y.: U. Books.

Freud, A. 1946. *The Ego and Mechanisms of Defense.* New York: Int. Pubs.

Freud, S. 1930. *Civilization and Its Discontents.* Reprinted, New York: Norton, 1961.

Freud, S. 1933. *New Introductory Lectures on Psychoanalysis.* New York: Norton.

Friedman, N. 1967. *The Social Nature of Psychological Research.* London: Basic Books.

Gagne, R. 1965. *Conditions of Learning.* New York: Holt.

Goldstein, K. 1939. *The Organism.* New York: Am. Bk. Co.

Gordon, W. 1961. *Synectics: The Development of Creative Capacity.* New York: Harper.

Haigh, G. 1968. A personal growth crisis in laboratory training. *Journal of Applied Behavioral Science* 4: 437–52.

Haley, J. 1967. Personal communication to N. Friedman. Quoted in N. Friedman, 1967.

Harrison, R. 1965. Cognitive models for interpersonal and group behavior: A theoretical framework for research. *Explorations, NTL-NEW Journal,* 2.

Hartmann, H. 1958. *Ego Psychology and the Problem of Adaptation.* New York: Int. Univs.

Harvey, O., Hunt, D., and Schroder, H. 1961. *Conceptual Systems and Personality Organization.* New York: Wiley.

Hebb, D. 1969. The mind's eye. *Psychology Today* 2: 54–57.

Hilgard, E., and Bower, G. 1966. Theories of Learning. 3d ed. New York: Appleton.

Hill, W. 1952. Learning theory and the acquisition of values. In *Psychological Studies of Human Development,* ed. R. Kuhlen. New York: Appleton.

Hobbes, T. 1651. *Leviathan.* Reprinted, Oxford: Blackwell, 1960.

Holmer, P. 1970. Review essay: Polanyi and being reasonable. *Soundings* 53: 95–105.

Husserl, E. 1962. *Ideas.* New York: Collier.

Husserl, E. 1965. *Phenomenology and the Crisis of Philosophy.* New York: Harper, Torchbooks.

Ichheiser, G. 1968. Analysis and typology of personality misinterpretations. In *Interpersonal Dynamics,* ed. W. Bennis, E. Schein, D. Berlew, and F. Steele. 2d ed. Homewood, Ill.: Dorsey.

Jourard, S. 1968. *Disclosing Man to Himself.* Princeton, N.J.: Van Nostrand.

Jung, C. 1962. Commentary in R. Wilheim, *The Secret of the Golden Flower.* New York: Harcourt.

Jung, C. 1963. *Memories, Dreams, Reflections,* ed. A. Jaffé. New York: Pantheon.

Jung, C. 1964. *Man and His Symbols.* New York: Dell.

Kahn, R., and Katz, D. 1963. Leadership practices in relation to productivity and morale. In *People and Productivity,* ed. R. Sutermeister. New York: McGraw-Hill.

Kaplan, A. 1964. *The Conduct of Inquiry*. San Francisco: Chandler Pub.

Kobler, R. 1965. Contemporary learning theory and human learning. In *Humanistic Viewpoints in Psychology*, ed. F. Severin. New York: McGraw-Hill.

Koestler, A. 1945. *The Yogi and the Commissar*. New York: Macmillan.

Koestler, A. 1964. *The Act of Creation*. New York: Macmillan.

Kubie, L. 1960. Some unsolved problems of the scientific career. In *Identity and Anxiety*, ed. M. Stein, A. Vidich, and A. White. New York: Free Press.

Kuhn, T. 1962. *The Structure of Scientific Revolutions*. Chicago: U. of Chicago, Phoenix.

Laing, R. 1967. *The Politics of Experience*. New York: Ballantine.

Langer, S. 1967. *Mind: An Essay on Human Feeling*, vol. 1. Baltimore: Johns Hopkins.

Lawrence, D. H. 1923. *Studies in Classic American Literature*. Reprinted, New York: Viking, 1961.

Locke, E., Cartledge, N., and Koeppel, J. 1968. Motivating effects of knowledge of results: A goal-setting phenomenon? *Psychological Bulletin* 70: 474–85.

McDermott, J. 1969. Technology and the intellectuals. *New York Review of Books*, July 31.

McGchee, W. 1967. Learning theory and training. In *Studies in Personnel and Industrial Psychology*, ed. E. Fleishman. Homewood, Ill.: Dorsey.

MacIntyre, A. 1962. Mistake about causality in social science. In *Philosophy, Politics, and Society*, 2d ser., ed. P. Laslett and W. Runciman. New York: Barnes & Noble.

MacMurray, J. 1953. *The Self as Agent*. London: Faber.

Mann, R. 1966. The development of the member-trainer relationship in self-analytic groups. *Human Relations* 19: 85–115.

Mannheim, K. 1936. *Ideology and Utopia*. New York: Harcourt.

Maritain, J. 1954. *Creative Intuition in Art and Poetry*. Cleveland: Meridian.

Maslow, A. 1954. *Motivation and Personality*. New York: Harper.

Maslow, A. 1968. Some educational implications of the humanistic psychologies. *Harvard Educational Review* 38: 685–96.

Merleau-Ponty, M. 1963. *The Structure of Behavior*. Boston: Beacon.

Miller, G., Galanter, E., and Pribram, L. 1960. *Plans and the Structure of Behavior*. New York: Holt.

Mills, T. 1964. *Group Transformation*. Englewood Cliffs, N.J.: Prentice-Hall.

Mills, T. 1965. *Sociology of Small Groups*. Englewood Cliffs, N.J.: Prentice-Hall.

Mowrer, O. 1960. *Learning Theory and Behavior*. New York: Wiley.

Murphy, G. 1958. *Human Potentialities*. New York: Basic Books.

Northrop, F. 1959. *The Logic of the Sciences and the Humanities*. New York: Meridian.

Ouspensky, P. 1949. *In Search of the Miraculous*. New York: Harcourt.

Perls, F., Hefferline, R., and Goodman, P. 1965. *Gestalt Therapy*. New York: Delta.

Polanyi, M. 1958. *Personal Knowledge*. New York: Harper.

Priestley, J. 1964. *Man and Time*. New York: Dell.

Rapaport, A. 1966. *Two-Person Game Theory*. Ann Arbor, Mich.: U. of Michigan.

Rapaport, A. 1968. The promise and pitfalls of information theory. In *Modern Systems Research for the Behavioral Scientist*, ed. W. Buckley. Chicago: Aldine.

Reymond, L. 1971. *The Life Within*. New York: Doubleday.

Rhine, J. 1947. *The Reach of the Mind*. New York: Sloane.

Riesman, D. 1950. *The Lonely Crowd*. New Haven, Conn.: Yale.

Rogers, C. 1961a. A process conception of psychotherapy. *On Becoming a Person*. Boston: Houghton.

Rogers, C. 1961b. *On Becoming a Person*. Boston: Houghton.

Rogers, C. 1963. The actualizing tendency in relation to "motives" and to consciousness. In *Nebraska Symposium on Motivation*, ed. M. Jones. Lincoln, Nebr.: U. of Nebr.

Rogers, C., and Skinner, B. 1956. Some issues concerning the control of human behavior: A symposium. *Science* 124: 1057–66.

Rosenthal, R. 1966. *Experimenter Effects in Behavioral Research*. New York: Appleton.

Roszak, T. 1969. *The Making of a Counter Culture*. Garden City, N.Y.: Doubleday.

Russell, B. 1927. *An Outline of Philosophy*. London: Allen and Unwin.

Schachtel, E. 1959a. Focal attention and the emergence of reality. *Metamorphosis*, chapt. 11. New York: Basic Books.

Schachtel, E. 1959b. Memory and childhood amnesia. *Metamorphosis*, chapt. 12. New York: Basic Books.

Schein, E., and Bennis, W. 1965. *Personal and Organizational Change through Group Methods.* New York: Wiley.

Schoeninger, D. 1965. Client experiencing as a function of therapist self-disclosure and pre-therapy training in experiencing. Ph.D. dissertation, University of Wisconsin.

Schroder, H., and Harvey, O. 1963. Conceptual organization and group structure. In *Motivation and Social Interaction,* ed. O. Harvey. New York: Ronald.

Schroder, H., Driver, M., and Streufert, S. 1967. *Human Information Processing.* New York: Holt.

Schuon, F. 1963. *Understanding Islam.* New York: Roy Pub.

Schutz, A. 1962. *Collected Papers,* vol. 1, ed. M. Natanson. The Hague: Martinus Nijhoff.

Schutz, A. 1964. *Collected Papers,* vol. 2, ed. I. Schutz. The Hague: Martinus Nijhoff.

Schutz, W. 1967. *Joy: Expanding Human Awareness.* New York: Grove.

Shepard, H. 1965. Changing interpersonal and intergroup relationships in organizations. In *Handbook of Organizations,* ed. J. March. Chicago: Rand McNally.

Silverman, J. 1966. The problem of attention in research and theory in schizophrenia. In *Attention,* ed. P. Bakan. Princeton, N.J.: Van Nostrand.

Skinner, B. 1960. *Science and Human Behavior.* New York: Macmillan.

Slater, P. 1966. *Microcosm.* New York: Wiley.

Sturtevant, W. 1969. Studies in Ethnoscience. In *Transcultural Studies in Cognition. American Anthropologist* 66, no. 3, pt. 2: 99–132.

Suzuki, D. 1955. *Studies in Zen.* New York: Delta.

Teilhard de Chardin, P. 1959. *The Phenomenon of Man.* New York: Harper.

Truax, C., and Carkhuff, R. 1967. *Toward Effective Counseling and Psychotherapy.* Chicago: Aldine.

von Bertalanffy, L. 1967. *Robots, Men and Machines.* New York: Braziller.

von Bertalanffy, L. 1968. General systems theory—a critical review. In *Modern Systems Research for the Behavioral Scientist,* ed. W. Buckley. Chicago: Aldine.

von Weizsacker, C. 1957. *The Rise of Modern Physics.* New York: Braziller.

Watts, A. 1963. *Psychotherapy East and West.* New York: Mentor Books.

Watzlawick, P., Beavin, J., and Jackson, D. 1967. *Pragmatics of Human Communication.* New York: Norton.

Webb, E., Campbell, D., Schwartz, R., and Sechrest, L. 1966. *Unobstrusive Measures: Nonreactive Research in the Social Sciences.* Chicago: Rand McNally.

White, S. 1940. *The Unobstructed Universe.* New York: Dutton.

Whyte, W., and Hamilton, E. 1964. *Action-Research for Management.* Homewood, Ill.: Irwin-Dorsey.

Wiener, N. 1954. *The Human Use of Human Beings.* Garden City, N.Y.: Doubleday, Anchor.

Wilson, C. 1956. *The Outsider.* New York: Delta.

Wilson, C. 1967a. Existentialist psychology: A novelist's approach. In *Challenges in Humanistic Psychology,* ed. J. Bugenthal. New York: McGraw-Hill.

Wilson, C. 1967b. *Introduction to the New Existentialism.* Boston: Houghton.

Winer, B. 1962. *Statistical Principles in Experimental Design.* New York: McGraw-Hill.

Yogananda, P. 1968. *Autobiography of a Yogi.* Los Angeles: Self-Realization.

NAME INDEX

SUBJECT INDEX